Violence and Order
on the Chengdu Plain

Violence and Order on the Chengdu Plain

The Story of a Secret Brotherhood in Rural China, 1939–1949

DI WANG

Stanford University Press
Stanford, California

Stanford University Press
Stanford, California

This book has been published with the assistance of a Research & Development Grant for Chair Professor (CPG) of University of Macau.

Library of Congress Cataloging-in-Publication Data
  Names: Wang, Di, 1956– author.
  Title: Violence and order on the Chengdu Plain : the story of a secret brotherhood in rural China, 1939–1949 / Di Wang.
  Description: Stanford, California : Stanford University Press, 2018. | Includes bibliographical references and index.
  Identifiers: LCCN 2017032564 (print) | LCCN 2017037897 (ebook) | ISBN 9781503605336 (epub) | ISBN 9781503604834 (cloth : alk. paper) | ISBN 9781503605305 (pbk.)
  Subjects: LCSH: Ge lao hui—History—20th century. | Brotherhoods—China—Sichuan Sheng—History—20th century. | Secret societies—China—Sichuan Sheng—History—20th century. | Power (Social sciences)—China—Sichuan Sheng—History—20th century. | Filicide—China—Sichuan Sheng—History—20th century. | Sichuan Sheng (China)—Rural conditions—20th century.
  Classification: LCC HS310.Z7 (ebook) | LCC HS310.Z7 W36 2018 (print) | DDC 369.0951/38—dc23
  LC record available at https://lccn.loc.gov/2017032564

Typeset by BookMatters in 10.5/12 Bembo

*To Bill Rowe, who has taught, inspired,
and supported me to do my best work*

Contents

Maps and Figures

Preface and Acknowledgments

ABOUT A DECADE AGO, when Professor Li Deying, a friend of mine at Sichuan University, was doing research in the Peking University Library, she found a sociological report on a Paoge family in 1940s Sichuan by Shen Baoyuan, a female student in the Department of Sociology at Yenching University. Deying knew that I was working on materials related to the Paoge, so she made me a photocopy of the report. Shen's thesis was useful, but at the time I was concentrating on another project—public life and teahouses in twentieth-century Chengdu—so I gave it no immediate thought. It stayed on my shelf for nearly a decade.

Since the 1980s, I have wanted to write a book on the Paoge. In 1989 my research project on the Paoge received a Chinese Studies Fellowship Award from Wang Laboratories, Inc. (USA), but because of many factors—especially the lack of systematic sources—I did not complete the project. I never stopped collecting relevant materials, however. During the spring of 2009, while I taught in the Department of History at the University of California at Berkeley, I read through all "cultural and historical materials" (*wenshi ziliao*) from Sichuan's provincial and county levels to district administrations on the shelves of the C. V. Starr East Asian Library. In 2014, after my second teahouse book was nearly completed, I began to give serious thought to the Paoge project. That summer, while reading through the documents I had collected for years, I taught a graduate seminar at East China Normal University in which I used several classic works of microhistory such as those by Natalie Davis and Robert Darnton. These books inspired me to attempt a microhistory of my own based on Shen Baoyuan's 1940s investigation of the Paoge in Hope Township.

Deciding to use Shen's fieldwork report as a historical source, I wanted to answer the following questions: (1) What is the true geographical location of Shen's investigation? (2) What is the real name of Lei Mingyuan, Shen's main interview subject? (3) Does Shen know Lei Mingyuan's situation after

1949? If I could find Shen, I thought, these puzzles could easily be solved. In early July 2014, I started to look online for Shen, who would have been at least ninety years old by then, so I felt a sense of urgency. I found out that she was the daughter of the American-educated scholar Shen Zurong (Samuel T. Y. Seng), who is considered the father of library science in China. The Shen family had established a scholarship at Sun Yat-sen University. The latest news on Shen Baoyuan was from 2012 about her attendance at the university's scholarship award ceremony. From a blog essay by Professor Cheng Huanwen, library director at Sun Yat-sen University and the author of Shen Zurong's biography, I knew that Cheng had communicated with Shen Baoyuan. I contacted Professor Ma Guoqing, a friend in the Department of Anthropology at Sun Yat-sen University. With his help, I connected with Cheng and ultimately gained Shen's telephone number. Finally I was able to speak directly with Shen Baoyuan.

The result was disappointing: the entire conversation probably lasted only two or three minutes. After I told her the purpose of my contacting her, Shen said, "I have been suffering from Alzheimer's and cannot remember anything in the past. I do not want to waste your time." She did not want to be disturbed with this matter. If I had started to write my book ten years earlier, perhaps the situation would be different. I tried not to feel so disappointed; it was unlikely for anyone, much less a ninety-year-old, to remember what had transpired seventy years earlier. I tried to move on without regret, although I did not completely give up hope. I attempted to obtain some information through Shen's daughter and asked if her mother had talked about the sociological investigation in 1945. But, again, I was disappointed. She told me that her mother had never mentioned the experience; in fact, Shen's daughter had only learned about the investigation from me. I was, however, able to confirm that Shen Baoyuan was born in February 1924. Therefore, I knew that when Shen traveled to Hope Township for her fieldwork that summer, she was twenty-one and a junior studying sociology. In 1946 she graduated from Yenching University at twenty-two, the typical age of most college graduates.

I would not be able to check the historical facts with Shen herself—a reality that might not be entirely disadvantageous. Even without the problem of her having lost memory, whatever she could tell me today about events from the 1940s might be a "reproduction" of history. Largely relying on Shen's fieldwork report—a real record of the original sociological investigation—while digging deeper into other historical sources might therefore be the best outcome. This book explores history in two voices: the first is that of protagonist Lei Mingyuan and his family; the second is that of Shen Baoyuan, who recorded their stories and observable patterns to document Paoge activities and Paoge families from a Western-trained sociological student's viewpoint. In a third layer of interpretation I seek to understand these two stories joined in the Chengdu plain.

I would like to especially thank Li Deying for providing me with Shen Baoyuan's 1946 bachelor's thesis, which is the core source for this book. I am grateful to Howard Goodman, who thoroughly edited the manuscript and helped improve it by asking clarifying questions and offering insightful suggestions. My thanks go to Bill Rowe, Madeleine Zelin, and Cynthia Brokaw for supporting my grant applications for this project. More than twenty years ago, Bill recommended Carol Ginzburg's work, which simulated my interest in microhistory. Special thanks to Cynthia, who provided photocopies of two versions of *Haidi*, printed in 1920s and 1930s Chengdu, both of which are very valuable to this book. Thanks to Cui Rong, who helped me type Shen's entire report into an electronic format as the starting point for this book, and An Shaofan, who helped me check the errors of pinyin in the bibliography and character list as the ending point of the project. For their constructive comments, I thank Huaiyin Li and a anonymous scholar, who served as reviewers for Stanford University Press. For their expert direction throughout the publication process, I would like to express my gratitude to SUP editors Jenny Gavacs, Margo Irvin, and Marcela Maxfield, who successively were in charge of this book, and to independent editor Amy Smith Bell for her meticulous copyediting of the final manuscript.

This project received the following financial support: the College of Liberal Arts Seed Grant of Texas A&M University, the Fulbright Senior Research Scholarship, and the Research and Development Grant for Chair Professor of the University of Macau. My thanks go to the C. V. Starr East Asian Library of University of California at Berkeley, the Sterling C. Evans Library at Texas A&M University, the Sichuan Provincial Archives, the Library of East China Normal University, and the Wu Yee Sun Library of University of Macau. I thank the David M. Rubenstein Rare Book and Manuscript Library at Duke University for providing permission to use the photographs taken by Sidney D. Gamble from 1917 through 1919. I also thank the Needham Research Institute at Cambridge University for providing permission to use the photographs taken by Joseph Needham from 1943 through 1946.

During the years when the manuscript was taking shape, several institutions invited me to give talks on Sichuan's secret societies: the University of California at San Diego, L'École des hautes études en sciences sociales (EHESS, Paris), the University of Arkansas, Sichuan University, Nanjing University, Central China Normal University, Fudan University, Shanghai Jiaotong University, and Peking University. I thank the scholars and students who attended my presentations for their stimulating comments and questions. Some material in the introduction as well as in Chapter 11 has been previously published in the journal *Frontiers of History in China*. I thank the publisher for permission to reuse the material here.

Finally, this book would not have been possible without the support of my family. My deepest gratitude goes to all of them.

D. W.

Violence and Order
on the Chengdu Plain

Two Voices Joined in the Chengdu Plain

THIS BOOK INVESTIGATES, and to some extent reconstructs, a story comprising two intertwined voices. Two different groups share and act upon certain common interests: One voice exhibits the shape of work, ideas, and itineraries among certain sociological investigators in 1940s China. Theirs was an academic platform—the privileged elite. We see them mainly through the writing of Shen Baoyuan, a twenty-one-year-old female college student in the Department of Sociology at Beijing's Yenching University. Like other universities at the time, Yenching was forced to transfer its daily operations to China's West—in this case, to Chengdu. Shen's writing concerned events of the summer of 1945. As part of her academic requirements, she and others went to the northwest suburbs of Chengdu, in particular to a village in Sichuan Province she refers to as Hope Township (Wangzhen). There, Shen established a relationship with the Lei family, whose male head of household was a local "master" of a secret society known as the Paoge (the Gowned Brothers).[1] Shen's voice blends into the story's other voice: the Lei family organization. She recorded what she saw and heard and along the way became emotionally and intellectually committed to their lives and fates. Shen's academic world combined with the wider net she cast, centered on the Lei family organization. People in their networks ranged from rich to poor and from urban to rural, living in an ongoing process of financial and social stress.

In my analysis, the story's two voices—that of Shen Baoyuan and the Leis—explore larger concepts of morality, laws, governance and disorder, fairness and oppression, and the meanings that these realities projected onto individual lives. The book poses the question of whether a fruitful and enduring harmonizing of voices occurred, or whether the rarefied world of ideas failed to produce. Two basic positions—Shen as an urban educated woman; Lei as a leader of a rural local secret society—underlie the complex story of Shen and the Leis. The methodological theses concern how we can better develop and enrich the historiography of local control and social patterns in modern China. The history of local governance in wide areas of China—before, during, and after the Japanese invasion and into the Japanese collapse in late summer of 1945—must involve analysis of local secret societies. Emerging with anti-Manchu sentiments in roughly the seventeenth century and continuing into the 1940s, secret societies were all over China. These organizations often operated as gangs that provided belief systems around the bonds of male loyalty; they also acted as profit-oriented crime syndicates with corrupt links to hundreds of local governments that were institutionally linked to China's center. Without a knowledge of secret societies, we cannot truly understand how China worked outside of the national metropolitan and provincial seats of government. The focus in this book is on the Paoge—a secret society with a long history that operated throughout Sichuan. The geographical framework of this microhistory is situated in the Chengdu Plain.

Names for secret societies were quite ambiguous and changeable, and they could be called different things by different actors, even by the organizations themselves. This book concerns a loose but loyal group of individuals in Sichuan called the Paoge, also known as the Gelaohui (the Sworn Brotherhood Society). An illegal organization that struggled with state authority for a long time, the Paoge depended on their solid historical and cultural roots in local soil, their organizational structure, wide social network, and members' bonds of brotherhood. The organization developed into such a powerful rural-urban civil force that by the 1940s local governments had to work with them to handle local affairs. Paoge masters (*daye* in Chinese, literally "elder uncle" or alternatively *duobazi,* "helmsman"; the rankings are discussed in more detail in Chapter 2 and Appendix 1) were de facto leaders of their local places. Known to have preserved stability in everyday interactions, while simultaneously serving their own power structure, the masters became a tenacious force that could (and on occasion did) resist various state incursions and controls.

To enrich the historiography of local control, we must assess groups of people and narrate their stories. We cannot become overly reliant on the structured data that emerge from government archives; we must not forget to shape and frame the narratives that give us human scenes motivated by human needs and desires. Stories of secret societies are not easily come by; they are not well larded in the archives nor consistently published in private memoirs and books. If we accept what has been laid at our feet—for example, Shen's startling piece of sincere, even emotional academic reporting from the field—and enrich it by making groups of individuals to chart their needs, we can ultimately suggest the nature of people's motives for their social actions and reactions. New links can be found. By compiling academic biographies, we can further the understanding of the Paoge, as it was a certain group of like-minded leaders in sociology and anthropology who brought about analytic work on secret societies and rural life in China from the 1920s through the 1940s. These sociologists and anthropologists, many of them Western-educated, were quite influenced by the West. We often encounter the label "rural activists" (*nongcun gongzuo zhe*) for these academics, as they believed that to understand China, they had to understand its rural areas and peasants. Investigations of rural society became an important part of their Rural Construction and Rural Education Movement. These scholars entered the countryside and left us many precious records.

This book takes advantage of what I contend is a convincing trove of new source material, which transcends its role as historiographic tool to become a precious testimonial about people as well as a piece of continuing historical memory for understanding the Paoge and local control and society in China. Along the way, the following questions find partial answers: How did the Paoge and their organizations play a role in the rural community? How were people's lives affected by the organization? What is clarified about everyday life and patterns by the stories of a local secret society and its members? What do we learn by pursuing secrets of passion and rage, and are those useful in a historiography? How can we assess the work and life of Shen Baoyuan as well as the strivings and achievements of families like the Leis? Was Shen a pure and neutral innocent? Was master Lei a creature of his bathetic passions?

This Introduction provides a framework for this line of questioning. First I summarize recent achievements in historical scholarship concerning China's secret societies as they operated in local areas from the late Qing to the Maoist era. Next I frame a reliable overview of the intellectual influences on Shen and on the trends in sociology in China's universities at the time. The Introduction ends with a discussion of Shen's written report, her bachelor's thesis. Looking at several passages clarifies her motives and personal horizons, laying the stage for my examination of the Paoge and Shen's confrontation with their local world.

★　★　★

My interest in the Paoge began in the 1980s. Since then, I have collected all kinds of relevant sources. In my 1993 book on the social history of the upper Yangzi region, I gave a preliminary description of this secret society. In my 2003 book on street culture in Chengdu, I discussed the relationship between the Paoge and street politics. I analyzed the Paoge role in the conduct of "negotiations over tea" (*chi jiangcha*) and their role in social control in my 2010 book on Chengdu teahouses before the Mao era.[2] When I began the careful analysis of Shen Baoyuan's investigation, I was intensely drawn to the obscure details of the Paoge. Gradually I began to use her materials as a primary source for a microhistory dealing with local society and social work activism in rural Sichuan.[3]

Over the past four decades, especially since the 1990s, there has been a good deal of scholarship on secret societies in general.[4] Dealing with this political phenomenon has not been an easy line of academic research to follow. Part of the problem has been in correctly perceiving the different contexts in which the societies worked: sometimes as antistate secret rebel societies (as was the case in late Qing times) and other times as purveyors of organized crime who occasionally exuded Western gangster traits. In other words, the secret societies and their members have been chameleon-like. The initial look at the political nature of the Paoge was actually as far back as the 1940s—even before Shen produced her thesis. These early observers saw the Paoge as a complex society that showed both positive and negative impacts on local communities; they regarded the Paoge as a mysterious organization with a complex mode of membership.[5] These were mostly surface observations, however, and few researchers actually entered deeply into the groups, as Shen did. Another later problem was the code that one had to crack to separate out veritable Paoge actions and records from the "cultural and historical materials" (*wenshi ziliao*) created in the post-1949 era to serve the thinking of the Maoist state, whose conceived roles for these groups wavered from counterrevolutionaries to local bullies and forces of evil.[6]

We have seen quite a breakthrough since the late 1990s, with discoveries of new sources, the opening of archives, and the introduction of other disciplines. Some excellent studies of the Sworn Brotherhood Society have been published in both the West and in China, but as leading scholar David Ownby has noted, these works mainly concentrate on the origin of the Heaven and Earth Society and popular religions.[7] To date, no Western-language monograph on the Paoge has been published. The Paoge was the most fascinating branch of the Sworn Brotherhood Society, and the most influential among commoners. Furthermore, before this book, there has never been a sociological or historical study that dealt with a Paoge-oriented family like the Leis of Hope Township. Paoge master Lei Mingyuan generally operated according to basic templates of the Paoge organization that had been in place for near three centuries in his area of Sichuan.

Let us frame, as effectively as the facts allow, what is known of Shen Baoyuan before her time at Hope Township. What was her back story—that is, what formed her intellectual search upon arriving in the western province of Sichuan? Her choosing a Paoge family as her subject of survey was very discerning. She regarded herself as a rural activist, as numerous scholars concerned with rural issues self-identified.[8] Some of these academics became the pioneers of Chinese sociology and anthropology. From the outset, such scholars had the goal of understanding and transforming rural China. Shen Baoyuan's choice of investigating the Gowned Brothers was not accidental; rather, it was part of the rural educational movement, a result of an academic trend that emphasized fieldwork dealing with Chinese rural sociology and anthropology. At that time, there was not a clear distinction between sociology and anthropology. Today, when we look back at works from the Department of Sociology at Yenching University, we find that their methodologies and research subjects are hardly to be distinguished from those of anthropology. This tradition has persisted: anthropology in many Chinese universities is currently part of the Department of Sociology (including Peking University). The sociology professors of Yenching University mentioned throughout this book were therefore also anthropologists.

It is important to detour briefly, to give a sense of the way that theoretical and data-oriented social research in the West from about 1880 to 1910 was received academically and put to unique uses in China in the early twentieth century, well before Shen's time. The Chinese experience was chiefly led and influenced by several foreign professors, especially those working at missionary universities. In 1917, C. G. Dittmer, an American professor at Tsing-hua College, guided student research into the costs of living of 195 households in Beijing's western suburbs. In 1918 and 1919 the missionary Sidney D. Gamble and Professor John Stewart Burgess of Yenching University launched a survey of Beijing's social conditions, published in 1921 as *Peking, a Social Survey*. In the same year, Professor Daniel H. Kulp of Shanghai College (Hujiang daxue) took students in the Department of Sociology to Phoenix Village (Fenghuangcun), located in Chaozhou, Guangdong Province, where they investigated 650 households and later published their 1925 report *Country Life in South China*.[9] In 1922 the Federation of International Famine Relief Commission (Huayang yizhen jiuzai zonghui) invited C. B. Malone and J. B. Tagler to lead 61 students from 9 universities in an investigation of 240 villages in Hebei, Shandong, Jiangsu, Zhejiang, and other provinces and published *The Study of Chinese Rural Economy* in 1924.[10] From 1921 through 1925, Professor John Lossing Buck at the University of Nanking (Jinling daxue) organized students to survey 2,866 farms in 17 counties in 7 provinces and eventually published *Chinese Farm Economy* in 1930. Buck organized an even larger investigation of 16,700 farms in 22 provinces and published *Land Utilization in China* in 1937.[11]

Chinese sociologists conducted other social projects during the 1920s. The board of the Chinese Educational and Cultural Foundation (Zhonghua jiaoyu wenhua jijin dongshihui) established the Office of Social Surveys (Shehui diaocha bu), which was renamed Beiping Institute of Social Surveys (Beiping shehui diaochasuo) in 1929. Beginning in 1926, with funding from the United States, the institute conducted many social studies led by Tao Menghe and Li Jinghan and published more than two dozen books. During 1929 and 1930 the Institute of Social Sciences (Shehui kexue yanjiu suo) of Academia Sinica, headed by Chen Hansheng, investigated the rural areas of Wuxi, in Jiangsu Province, and Baoding, in Hebei.[12] In 1926 the Association to Promote Chinese Common Education (Zhonghua pingmin jiaoyu cujinhui), led by Yan Yangchu (Y. C. James Yen), conducted experiments in rural education in Ding County, Hebei Province. In the early 1930s, with funds raised in the United States, Yen moved the headquarters from Beijing to the city of Dingzhou and recruited college students to participate.[13] Yen's experiments drew people's attention to administration at the county level and provided many ideas on how to reform rural society in China. In 1928, Li Jinghan took over Yen's experiments and later edited *Investigation of the Social Conditions in Ding County* (Dingxian shehui gaikuang diaocha), which became one of the earliest large-scale county-level surveys.[14] Developments in academic sociology and anthropology in China were inseparable from studies conducted directly in the countryside. Yenching University sociology pioneers—such as Yang Kaidao, Li Jinghan, Wu Wenzao, and Fei Xiaotong (Wu's student)—emphasized rural fieldwork.[15] They published a number of textbooks on rural sociology, such as Yang Kaidao's *Rural Sociology* (Nongcun shehuixue).[16] These works dealt with the realities of rural China's society, population, land, economy, finance, education, self-governance, and other issues.

Yenching University's sociology department was founded in 1922 by John Stewart Burgess and D. W. Edwards, whose purpose was to train experts to engage in social welfare and social services.[17] This accompanied a larger wave of Western progressivist thinking about the improvement of humanity through reformed education, alcohol prohibition, urban architecture, eugenics, and government guidance and controls upon various facets of the economy and finances. Graduate programs in "social work," seen as somewhat distinct from the relatively more theoretical sociology, were introduced in major US universities. After earning a doctorate in sociology from Columbia University, Wu Wenzao took a position at Yenching in early 1929 and began to devise a methodology of training students who would work in China. In 1933, Professor Robert Ezra Park (1864–1944) from the University of Chicago—a major center of sociology, early learning, and the new field of social work—was invited by Yenching to teach methodologies of community surveys. Considered one of the most influential figures in early US sociology, Park taught at Chicago from 1914 to 1933, where he played a leading role in the development of the Chicago School within the field of sociology.[18]

Aiming to bring together the best practitioners to form the department at Yenching, Park suggested that Wu invite Alfred Reginald Radcliffe-Brown (1881–1955), an English social anthropologist and one of the founders of structural functionalism, to give talks at Yenching for three months.[19] Subsequently, Wu arranged for Li Anzhai to study anthropology at the University of California at Berkeley, then Li transferred to Yale University. Wu also sent Lin Yaohua to Harvard for doctoral studies in anthropology (Li and Lin are discussed later in this Introduction) and Fei Xiaotong to the London School of Economics to study under Polish anthropologist Bronisław Malinowski. Fei earned a doctoral degree from the University of London in 1938. All of these men completed their degrees, returned to Yenching, and became influential.[20] Under Wu Wenzao's leadership, faculty members and students in sociology, guided by the theories and methodologies of social work and social anthropology, traveled to a wide range of rural areas for their surveys. In 1936, Fei Xiaotong studied Kaixuangong Village (Kaixiangong cun) and completed *Peasant Life in China: A Field Study of Country Life in the Yangzi Valley*.[21] Shen Baoyuan's adviser, Xu Yongshun, published an article titled "Migrants and Crime in Northeastern China" (Dongsansheng zhi yimin yu fanzui).[22] The research of department chair Lin Yaohua, dean of the law college Zheng Linzhuang, and professor of education Liao Taichu focused on the countryside. It is safe to surmise that their work influenced Shen's investigative methods and techniques.

Since the Yenching program would open a rural school in Hope Township, we might mention something about work toward education reform and local self-governance in the preceding decades, as a part of China's overarching rural reconstruction movement. In 1929, Liang Shuming founded the Institution for Village Governance (Cunzhi yanjiu yuan) in Hui County (Huixian), north Henan Province, for the purpose of "rural reconstruction" (*xiangcun jianshe*). In 1931 he established the Rural Research Reconstruction Institute (Xiangcun jianshe yanjiuyuan) in Zouping County, Shandong Province, and published the journal *Village Governance* (Cunzhi) in Beijing. These institutions had the direct purpose of developing rural reconstruction, and the journal offered instructions for the movement in local places and provided a platform for information exchange. Liang wrote several books to express these ideas of rural reconstruction.[23] Entrepreneurs such as Lu Zuofu, who launched an experiment in Beibei (a part of today's Chongqing), also took part in this movement. The project emphasized education as the highest priority for rural areas. In 1934, Lu Zuofu laid out the blueprint for rural reconstruction in his article "The Movement of Rural Reconstruction in Jialing and the Three Georges Areas" (Sichuan Jialingjiang Sanxia de xiangcun jianshe yundong).[24] His main point was that it was possible in a short period to fashion this remote and "backward" area into a developed region.

After the start of the War of Resistance against the Japanese (1937–45), the so-called Great Rear Area became an important base for the reconstruction movement. Known as Dahoufang (the areas behind the frontlines), the region comprised southwest and northwest China under the Nationalist government during the war. James Yen's Association to Promote Chinese Common Education shifted its focus to Sichuan. In the spring of 1936 the association worked with the Sichuan provincial government to establish a committee devoted to this goal. In April 1937 the Sichuan provincial government set up Xindu as an experimental county governed directly from provincial offices. In September 1939 the Nationalist government announced the "Outline of County Organization at All Levels" (Xian geji zuzhi gangyao), which adopted the experiences of Yen's work in Ding and Xindu counties. Given the special circumstances and the important position of Sichuan in the war, the Nationalist government decided, on March 1, 1940, that with the association's assistance, Sichuan would be the first province to implement the new organization.[25]

During the 1920s and 1930s there were more than six hundred organizations and institutions engaged in the activities of rural reconstruction, with over a thousand locations and a variety of experiments, such as Yen's area in Ding County, Liang Shuming's work in Zouping County (Shandong), and Qinghe (Beijing) undertaken by Yenching University—most of these dealing with education.[26] In addition to rural education, the experiments involved rural self-government and such agricultural reforms as seed-stock improvement, pest control, and other activities. There were attempts to solve the problem of farm debts by establishing cooperatives and credit unions, rural hospitals, and rural public health-care systems. They also rolled out slogans and teachings aimed at the rural residents to reform such "evil" social customs as foot-binding, drug abuse, gambling, child marriage, mercenary marriage, infanticide, and other "bad habits." During the summer of 1945, Shen Baoyuan was in Hope Township, where Yenching University had opened a summer school. This would be the portal through which Shen connected with Lei Mingyuan and his family.

★   ★   ★

It is not a coincidence that Shen Baoyuan's academic work occurred during the national crisis. After war broke out, many colleges and universities closed, and the Nationalist government began to relocate them to the interior. In the early years of the war (1937–40), almost all universities along

China's southeastern coast, except certain missionary institutions such as Yenching and Fu Jen Catholic, moved to southwestern and northwestern China. According to the statistics of the Nationalist government's Ministry of Education, seventy-seven colleges and universities moved to these rear areas and resumed classes, but seventeen quickly closed. After World War II broke out in the Pacific in December 1941, Yenching University moved from Beijing to Chengdu, where it resumed classes in 1942 under the English name "Yen Ching University in Chen [*sic*] Tu."[27] The university experienced some difficulties finding a new location, but it finally selected the site of a middle and elementary school on Shaanxi Street as its campus.[28]

Emphasizing social service, Li Anzhai (1900–1985) and Lin Yaohua (1910–2000) served as successive chairs of Yenching's sociology department. Li was a scholar of ethnology and sociology. From 1934 to 1936 he studied anthropology at the University of California–Berkeley and Yale University, and after returning to China in 1936, he taught at Yenching. Li's major works include *Aesthetics*, *A Sociological Study of the Book of Rituals and the Book of Rites*, and *Significs*.[29] Lin was one of the pioneers of Chinese anthropology, and his major works were on clans and families.[30] The department encouraged and organized students to participate in social surveys and services. Professors thought this would lead students to partake in activities that would aid in the necessary organization of people during the war and to develop a better understanding of their social responses in general. Given this backdrop, it seems a matter of course that Shen Baoyuan chose a Paoge-oriented family whom she might help and study.

Yenching students at the time were also deeply influenced by the Chinese Communist Party (CCP). On October 15, 1944, "the progressive students" (*jinbu xuesheng*)—namely, leftists from various universities, including Yenching—established an Association for Democratic Youth in Chengdu (Chengdu minzhu qingnian xiehui). The Chinese Communist revolution was already a force based in numerous parts of the south-central, western, and northwestern countryside, and the CCP was encouraging young people to go to rural areas to better understand the peasants, who were beginning to function, through indoctrination and training, as a key part of Mao's radical formation of local, revolutionary militias. The Yenching students who went to the countryside were not only influenced by their professors; they were also responding to the CCP's call. In the spring of 1945 the Association for Democratic Youth in Chengdu arranged for the performance of various services during the summer break; members of rural work teams (*nongcun gongzuo dui*) provided medical service and medicines, organized evening classes, gathered people in support of the war, and looked into landlord-tenant relations.[31] I did not find direct information to determine whether Shen Baoyuan's investigation in Hope Township was organized by the CCP, but a connection is not implausible. Her leftist ideology (explored in future chapters) would have had common ground with party thinking.

★   ★   ★

Let us look further at Shen's intellectual positions, her habits of expression, as a young academic. We can take the first step visually, by observing the title page of her bachelor's thesis. It reads:

Thesis for Bachelor of Laws, Department of Sociology, the Privately Established Yenching University

> Examiners:
>   Supervisor: Xu Yongshun
>   Chair: Lin Yaohua
>   Dean: Zheng Linzhuang
> Name of the student: Shen Baoyuan
>   Student number: W42039
> April 1945
> Title: "A Family of the Rural Social Organization"

Chapter 11, "Looking for the Storyteller," examines the academic stances of Shen's mentors (those mentioned on the title page). What emerges is the activist nature of China's first sociologists and anthropologists. In addition, Shen's use of the term *shetuan*—a contraction of *shehui tuanti* (literally, a band or group emerging from and/or advocating for a local society)—is quite purposeful, revealing a facet of her thinking that I delve into later. She was careful to use what her profession would have considered to be an accurate term as well as a sociologically acceptable point of view—one that aligned to some extent with newly developing Communist Party attitudes toward revolutionary society and the operations of unsanctioned "bands of brothers" (arguably an acceptable way of taking *shetuan*). What the outside world was calling "secret societies" in this way became more neutral and possibly ideologically trainable. Next, we sort out the effectiveness of that line of thinking.

Shen's abstract preceding her thesis reveals more. She reverts to the blunt term "secret society." It begins:

This thesis aims at a dissection of the Paoge, a society that currently exists in China; it analyzes the history of a Paoge leader's life in order to explain the functions as well as the fluctuations and flourishing of a secret society's local community control.

    To match up theory with practice, I chose a head of the Paoge who was very active ten years ago in a farm village. I would like to examine the everyday life of this lower-level leader in a local place, and the relationship between his family and the locale in order to advance by one more step our understanding of the goals and capabilities of that society. Therefore, what I draw on includes the case-study methodology, an examination of the relationship between his social background and community, and a portrait of the typical circumstances of a Paoge member. In addition, I draw on a new socio-anthropological methodology—the Operational Method.[32] From a functionalist viewpoint, it studies the phenomenon of Paoge society.

The Paoge society is the foremost one of the secret societies, always hiding its secrets from the outside, and maintaining an oblivious distance from other organizations. It is a unique specimen and becomes a special form of the secret society because it has its "secrecy" and "sacrality" while also being "quasi-overt" and "tainted," which internally expresses a complexity and richness. Out of my own curiosity and interest, and after careful consideration, I decided to choose this topic.

Here we see that Shen Baoyuan was not rigid about terminological correctness. Perhaps she simply desired to be truthful to her mentors and at the same time reveal her own commonsense approach to everyday life in China and its dramatic implications. We encounter another term from academic jargon: "operational method." It is safe to deduce that this is Shen's English for "structural functionalism"—an important theory of sociology that had been acutely noticed and taken up among China's first sociologists. She took care to keep her rather bold and personalistic approach contained within the profession and its accepted tools.

Looking further into Shen's habits of thought, let's examine the first paragraphs of the main text of her report:

Since childhood I yearned for rural life very much and appreciated the natural scenery much more than the manmade cities. I loved the naive smiles on the faces of rural companions, who were far and away better than the cunning boys and girls in the city. My heart often stayed behind on the far shore of life, with its blue mountains and green rivers and quietly fell in love with the naturally shaped, beautiful countryside.

Today, however, as a rural activist, my appreciation for the beautiful scenery has been transformed into sympathy and respect for rural people. When I think of the farmers' hardships, I always feel a deep apology for them, so I want an opportunity for living, playing, and working with peasants. I have a selfish reason: I cannot gain peace in the noisy city and miss the quiet life in the countryside. I want to practice simplicity, to work hard to change for the better my bad habit of boastfulness in order to return to the natural state of mankind. Therefore, out of a preference and a hope present from birth, I have decided to serve rural areas from now on.

In the summer of 1945, the slogan "The Intellectuals Go Down to the Countryside" was seen everywhere. By using our summer break, we want to spread around the fruits of rural labor. On the one hand, we can express our highest respect to peasants, and to gain knowledge that one cannot get from books, and on the other hand, we repay those uncrowned kings, the kind-hearted peasants, for their hard work and suffering.

Shen enthusiastically welcomed the notion that students needed to link their learning to practice in the field and to mingle with ordinary people. Since childhood, she notes, she had yearned for the rural life and its environment: the hustle of urban life held little interest for her. Noting that rural people were honest, Shen did not trust "cunning" city residents. In fact, she admitted that her participation in the investigation was "for a selfish reason": she could derive no peace in the city, and she longed for "the quietude of the village life."

Yet we must also grant Shen the bravery to say that those childish thoughts have been supplanted by more socially minded ones. She has transformed from a frilly dreamer into what today we might call a "social justice warrior." She has dared to attack her own naivety and self-imposed guilt concerning social worlds not her own and thus thought to take on the harshness encountered by the suffering "other"—a class of people identified as potential leaders of an idealized new society. Shen sympathizes with that so-called lower class, revealing guilt over her privileged life. She has "sympathy and respect" for the peasants and a desire to "live, play, and work with them."

Shen was an idealist, obviously, and felt uncomfortable with her own background. She wrote that fieldwork was a response to the current slogan about "going down to the countryside" and thus she will use her vacation to work with farmers, express her respect, and learn beyond mere books from them.[33] Shen's professors at Yenching offered direct examples of this idealism. Professor Liao Taichu in the Department of Education had established a rural service station in Hope Township. During four years at the Chengdu campus, Lin Yaohua, sociology department chair, had spent three summer breaks in the minority areas of Liangshan and Xikang (Map 1).[34] Shen's investigation followed such practices and shared the class-oriented values that were regularly preached through Communist ideology.

This look at Shen Baoyuan's academic environment better frames the rural fieldwork and activism that we encounter moving forward. Her thesis may be regarded as a product of early Chinese sociology and anthropology and a result of influential academic trends since the 1920s and 1930s. She briefly mentions in her work that Lin Yaohua taught her the viewpoint of structural functionalism, an academic theory that regarded society as a complex structure whose parts (births, deaths, schools, work, rituals, associations, and so forth) work together to function as an organism. This theory tended to observe the everyday outcomes of the parts to correlate the data. One may surmise that, to a certain extent, Lin's study of families influenced Shen's own topic choice. The theory of structural functionalism had become popular in 1930s and 1940s China and went on to dominate Western academic sociology, as seen in the work by Harvard University's Talcott Parsons in the 1930s through the 1960s and beyond (through his students).

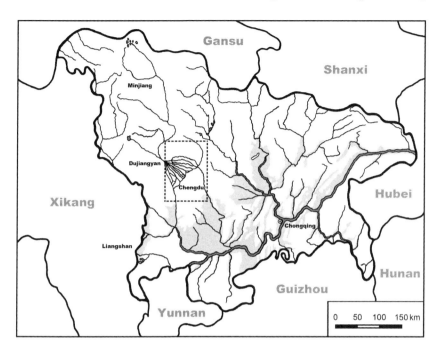

MAP 1.　Sichuan in the 1940s (Map 4 is the inset area in Map 1).

When the University of Chicago's Robert Ezra Park visited Yenching, he taught field investigation and community studies, inspiring Wu Wenzao, Lin Yaohua, and Fei Xiaotong to combine the methodologies of sociology and anthropology. During his visit in China, Radcliffe-Brown was the adviser for Lin Yaohua's master's thesis, and under Radcliffe-Brown's influence Lin advocated the new sociological and anthropological methods of structural functionalist research for the study of families. This advocacy turned immediately to village families in the west, due mostly to the fact that the war had pushed everything away from the northern and eastern cities.[35]

Shen Baoyuan came to Hope Township during this academic environment. The training she had received from Yenching University and the political and ideological currents there no doubt impacted her investigation. She held onto her original, if naïve, intentions concerning rural areas and rural problems, and she sympathized with peasants and their situations. Such intentions apparently played a crucial role in her observations of rural reality. These simplistic intentions were melded with some more complex strains of theory—the result of academic sociological and anthropological developments from before her time, developments that have escaped thorough investigation and retelling.

⋆   ⋆   ⋆

In April 1946, Shen Baoyuan completed the report and titled it "Yige nongcun shetuan jiating" ("A Family of the Rural Organization") as her bachelor's thesis for the Department of Sociology at Yenching University. The report consists of forty-three pages, plus a three-page abstract. The thesis is written on the special stationary printed for Yenching University that provided spaces for 576 Chinese characters on each page. Each page is folded along the center line, where "Yanjing daxue biye lunwen" (Graduation thesis of Yenching University) was printed, resembling the A and B folded pages of traditional woodblock printed books. The thesis has a total of twenty-four thousand or so Chinese characters for the main text. A three-page appendix contains approximately a thousand characters and covers six parts: (1) discussion of the origins of the Paoge and the Paoge's canonical book *Haidi* (further discussed in Chapter 4); (2) definition of the Paoge and its other names; (3) examples of Paoge secret codes; (4) Paoge internal regulations; (5) examples of Paoge argot; and (6) a bibliography of Paoge canonical writings.

Shen's title page tells us more about other people who inhabited this academic world—namely her Yenching University mentors, including thesis adviser Xu Yongshun and two reviewers, Lin Yaohua and Zheng Linzhuang.[36] In addition, in the preface Shen offered a special appreciation to Liao Taichu (Liao T'ai-ch'u) for providing her with his English-language paper on secret societies in Sichuan titled "The Ko Lao Hui in Szechuan." Although Shen Baoyuan did not mention the title per se, Liao published only one article on the Paoge. Shen completed her thesis in 1946, but Liao's article was published in 1947. What Shen read, apparently, was the manuscript of the Liao's article before its publication. Since the completion of Shen's report in 1946, although it has always been listed in Yenching University's catalog of sociological theses, no later scholar or any other writer to my knowledge has recognized its value.[37] Shen's academically oriented report, coupled with contemporary social surveys, archives, novels, and memoirs, shows us that the rural activists in Republican-era China made outstanding contributions to our current understanding of rural China. From their particular perspectives, they all have contributed to a picture of the Paoge in 1940s Sichuan.

PART ONE

The Haunted Past of Hope Township

CHAPTER 1

A Public Execution

A TRAGEDY TOOK PLACE IN 1939. Many years later, the villagers still clearly remembered the cruelty of the murder: a father's anger had turned into a criminal act. The death on the riverbank lingered unpleasantly, and the people could not understand "his vicious heart, as a father."[1] This was the kind of utterance that we find in Shen Baoyuan's retelling of the incident. She must have gleaned the narrative from villagers' stories, bit by bit, adding along the way her own analysis and emotion. There seems to have been no report of it in Chengdu-area newspapers, even though the story, with its many tendrils, took place in nearby Chengdu, in little Hope Township (Wangzhen).

Before we move another step toward Shen's (and in part my own) reconstruction of the morbid execution carried out by a Paoge master named Lei Mingyuan, we ought to physically locate the man, his daughter Shuqing, and Hope. The wide setting is rural Sichuan's small locales, where secret societies ran untrammeled and free to exert power. The fine details of the incident played out not just anywhere in Sichuan, but around the Chengdu Plain. The area in general, although relatively isolated in earlier times, has been and still is one of the most densely populated areas of inland China. It was also one of the most affluent, and in an earlier time the province of Sichuan was one of only two provinces with a dedicated governor-general: other provinces shared such administrators. Rice production was the largest in the upper Yangzi region, benefitting as it did from the Dujiangyan irrigation system, which was originally constructed in the third century BC and still helps to control the Min River. The result was (and is) an ecologically stable and attractive region (see map in the Introduction).

In modern scholarship the most important and influential study of

Sichuan was made decades ago by anthropologist G. William Skinner. It deals mainly with marketing structures in the Chengdu Plain and provides an analytical model of the way local markets fit into local people's needs and how everyday economic life was tied at many different levels to these market structures.[2] After Skinner, a glaring need for a social-historical analysis of this area of Sichuan resulted in a new sort of research. My own work, published in 1993, answers a part of this need. I have provided a general picture of developments starting in the early Qing period, and my findings have focused on both the rising world of migrants at that time (a situation that has been characterized through the expression "filling up Sichuan with Hunan and Hubei people" [*Huguang tian Sichuan*]) and the related problem of shortages of arable land factored with steep population growth since the mid-Qing era.[3] Thus few people in the last century can have claimed they were descendants of Sichuan natives.[4]

In late Ming and early Qing times the area was plagued by war. In 1644, for example, Zhang Xianzhong, leader of the peasant rebellion, took Sichuan and established a regime when so many people were killed during the war.[5] But by the early 1700s, Sichuan's economy recovered and the immigrants poured in. The newcomers, despite their other dialects and ingrained duties to their native lineages and temples, tended to be active and striving; they set up guilds and native-place associations; they built shrines, temples, and association halls to service their gods, sages, and ancestors.[6] They became heads of their associations as well as leaders of their local communities; they established connections with court-appointed officials and helped to provide for security, militias, granaries, relief and orphanages, philanthropy, and so on. These associations and the endemic populist, charitable programs that drove them became in some sense more important than clans or even the state itself, making the area a fertile ground for secret societies like the Paoge.

By way of contrast to the warm and productive Chengdu Plain, it is easy to imagine that in North China in the harsh winter it became increasingly difficult for households the more isolated from each other they were. Farming settlements in the north were therefore arranged cheek to jowl to fend off the demands of the environment. But people in the Chengdu Plain did not have such a problem. Settlement patterns in the more dispersed and much more commercialized Chengdu Plain saw looser relationships, and families lived relatively more independently. Strictly speaking, grouped families there should not be called villages; the term *settlements* might be more appropriate.[7] Such interrelationships among settlements provided advantageous conditions for trade in the Chengdu Plain. In addition, the ubiquitous bamboo groves created a stable living environment, and good wells were plentiful. At the edges of the groves, other trees and crops

FIGURE 1.1 A typical scene in the Chengdu Plain in the 1940s: Farmhouses scattered around farmland. *Source*: Photograph by Joseph Needham, 1943–46. Reproduced courtesy of the Needham Research Institute, Cambridge University.

were also planted, such as fruits and vegetables, offering a variety of agricultural products for trade in cash and food. Chickens prowled for food in the bamboo groves; ducks and geese wandered in paddy fields or ditches. If a stranger approached a house, a dog would bark. And out at the edges of the groves, farmers buried their venerated dead. The pattern of life, close to the fields, was an expected combination of work, daily routines, and tending to ecological systems (Figure 1.1). Lu Yongji, magistrate of Mianzhu county (Mianzhu xian) during the Kangxi period (1662–1722), wrote in one of his poems that "villages were withered and fallen after the war, and half the residents came from Hubei. Houses were built in the bamboo groves, and neighbors could see each other over the short distance."[8] On every anniversary of the death of their ancestors, family members and relatives went to the graves for rituals.

A classmate of Shen Baoyuan, Bai Jinjuan worked in a rural social survey project. She described a farmer's house only a few miles away from Hope Township:

Woman Fu's house is located on a small path three miles from the local market, surrounded by rice paddies, lush bamboo trees, and a bamboo-fence wall. The main gate of the house faces south. There are eleven to twelve rooms in the north, east, and west sections. Three north rooms have pass-through doors, and three east rooms have the same. An east side-room contains a kitchen, and the south room is the family hall for worship of the Buddha. A big west room is as large as four; it is a storage for grain and tools. In both the northeast corner and the kitchen, there is a small door going to the backyard, which has a stream dividing if from the paddy field. Along the stream there is a fence with a door leading to the stream for fetching water. By the stream there are large stones for washing clothes. In the yard also are bamboo trees and a line of pigsties, feeding eight pigs. The toilet is south of the pigsties. At two sides of the main gate, straw sheds are built for the water buffalos.[9]

If we think that Woman Fu was a landlord or at least a rich peasant, we would be wrong. Fu was actually a tenant, a widow over fifty, still with several children.[10] People like her, toward the poorer end of the spectrum, had numerous ways to earn cash, see profits, and stay afloat. A high-density network of rural markets was established in the Chengdu Plain by which farmers traveled an average of fewer than five kilometers to reach a market. Chengdu was the commercial base of the whole region, and a well-developed trading system was established centered on it, including regional centers, local towns, town markets, and rural markets.[11] There were market regulations that prohibited "bad practices" such as cheating and monopolizing. If a dispute occurred, mediation would occur to avoid violent conflicts. The area Shen Baoyuan investigated was very close to the place Skinner studied (Zhonghechang in Map 2).[12] According to Skinner, the market network schedule, which avoided conflicting trading days, encouraged small traders. Rural peddlers traveled the market schedule, circulating goods between the central market and the small markets. Rural markets were an important place for socialization, where people could use wine shops and teahouses; peasants gathered for business or met friends, or discussed local news and events, official decrees, and gossip (Figure 1.2).[13]

The smallest rural settlement in the Chengdu Plain was called a *yaodian* (or *yaodianzi*); this rural shopping and trading nexus included such establishments as small grocery stores, teahouses, wine shops, and restaurants; usually these places had no more than one room for business. *Yaodian* often became social centers for rural areas. People always went to them for their pastimes, and the Paoge master Lei Mingyuan himself spent countless days in a *yaodian* in the Hope Township area. In slack seasons people spent a lot of time at low-class teahouses. In the Chengdu Plain many landlords lived in the market towns, where entertainment was limited, so teahouses were centers of amusement for them as well.[14]

In Sichuan many such places were run by the Paoge. This brings us to the question of Hope Township, a small settlement dotted just outside Chengdu, on the large, well-settled plain. We do not know with absolute

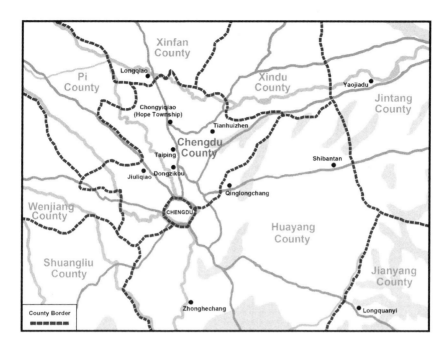

MAP 2. Chongyiqiao (Hope Township) and the surrounding area

certainty what or where this town was. One of the purposes of this chapter is to arrive at the best possible answer. We know that Shen Baoyuan did not use real names in her report. In the preface she wrote: "Because this thesis is a study of a secret society and its leaders, it is not necessary to disclose the objects of study; this is the professional ethic of social workers." Shen wrote about "Hope Township outside the West City Gate of Chengdu," but one notices that there does not seem to be a "Hope Township" on any historical record or today's maps. Shen did not state that she changed the place-name, but it is quite probable that she did. Fortunately, a locatable village may be the right candidate.

Chapter 11, "Looking for the Storyteller," recounts my contact with the elderly Shen Baoyuan, who now lives in Guangzhou. I failed to get useful information from her about Hope Township, however, so I pressed on in my hunt. I gathered information about Yenching University's campus in Chengdu and found the following passage in the entry of 1945 from the appendix of a chronicle of events given in a 1999 book titled *A Draft History of Yenching University* (Yanjing daxue shigao): "When the summer break started in mid-July, student organizations of Yenching University organized and funded two rural service groups (*xiangcun gongzuo fuwutuan*), working

FIGURE 1.2   A street in a rural market town in Sichuan. *Source*: Photograph by Joseph Needham, 1943–46. Reproduced courtesy of the Needham Research Institute, Cambridge University.

with West China University (Huaxi daxue) and Ginling College (Jinling nüzi daxue). They traveled to Longquanyi and Yaojiadu (see Map 2), in Jintang County for one and a half months' activities of rural education, hygiene, anti-Japanese propaganda, and surveys of rural society."[15]

This time frame is consistent with that described in Shen's 1946 report: "The first day we arrived in the village was July 14, and during five days, until July 19, we visited all kinds of people, especially local leaders and leaders of the [Paoge] society.... For one month and five days, from July 19 to August 24, I collected materials every day for my thesis."[16] Shen's investigation of Hope Township therefore might have been a direct part of that summer agenda detailed in the *Draft History of Yenching University* appendix. She wrote: "At that time, through the support of the rural service from the student relief association (Xuesheng jiuji hui) and the Department of Sociology, I and two other classmates, and an assistant of our school, carried out pioneering work. We were ready to work hard in this place." Shen revealed specifics about the project: "Our first work was to establish friendships with local people. Then we wanted to know the general condition of rural life, the situation of peasant families, and information about local power, etc. We planned to do work that included a peasants' school [*nongmin xuexiao*], tutoring, medical service, epidemic prevention, health guidance, letter writing, lectures about current events, exhibitions of news and pictures, and screening of movies."[17] Here the "peasants' school" was no doubt the "rural summer school" (*nongcun buxi xuexiao*) mentioned several times in her report.

The market town Longquanyi, mentioned in the *Draft History of Yenching University*, was in fact located southeast of Chengdu. Photographer Carl Mydans (1906–2004), connected with *Life* magazine, took many photos of Longquanyi in 1941. Shen made clear in her thesis that when she first went to "Hope," or perhaps on other days when she had to go there from Chengdu, she would travel out of the city via "North Alley through the West City Gate" (Ximen beixiangzi). However, a 1940s Chengdu map shows that North Alley was near the North City Gate (Map 3). If she traveled specifically to Longquanyi, then she actually would have exited Chengdu through the East City Gate and then traveled southeast. Therefore, Hope Township was surely *not* Longquanyi. Moreover, because North Alley was in the direction of Jintang County, I guessed that Hope Township might be Yaojiadu, in Jintang County. Some other early memoirs also mentioned this village. A woman named Su Yu, for example, wrote: "I spent my whole summer break in Yaojiadu, Jintang County, where I participated in rural service activities organized by the Democratic Youth Association led by the underground CCP [Chinese Communist Party]. At the time I had finished the first year of journalism at Yenching University and returned to school ahead of schedule after the Japanese surrender."[18]

For some time I assumed that Shen's "Hope Township" was Yaojiadu, thus I was puzzled that several times in her investigation she mentioned going out from West City Gate to reach "Hope Township." Had she erred in her report? Was she perhaps not familiar enough with the layout of Chengdu? By putting certain details together, however, I now am satisfied with another candidate—the township of Chongyiqiao, a northwestern suburb of Chengdu. This was the site of Yenching University's Rural Research Service Station (Nongcun yanjiu fuwu zhan), one of those projects rolled out after the university moved to Chengdu. According to an essay titled "Thirty Years of the Department of Sociology of Yenching University," given the university's major difficulty in keeping students on track during wartime, they realized that the new locale provided opportunities.[19] The essay defines three kinds of places for student research activities: the borderland, rural sites, and cities. In the *Draft History of Yenching University*, we find out that in the spring of 1943, Professor Liao Taichu in the Department of Education led a team teachers and students, who joined up with Law School students, to set up a "station for rural research" at the Xia Family Temple (Xiajiasi) in Chongyiqiao.[20]

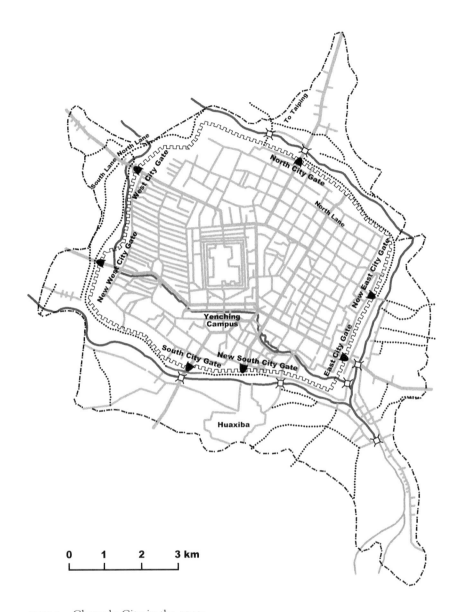

MAP 3. Chengdu City in the 1940s

The Law School had received financial support during these years from the Rockefeller Foundation to establish rural services in Chongyiqiao, to effect social investigation and social services. The station offered peasants continuing education, publication of monthly peasant news (titled *Nongmin xiaoxi yuekan*), small loans, instructions for visitors of peasant families, and training for rural youth.[21] The students and faculty conducted in-depth investigations of local political, economic, and social conditions, and they wrote reports and research papers on the Gelaohui (that is, the Paoge), private schools, Chinese medicine, apprenticeships, and so on.[22] Liao remarked that even near Chengdu, the culture of the countryside was "very backward," and an "evil force was very powerful in the local places." Therefore, he had selected Chongyiqiao to bring uplift to the rural populace.[23] The busy and ideologically promising mission that was set out for Professor Liao's project might have inspired Shen Baoyuan to choose Chongyiqiao. In addition, Liao had written significant research on the Paoge. Before its publication in *Pacific Affairs*, Liao offered the manuscript to Shen Baoyuan for her reference, as Shen mentioned in her thesis report.[24] In all, Shen would have gained certain advantages by taking up her work in Chongyiqiao. She mentioned in her report that the site had a "Yenching University Office of Services," seemingly the one organized by Liao Taichu.[25]

Another discovery confirmed the viability of Chongyiqiao as the actual site of Shen's Hope Township. I found the following in the *Gazetteer of Chengdu Streets* (Chengdu jiexiang zhi): "The location of today's North Alley and South Alley was a route outside the city wall of the Old West City Gate; it connected northern and southern routes."[26] This description led me to look more closely at the same 1940s map, and I found a small alley outside the Old West City Gate that was a south-north route. Divided by the city gate, the alley going north is called North Alley and one toward the south, South Alley (see Map 3). Apparently, the North Alley that Shen mentioned is this one rather than that running near the North City Gate.

With that evidence, Shen Baoyuan's description of the location of Hope Township is easier to understand: "Going out from the West City Gate and traveling through North Alley, passing Ping Hamlet (Pingxiang), and then walking five *li* [3.2 *li* = 1 mile] one arrives in Hope Township." Because North Alley was south-north, although Shen went out from the West City Gate, she actually went northward, not westward. Here Ping Hamlet should be Taiping Hamlet (Taiping xiang), one of fourteen townships in Chengdu County. Shen mentioned that Ping Hamlet was an "area for wartime evacuation" that had become "crowded" and taken on a "mixture of urban and rural lifestyles." From there, "one walked forward for five *li* and reached the area of Hope Township."[27] Looking at Map 2, it became clear that this was in fact the location of Chongyiqiao. Based on a *Gazetteer of Sichuan* (Sichuan tongzhi) compiled during the Yongzheng period (1723–1735), "Chongyiq-iao Station (Chongyiqiao pu) was in Chengdu County, 20 *li* [6 miles or so] northwest of Chengdu City."[28] It is worthwhile to consider that the charac-ter *chong* has a meaning that softly resonates with that of *wang*. Thus when Shen devised a cover name, she could have given out some kind of clue.

Well-known scholar Ye Shengtao lived in Chengdu during wartime. In his diary Ye mentioned several times visiting the famous historian Gu Jie-gang in Chongyiqiao. For example, after breakfast on November 17, 1940, he went out Chengdu's South City Gate to see a friend, stayed there for half an hour, then they took the bus to Chongyiqiao. In about an hour and a half, they arrived in Chongyiqiao, then took a poultry wheelbar-row (*jigongche*, a one-wheel car in the Chengdu Plain) to the Lai Family Complex (Laijiayuan) (Figure 1.3). Ye stayed there for a night and went to Chengdu with Gu Jiegang in the afternoon. They took the wheelbarrow again and did not enter the city from the North City Gate but through the West City Gate, as Shen Baoyuan did on her route to the so-called Hope Township. "It was beautiful to see bamboo groves along the stream," Ye wrote. It took two and half hours to arrive at Chengdu, then they changed their mode of transport from *jigongche* to rickshaw.[29]

Chongyiqiao was just a small place. During the Kangxi period (1662–1722), it gradually was transformed into a market town and later one of fourteen townships in Chengdu County.[30] Because of its important location, Chongyiqiao had close economic relationships with the other market towns of Chengdu County, such as Xipuchang, Tuqiaochang, Qinglongchang, and Tianhuizhen, and some market towns in other counties, like Longq-iao of Xinfan County (see Map 2). Closer to modern day, a secretary of Mao Zedong named Tian Jiaying suggested during the Great Leap Forward (1958–1960) that the name of the place be changed to Dafeng (literally, "great harvest"). Tian, a native of Chongyiqiao, found that in February 1959 cadres were exaggerating harvest yields, which contributed to mis-management of the harvest and then massive deaths from starvation. He suggested the name change because the word *chongyi* meant "respectful of righteousness"; he felt the town was no longer worthy of that but should, perhaps sardonically, receive a fantastic "great harvest." Tian committed sui-cide after he was wrongly accused during the Cultural Revolution.[31] Shen's and Tian's investigations were only fourteen years apart. History seems to ridicule us: in a few short years, with a major regime change meant to clean up the brutality, tragic events continued to haunt such a little place.

Chongyiqiao was urbane enough, however, to have guild halls and na-tive-place associations.[32] There were also the ubiquitous teahouses. When Wang Qingyuan investigated teahouses in the Chengdu Plain in 1944, he saw "over thirty teahouses" in Chongyiqiao.[33] Lei Mingyuan, known for

FIGURE 1.3   A wheelbarrow with umbrella (*jigongche*) in the Chengdu Plain. *Source*: Photograph by Sidney D. Gamble, ca. 1917–1919. Reproduced courtesy of Sidney D. Gamble Photographs, David M. Rubenstein Rare Book & Manuscript Library, Duke University.

lounging in teahouses, might have been there in Chongyiqiao when Wang Qingyuan came to investigate. Lei might even have come into contact with the family of dissident intellectual and writer Tie Liu. Tie's long autobiography, describing his life's ups and downs, recalls his hometown—Chongyiqiao. Tie's family was poor and lived in an area in Chongyiqiao called Gao Family Alley Village (Gaojiaxiang cun), but in the late 1930s, when Tie was a boy, his family moved to Chengdu.[34] When Tie's family resided in Chongyiqiao, it was the period during which Lei Mingyuan's power over the wider area had reached its peak.

★   ★   ★

Hope Township (Chongyiqiao) was just this sort of rural market town where the murderer, Lei Mingyuan, lived with his family. Lei, naturally in those times, was the head of the household. Although he was only a tenant in his property, he was deputy chief of the local branch of the Paoge and was thus called the vice helmsman (*fu duobazi*). Later in this tale, we learn about the man who was a rank above Lei—that is, the helmsman (Appendix 1 details the Paoge ranks). Even though Lei was not exactly a full helmsman, the title made him an important man.

At this time, his daughter Shuqing was a teenager. She was Woman Lei's stepdaughter, born by Lei Mingyuan's first wife, Woman Huang. Huang did not live in Hope Township but in another market town nearby, taking care of Lei's father (Chapter 7, "Entering the Paoge," provides more details about the wives and children of Lei Mingyuan's two families; see Appendix 2 for the Lei family tree). After finishing a village private school, Shuqing's opportunities to receive further education were complete; she stayed at home doing needlework, a common skill for Chinese women to pursue. It was almost 1940, a time of increasing modernization in China and of a certain Westernization of mores and social horizons—even in out-of-the-way places. Nevertheless, Lei did not think that education was important for his daughter.

Earlier in that disturbing year of 1939, the family had hired a young tailor to make clothes for the family. He was known to chat with the young Shuqing, and as time went by their relationship became closer. We will likely never know what stage of their relationship had developed, but a rumor began to spread accusing them of having done "a shameful thing." When the gossip reached Lei Mingyuan's ear, he exploded and vowed to punish them both. Woman Lei—we do not know her real name, as Shen Baoyuan called her "Lei Daniang" (Woman Lei)—recognized that the situation was dangerous and managed to help Shuqing to quickly run away from home. The young couple fled to Chengdu, hiding at the home of the tailor's family. However, Lei led his Paoge brothers there, rushed into the house, and caught the two. They tied up the couple and brought them back to Hope, where they were taken straight to the riverbank at gunpoint. Lei was enraged. Terrified and shivering, Shuqing and the young tailor were "without even a word to defend themselves."[35] They may have known Lei's temper well and that no matter what they said, they could not save themselves.

Shen detailed snippets of people's memories of the incident in her report, building on how each recounted their versions:

This was an execution procession: a father marches off to shoot his daughter. Many villagers were too scared to come out to watch the tragic scene, and they wept, whispered, and prayed. Some good-hearted men rushed to the site to try to stop the enraged father, but Lei shouted: "Damn, I am going to kill anyone who tries to stop me, and my pistol is not merciful!" Thus they had to step back with their anger and some were so afraid of saying anything. At this moment, people could do nothing but watch the killing begin, because villagers knew his vicious temper very well.

People quietly watched the "death procession" led by the young girl's father, but many did not want to come out for the "tragic scene." Sad and hopeless, some prayed silently while a few courageous people tried to stop the murder. The angry Lei easily thwarted their attempts.[36] The procession walked closer and closer to the riverbank. Shuqing and the young tailor trudged toward death at Lei's gunpoint. Woman Lei followed, crying, carrying candles and "paper money" for burning later on, as an offering to the dead. Although Woman Lei was usually an active person, as Shen described her, she felt helpless as she watched her stepdaughter's final movements. Facing her tyrannical husband, perhaps Woman Lei lost courage and could merely acknowledge that her stepdaughter's death was inevitable.[37]

Shen's report included this dialog between Master Lei and his young daughter, from just before the execution:

"Big girl, don't come back here when this is all finished!"

"No, I won't," she answered.

The father added: "Do not come back and haunt us by making banging sounds above the house!"

"I won't."

"If you want revenge, you should find the one who harmed you and do not look for me!"

"Oh I won't."

As recorded in Shen's report, the daughter lowered her head and did not look at her father's face when she answered. Apparently, this cruel man was afraid of her ghost coming back to haunt him. In traditional China many believed that a person's soul after death could, if disturbed for some reason, return to its home.[38] Most disturbing is reading about Lei's negotiation for his future peace of mind with his victim (his own daughter). It is difficult to rationalize such premodern beliefs about ghosts with modern notions about death.

It is no doubt right to imagine that Shuqing, at that moment, had no hope she would survive. She would likely have been familiar with her father's weak character: he would not yield to bonds of kinship. To save face and to maintain his reputation and authority were more important than his own daughter's life. Given Shen's description of Shuqing meekly agreeing not to haunt her father, Shuqing probably did not beg for her life; rather, she likely just waited for her last moment. Perhaps frightened about her life's miserable prospects after being branded with an "immoral relationship," Shuqing thought herself better off dead. How, living such a life, would she face her tyrannical father every day? How would she deal with villagers' looks and continuing rumors? If she really loved the young man, it was now useless, since her lover was dead. It seems likely that she wanted to die simply to gain relief from a life of potential suffering. Keeping silent and weeping were the only stance she could assume.

Shen Baoyuan's report continues her rendition of the violent incident:

Bang! With the sound of a gunshot, the first one struck was the boy, who fell into the waves. Then, the second shot, and the girl immediately fell into the river. Two kind-hearted villagers cried out anxiously: "I've come to save them! I would like to pay! I would like to pay!" "Please anyone around here: do the good thing!" However, two of Lei's men jumped into the rushing river and pressed the girl's head into the water. They looked like they had a real grudge against the departed. The river, sounding urgent and its waves rolling swiftly, carried away the tragic boy and girl, both pitiful creatures buried by the old code of ethics.

This occurred under the public's eye. Some good folk did step up to beg that Master Lei and his Paoge brothers spare the two youngsters. Surely the villagers could not believe what they saw next, after the shots: Lei's men went into the river to "press the girl's head into the water."[39] Shuqing struggled but soon lost her strength, and her body floated away with the waves. After Lei and his followers left the riverbank, a morose Woman Lei, alone, burned the paper money for her stepdaughter. The riverbank calmed, and the river kept rushing by in rolling waves. After that, everything almost seemed not to have happened.

A few miles away, Woman Huang—Shuqing's biological mother, Lei Mingyuan's first wife—heard the bad news and fell into deep grief. She could not imagine how Lei could have killed his daughter by his own hand. However, Huang could not openly express her grief; she had to protect the "family honor" and "husband prestige." She could not even cry, so she secretly sobbed, to bury her "infinite pain and endless bitterness in her heart."[40] From Shen's report, we see that Huang did not dare defend her daughter and only quietly endured the deep pain. In Chengdu the young tailor's parents, also feeling threatened by Lei Mingyuan's tyranny, did not dare to fight for their son's justice. They simply went out to Hope Township and buried him, after the body was carried out from the river. They might have felt that their son had indeed done something wrong, even if they could not say what that might have been. Rumors may have caused them to lose courage. To them, their son "had clearly succumbed to the control of the big man in the local brotherhood."[41]

People did not anticipate that this execution-style murder would have an unfortunate sequel. But it did. From Shen's report, what happened next concerned a local woman she refers to as Woman Li:

After the execution, Woman Li, kind-hearted wife of the principal of the local elementary school, could not relieve herself from the emotions of the tragedy. She fell into a deep sorrow and was unable to forgive Lei's treatment of his daughter's body—hastily burying it in the ground right near where it sunk. Since then, Woman Li's mind had become restless; she blamed herself for not being able to save the girl. Her nerves finally broke down: she often just sat, wept, or talked to herself. On a warm morning, she went to a nearby temple to burn incense for the dead and she claimed after she came back that she saw Shuqing's shadow in the mirror. After that, she developed a mental problem. Her husband was a gambler, and the family became increasingly poor but he made no effort. That Shuqing could not be saved from death, and furthermore that Woman Li's daughter got tuberculosis, this all wore her down. Six months later, in a stuporous madness, she jumped into the river to meet her own end.[42]

We have every reason to assume that the river was the same one that engulfed Shuqing and her lover. Although Woman Li's death brought back bad memories among other locals about the incident that had transpired there six months earlier, the impact and gossip in this case only lasted a few days, then everything was back to the usual. Time can erase people's memories. Those who do not witness wounds and blood perhaps tend more toward self-deception and choose business as usual.

★   ★   ★

Lei Mingyuan's killing of his daughter Shuqing was not a secret murder. In its own quasi-sanctioned way, the incident was a public execution. Lei did not face charges. The only explanation, according to Shen's report, was that such lynchings were to some extent recognized by society. The Paoge "did not feel anything wrong with such a punishment."[43] No villager reported the murder to the authorities. In fact, none thought Lei Mingyuan was guilty of the murder he committed. However, during China's Republican period, laws regarding the punishment for murder, including domestic murder, were clear. According to the "Criminal Codes" enacted in 1935, chapter 22 on "homicide" stated:

The murderer is sentenced to death, life imprisonment, or imprisonment for ten years or more; a penalty should be applied for an aborted crime; planning for a crime receives two years or less imprisonment (Article 271).

A person who kills a family member or relative is subject to the death penalty or life imprisonment; a penalty should be applied for an aborted crime; planning out a crime—three years or less imprisonment (Article 272).[44]

According to Articles 271 and 272, Lei's killing was a capital crime. Despite that, there was no legal action taken against him: he was not even sued. Villagers tacitly approved the Paoge's tyrannical power. This act in 1939 illustrates the social conditions in China at the time. A head of a social organization and a father could arbitrarily execute his family number. In the early twentieth century, numerous Western laws and principles of legal systems were being introduced into China. Lei's case revealed that in rural areas, even those close to big cities, modern concepts of justice were far from embedded in the local society.

Hope Township should be considered a microcosm of rural society. Similar tragedies took place all over China. The Republican government had been established for more than three decades, movements that promoted modernization had gone on for more decades—for example, the New Culture Movement (1910s and 1920s), the Rural Reconstruction Movement (1920s and 1930s), and the New Life Movement (1930s and 1940s). China's rural society may have seemed to some (the intellectuals perhaps) to have changed for the better, but it had really changed little.[45] Rural people in the Chengdu Plain were, to a certain extent, still cloaked in the past several centuries. Moreover, since the killing of Shuqing happened in the outskirts of the provincial capital—a place held up as a center of trends—the elite no doubt imagined even worse things deeper in the hinterland.

Qin Mu, famous writer in contemporary China, published an article in 1943 titled "Lynching, Marketing Humans, and Blood Lust" (Sixing, renshi, xue de shangwan) that criticized the not-too-rare phenomenon of lynching. He pointed out that in some places a man and a woman caught in illicit sexual activity could be tied together, placed into a bamboo cage, and weighted down to the bottom of a river. In remote areas, Qin said, people ate their enemy's heart and liver. As a child, Qin was eyewitness to villagers who had killed a robber, cooked his heart and liver, and ate them with wine. In some places, Qin noted, after catching a thief who stole vegetables from a garden, villagers would cut his hamstring, so that the thief became crippled for life. Most thieves who stole food were hungry and poor, but they could be given brutal punishment. Qin condemned these harsh tactics, adding they were "regarded as normal even among the good country folk." Inhuman punishment was "rarely opposed by villagers," he wrote, and "it was a great pity that people did not stand against it and that laws did not forbid lynchings of all kinds."[46]

Given the reality of traditional Chinese family punishments and clan regulations, which were often sanctioned as "correct" within the local community, people felt powerless in the face of a lynching. The elite of a locale, usually gentry, for centuries had enjoyed various privileges under imperial laws; they simultaneously wielded authority to exercise domestic discipline and issue their own lineage rules, to protect their ancestral halls, private schools, cemeteries, and the like. Regulations were needed to bring lineage members together in their duties and ritual obligations. Domestic discipline was thus supported by the central state's laws; the state in turn relied on the clan and family to keep order. However, as historian Lü Simian has pointed out, in modern Chinese society there were often "social punishments that were not legal punishments," which existed partly from political instability. Therefore, in many places people relied less on poorly implemented and often locally confusing laws than on the traditional, widely acknowledged, social customs. Another impetus for unsanctioned punishments was the need of certain "evil powers" (namely the secret societies) to exert their own forms of discipline.[47] In this sense, Lei Mingyuan's public execution of his daughter was not a crime in terms of the state but merely an exercise in domestic discipline. The state did not interfere with clan and family, except when a figure was charged with a criminal offense. As a result, lynchings, seen as a form of discipline, could continue unabated.[48]

★ ★ ★

Six years after the murder of Shuqing, the young student Shen Baoyuan entered Hope Township and engaged with the Lei family. Without her investigation we would never know the tragic story, thus making it similar to the millions of forgotten tragedies throughout Chinese history. With grief and indignation, Shen wrote: "The river... carried away the tragic boy and girl, both pitiful creatures buried by the old code of ethics." The so-called old code in some sense meant Confucian ethics and moral injunctions. The two young people were arbitrarily killed, Shen sensed, just like ants; Shuqing was a victim of a "conservative social system, occlusive customs, and rumors." Her powerful father was not her protector but in fact the one who destroyed her. Lei Mingyuan regarded a woman's virginity so fetishistically that he killed his own daughter "without reasonable investigation and testimony."[49]

The murder would consolidate Lei's reputation in the local place: basically Shuqing's life was sacrificed for his own search for status. But some villagers at that time, in that rural place, were cynical in another way; they held unsanctioned murder to be bad simply because it would disturb the natural habits and movements of dead souls and the rules of the postmortem underground. Lei's murder of his daughter would have been thought of as a portal for the admittance of bad luck. Later, the Lei family's status declined socially and economically, tempting the locals to see fitting retribution. When we revisit this tragedy almost eighty years later, using modern ways of inquiry and scholarship, we want to know why it happened and what in the social and cultural soil may have engendered it. Therefore, we press ahead in Chapter 2, by entering the interior of the Paoge secret society.

CHAPTER 2

A Local Band of the Gowned Brothers

THE PAOGE (the Gowned Brothers) was one name for the Sworn Brotherhood Society (or the Gelaohui), which existed in great number in Sichuan; they were the most influential secret organization in that province, having risen as early as the Qing dynasty and continuing into the Republican era.[1] Although the earliest studies differed about the percentage of the province's total adult male population who were members, almost all stated it was very high. A 1946 article said, "The power of the Paoge in Sichuan is huge. It is said that in Chongqing alone more than half of the men have joined the organization, including people in various trades, especially among business and the military."[2] Other reports from the 1940s (including one by Liao Taichu, an academic mentor of Shen Baoyuan) and a work written later by a former Paoge member offer hefty percentages, ranging up to 90 percent.[3] Archival materials from the 1940s and early 1950s seem to support these estimates. According to a list of performing troupes who appeared in the Garden of Ease Teahouse (Suiyuan chashe) in 1955, as found in the Chengdu Municipal Archives, of a total of twelve folk performers (eleven men and one woman), eight were members of the Paoge. This is a tiny data sample (it is only an indicator), but other documents support the purported penetration of the Paoge membership in the general populace.[4]

If Paoge men so dominated towns and villages, to what extent did they influence Sichuan politics and local order? Consider, as an example, the election of Chongqing's City Council in 1946. From the forty or fifty candidates, "almost all were leaders of the Paoge." Without membership a person had no chance to win an election. Some candidates, in order to win, tried to join the Paoge right before the campaign. One candidate who had looked down on the Paoge in the past wanted to join at the right moment by offering a huge amount of cash; however, he was declined enrollment.[5] The Paoge generally were from the lower classes, but eventually their power in Sichuan had developed to such an extent that "all kinds of people and even the middle class, in order to adapt to the environment and to raise their reputation, were also happy to make a connection with the Paoge."[6] Zhang San, a writer in the 1940s, pointed out that the Paoge "were the most powerful people in the local society who could maintain prestige and leadership. As long as something was for the good, the Paoge would not act like other gangs but become an organization favorable to the masses."[7]

Another writer in the late 1940s, Li Mufeng, investigated the factors behind the Paoge's strong growth and found that "the Paoge possess a strong solidarity that has held for hundreds of years without a break, especially their righteousness." The most important credo promoted by the Paoge, as Li described them, was to forbid rape and adultery. Any such accused would be executed. In addition, the Paoge could help members lead a better life by "sharing happiness and overcoming problems together." But this sort of morality-boosting was not the chief selling point. The Paoge's expansion in Sichuan occurred "because of years of civil wars in this province, when the powerful men suppressed people, whose livelihoods were seriously affected. People hardly could survive if they did not have a strong organization to protect them." If a bullied person wanted to go to the court, but he knew nothing about the law and had little time or money for a lawsuit, he would invite a Paoge "big brother" as a mediator to settle the case. The so-called big brother had authority, and people "always obeyed his judgment" (I discuss this activity further in Chapter 5).[8]

How could an organization that had such a high percentage of members among the population be called a "secret society"? This book explores the people, actions, motives, and events that relate to rural families in general in Sichuan as well as one rural family specifically in the Chengdu Plain. It takes up their contacts and dealings with a social phenomenon we might call bands of illicitly operating, frequently criminal strongmen with pretensions to local administrative and social control above and beyond their plundering and shows of force. That is too long to be used as a convenient descriptor in the narrative, thus several shorter phrases have come into use in media, literature, and academic writing that discuss late-imperial and Republican rural Sichuan. They are (1) secret society; (2) the Paoge; (3) Gelaohui; and (4) the Sworn Brotherhood. They are not easily disambiguated, nor is it worth trying to do so except in a longer study devoted to that topic specifically. Allow me to clarify why I conveniently refer to these bands without hewing to precise distinctions. For more than three hundred years the Paoge maintained certain traditions such as their organizational structures, founding myths and rituals, and even language. Nevertheless, their ideologies (anti–Manchu resistance) and their political agendas (overthrow of the Qing dynasty) dramatically shifted from an anti–Manchu, truly secret society (because it was persecuted) to the popular (and thus relatively exposed) social organization in Sichuan that remained until 1950. The 1911 Revolution was a critical turning point; after that, the Paoge faced only loose control and pursuit by authorities, who did not carry out a consistent policy of suppression. After over three decades, especially under the environment of warlordism and wars, local governments lost all ability to control these groups.

In the 1940s the members of Sichuan organizations that called Paoge or Gelaohui at a certain point reflected a very high percentage of the adult male population. Therefore, it is not logical to call those groups "secret." Self-proclaimed Paoge were not truly a secret society that could be both widely spread and loosely coordinated. But contemporary newspaper and magazine writers, as well as contemporary Chinese academic researchers and sociologists, attached the term *mimi huishe* (secret society) to certain people who fit the description of a band of illicitly operating strongmen with pretensions to local administrative and social control. This was merely a convenient term used for creating legends, writing academic prose, and detailing everyday reportage. In hindsight, it probably would have been better to just call these groups illicit, organized gangs.

The writing of young academic Shen Baoyuan used the phrases "Paoge," "secret society," and "local populist band." The first sentence of her 1946 report states: "This thesis aims at a dissection of the Paoge, a society that currently exists in China. It analyzes the history of a Paoge leader's life in order to explain the functions as well as the fluctuations and flourishing of *a secret society*'s local community control" (my emphasis). When Shen did her investigation, she noted that the Paoge members were "very cautious about leaking secrets of the organization."[9] Her teacher Liao Taichu, in his study of the Paoge in Chongyiqiao (the same locale as Shen's fieldwork), pointed out that "of the various Chinese secret societies functioning in Szechuan province, the most prominent is the Ko Lao Hui [Brothers Society]."[10] Even earlier, in 1936, researcher Sha Tiefan wrote: "This organization [that is, the Paoge] is a secret society, and its members are various, from all classes and with different quality."[11] This mix of expressions can be found throughout publications of the time.[12] Thus throughout the book I use the term "secret society" but not in a restrictive way. More often I use Paoge or Gowned Brothers—actually the more proper names for the loosely organized network of strongman groups in Sichuan. I do not use "Sworn Brotherhood Society" specifically to separate the Sichuan sphere of the Paoge from that of Gelaohui in other provinces.

★   ★   ★

There is a much longer, richer history behind the Paoge. In the nineteenth century the organization was spread out widely and became one of the most influential of Sichuan social forces. During the 1911 Revolution the Gowned Brothers played the important role of allies to the revolutionaries. At that time, their activities went from underground to public. Although later the government tried to restrict them, the Paoge became more visible, and the restrictions were gradually loosened because of the organization's comprehensive roots, low and high, in society—from government officials to laborers. Throughout the organization's three-century history, various governments made efforts to destroy it but failed. Only the Communist regime after 1949 finally achieved this goal.

There are several explanations that concern the origins of the Paoge. In general, their origin is not entirely clear and provides some puzzles. Some writers, including Zuo Zongtang (1812–1885), leader of the nineteenth-century Hunan Army, thought they were connected with a gang network called the Guolu—arguably the early form of the organization known as the Gelaohui (Sworn Brotherhood Society) in Sichuan. The Gelaohui was widespread in China as an anti-Manchu organization, and "Paoge" was the name of the Gelaohui in Sichuan. The heads of Gelaohui (discussed in more detail below) and Guolu were both called *maoding* (caped men). Fu Chongju, who compiled *Investigation of Chengdu* in 1910, wrote that the Paoge were called *bangke* (stick men) in West and South Sichuan; in North Sichuan, they were known as *daoke* (knife men); and in East Sichuan, *guofei* (*guo* bandits).[13] In Qing documents the organization was described as *huifei* (organized bandits) or called *maoding,* who were sworn to brotherhood.[14] Shen Baoyuan's investigation mentioned *bangke* in Hope Township who belonged to the category of "muddy-water Paoge" (*hunshui* Paoge), indicating those Paoge who were criminal or bad in some serious way.[15]

Of course, the Paoge have their own origin story. In Appendix 1 of Shen's report there is a brief description based on the Paoge writing called *The Bottom of the Ocean* (Haidi). The story there is almost the same as Liu Shiliang's description in his *Complete History of the Hanliu* (Hanliu quanshi), which was published in 1939.[16] The parallelism indicates that all the Paoge organizations adopted one origin myth because members were also called "remnants of the Han" (that is, "Hanliu"). In this story they started out based on Zheng Chenggong's "sorrow at the fall of the Ming dynasty and the death of his father," when Zheng then gathered fellows at the Bright and Far Hall (Mingyuan tang) on Golden Terrace Mountain (Jintaishan) in 1661 to establish a secret society that would have more than four thousand members. This was the beginning of the Gelaohui's organization. *The True Record of the Golden Terrace Mountain* (Jintaishan shilu) was the canonical writing that "contained the history of Hanliu." In 1670 Sichuan native Chen Jinnan was sent by Zheng Chenggong to Ya'an, a town in West Sichuan, to open a lodge called Seminal Loyalty Mountain (Jingzhongshan), thereby launching the activities of the Sworn Brotherhood Society in Sichuan. In 1683, when Qing troops captured Taiwan, Zheng Keshuang, grandson of Zheng Chenggong, "out of fear that important documents would be taken by enemy, sealed them into an iron box and threw it into the ocean."[17]

According to Liu Shiliang, in 1848 the Sichuanese Guo Yongtai claimed that he had found the original copy of the *True Record of Golden Terrace Mountain* in the possession of a fisherman. Guo edited and issued the record as the canonic writ for the organization but under a new title—*The Bottom of the Ocean* (Haidi)—to support his claim that it was the document thrown into the ocean when Taiwan was captured by the Qing.[18] The most important fact is that the book provided models for the Gowned Brothers' rituals. We have no way to determine if Guo's claim about discovering the Paoge foundational text is true. However, there is no question that it boosted the power of the Paoge. Although its various local organizations had gradually expanded from the late seventeenth to the early nineteenth centuries, the Paoge experienced a surge of growth in numbers and influence in the second half of the nineteenth century, when the organization used this very same "retrieved" text as an ideological and spiritual foundation and a powerful communication tool (discussed further in Chapter 4). For a true late-nineteenth century Paoge member, to understand the language of *The Bottom of the Ocean* was proof positive of dedication. Despite the haziness of the book's provenance, it is clear that both a reincarnated type of ritual canon and a supporting organization were the results—and at the same time the agents—of the late-nineteenth-century anti-Manchu movement.

★   ★   ★

With *Haidi* Hanliu and the Paoge's origin story, we have what British Marxist historian Eric Hobsbawm has termed an "invented tradition"—namely, "a set of practices, normally governed by overtly or tacitly accepted rules and of a ritual of symbolic nature, which seek to inculcate certain values and norms of behaviour by repetition, which automatically implies continuity with the past."[19] In the case of Qing-era China the "invented tradition" became a tool of political struggles, which the Paoge used to explain their anti-Manchu actions and to tie their members together. For an authentic, believing Paoge, understanding *The Bottom of the Ocean* became a precondition of identity.[20]

For nearly three hundred years the organization struggled for local control, in conjunction with their establishing links with local elites, the *baojia* system, and militias. Because of the long tradition of immigration into the

Chengdu Plain, clan organizations were not as powerful as those in South China. The state implemented indirect control of rural areas through local elites, who played an important role in late Qing local politics. Historian Keith Schoppa examined the identities and social activities of local leaders, including local defense, public affairs, charity, local mediation, and education.[21] From the Qing era to the Republic, rural areas below the county level were controlled through the *baojia* system.[22] The *baojia*—consisting of a formula of organizing households and neighborhoods to achieve control in local places—had a long history in China (traceable to before the Song dynasty). During the Republican era every ten households were organized into a *jia* and every ten *jia*, into a *bao* (one hundred households, but the number was changeable). People watched out for each other to accomplish overall security.[23]

For example, according to the "Rules of the *baojia* in Baxian county," devised by local *baojia* in Baxian in 1813, in each market town a wooden support had to be set up with a gong and a wooden board on which was written "catch bandits" (*yanna feitu*); there were also four big sticks. Each household was required to prepare one or two sticks for neighborhood security and self-protection. If any bandits entered this area, watchmen would beat the gongs. As soon as the alert was made, the *baojia* heads would lead people who carried the sticks to fend off the bandits or to catch them. In 1850 the county office of Baxian issued the "Regulations for *baojia* organization" and required *baojia* heads to conduct surveys and to record information on the households under their jurisdiction, including properties and names of relatives and hired hands.[24]

Generally speaking, heads of *baojia* and militia (*tuanfang* or *tuanlian*) were the respected leaders of locales. A *baojia* head "should have no wrongdoing and no violation of laws and have high abilities." They "may not be a gentry or landlord" but "must have a good quality and be reasonable and respectable." In addition to *baojia* heads (*baozheng*), there were also heads of the local market (*changyue*) and heads of the market town (*xiangyue*), who were recommended by local gentry and approved by officials; they worked together to settle disputes among residents and to handle such local affairs as security and taxation.[25] Being a head of *baojia* was arduous, as the position was unpaid and it could be difficult to handle local affairs at the crack between local power and the state. When the government imposed an additional tax, or when people could not pay their taxes because of hardship, the *baojia* head would have to figure out a way to sort out the dilemma between state power and local interests. However, there were of course benefits and privileges, so local elites often chose to hold such positions. After a new county structure was created by the Nationalist government in Sichuan in 1935, the *baojia* system was similarly reorganized. By 1945, Chengdu

County, where Hope Township was situated, had 14 market townships (*xiangzhen*), divided into 255 *bao* and 2,511 *jia*.[26]

★   ★   ★

A strong development of the Paoge occurred after about 1820, under the Qing dynasty; an even more radical expansion happened during the 1850s and 1860s. Based on official reports, the organization's members were lower-class people, often working as groups of dozens or even hundreds. When Qing troops tried to suppress them, they hid among local residents.[27] The Paoge held ceremonies called "opening the mountain" (*kaishan*—that is, the ritual of recruitment). During such occasions, a few dozen, hundred, or even a thousand people would attend, some having traveled hundreds of miles.[28] Facing Paoge expansion, the government was without a working strategy to control them.

In the late Qing period, the Paoge formed their networks in Sichuan. One official pointed out that "the brotherhood has spread everywhere in Sichuan, and many of the members are robbers. When they commit a crime, the organization protects them. Since they are all over Sichuan, when one is caught, there are still many more."[29] They even infiltrated the Qing troops. In his *History of Hunan Army* (Xiangjun zhi), scholar Wang Kaiyun wrote: "The Gelaohui originated in Sichuan; they are vagrants as sworn brothers and support each other when needed. After the establishment of the Hunan Army, many Sichuan people joined." Zuo Zongtang had ten battalions of Sichuanese, "all of whom were Gelaohui members," and the heads of the battalions were called "big brothers"; this reveals that the organization had "deep roots in the army."[30] The Paoge were quite pervasive, "drawing people from all levels and professions such as gentry, merchants, scholars, officials, laborers, and criminals."[31] This wide range of social backgrounds laid a foundation for their enduring expansion.

Social unrest gave secret societies many opportunities to enlarge their power and influence. Although the Paoge were forbidden during the Qing, they were very active in teahouses, opium dens, restaurants, opera houses, and other public places. According to Liu Shiliang, "Hanliu [that is, Paoge] had the most achievements in Sichuan." By 1911 the "Benevolence Faction" (Renzi qi) in Chengdu alone had 374 branches. Paoge branches could be found along every travel route, even in the smallest settlements.[32] In the late Qing the police issued regulations that notified the populace they would investigate groups with "strange clothes, ferocious faces, and violent tendency."[33] This description illustrates what the police thought Paoge members looked like.

The Paoge were on the front lines in the 1911 Revolution. During the

Railroad Protection Movement in 1911, the Paoge worked with the Railroad Protection Army and openly conducted political action.[34] However, after the Revolution, local governments criminalized the Paoge once again. Despite the government's control, the Paoge gradually controlled local Sichuan communities. They often operated teahouses, taverns, opium dens, and lodges as headquarters, which became unofficial centers of power while at the same time they often engaged in such criminal activities as opium smuggling and gambling.

The phenomenon of local militias emerged from the *baojia* system, and therefore they overlapped with *baojia* in certain ways regarding structure and function. While *baojia* were managed by the government and officials, local militias (*tuanlian*) were mostly undertaken by local elites. The 1920s and 1930s in Sichuan were a time of turmoil, banditry, and social disorder. Local authorities were reduced in power and their ability to manage. In the face of increasing taxes and difficulties in collecting them, local officials had little choice but to recognize the Paoge as political operators, and therefore some Paoge masters became heads of local militia. Sometimes the official magistrate would not dare to travel to the countryside because he did not have sufficient protection and could be "insulted by powerful leaders of *tuanlian*," who were often Paoge. One man recalled that when he was a student in the middle school, he would observe how a few Paoge brothers could accumulate 300,000 to 400,000 *yuan* and own more than a thousand firearms. They always acted in groups of fifty to sixty and could exercise power over life and death.[35]

Local authorities avoided confrontation and did not dare to offend: they relied on the Paoge for fundraising and tax collecting. By the 1930s and 1940s the Paoge were taking over tax-collection responsibilities from local elites, who for a long time had assumed the role of guarantors of a local area's tax quota for the year. For instance, in Zhugao, under Jintang County near Hope Township, Paoge master He Song contracted with the local government on market taxes and subleased them to someone else. Except for a part of the take that went toward harbor maintenance and schools, He kept the rest.[36] Here we see an interesting phenomenon: As a banned organization (at least in theory), the Paoge could actually contract with the local government about tax farming and help government fulfill its tax needs, ultimately taking a profit. To a certain extent, the organization became an intermediary between the local government and peasants. Furthermore, the profits He Song gained were partially used for some local projects and schools. The local government had to depend on the Paoge masters even to effect beneficial local projects.

Zhugao was an important route for the transport of cloth, cotton, sugar, vegetable oil, rice, tobacco, and wine, and in 1945, He Song "set up customs passes to extort merchants." All merchants had to pay a protection fee but did not need to pay the government tax. Therefore merchants preferred to pay He. During the 1940s the land tax was paid by crops or products. As the head of the township (*xiangzhang*), He Song took over the management of the land tax and profited from it. It was reported that he got "a million of *dan* of grain" from this practice. Although there is no other source to support this claim, the case shows the extent that a Paoge master could be involved in handling and cutting into local taxes. They could even challenge local officials. In early 1945, for example, a chief in the county's land tax management office came to Zhugao for a land survey and gained a large amount of money during the process. He Song was upset that he did not share his take and forcefully took all of the money. The chief reported this to the magistrate, who did nothing about it.[37]

Most Paoge members came from lower-class families, who worked various trades and grifts. According to Liu Shiliang, they were fortunetellers, Chinese medical doctors, gamblers, swindlers, beggars, Buddhist monks, Daoist priests, soldiers, and folk performers, among other things.[38] It is no doubt that the Paoge had a complicated membership—that is, not an acutely categorizable or easily identified one. However, officials often deliberately overemphasized the connection with bandits and fraudsters so that they had excuses to attack the organization. Many local elites and landlords even joined the Paoge. Official documents showed: "The Paoge began with law-offenders but later local gentry and the wealthy joined in order to gain protection."[39] Some rich families joined the Paoge not just for protection but also to expand their social networks and power.[40] By the late Qing, even scholars and educators were in the organization. For example, Zhang Jiexian, a head of the Paoge in Guanxian, was a principal of an elementary school who became a leader of the Railroad Protection Army in 1911.[41]

Through their long development, Paoge organizational features and structures took a certain shape. An official document reveals that "the lower-class Gelaohui in Sichuan have many different factions, but can be divided into two major ones: the River-Lake Society (Jianghuhui) and the Filial Righteousness Society (Xiaoyihui). The former emerged first. Its members are rascals and evil gentry, who often harm the local people. As a result, the Filial Righteousness Society formed to resist the former." Paoge members could also be divided into two types: members who had no work profession or work habit but relied on crime, and those who had legitimate professions but joined for protection.[42] The former had the nickname "muddy water" (*hunshui*) and the latter "pure water" (*qingshui*). The pure-water faction had their own professions and livelihoods and did not involve themselves in criminal activities. The muddy-water members were in a sense professional Paoge.[43] In her report Shen Baoyuan pointed out that in Hope Township the pure-water members had good discipline and connections with the government and military, while the muddy-water ones were the targets of government agents. Lei Mingyuan belonged to the pure-water members, and his group had "restrictions and good manners." These members also held official positions.[44]

Shen Baoyuan found out about the Paoge's strict hierarchy. Such a structure, of course, was conducive to internal control and good communications top to bottom. The Paoge had many branches, factions, or lodges, called "mountain halls" (*shantang*). Generally, each branch had eight levels (*pai*), with the first, second, third, and fifth called "upper-four levels" (*shang-sipai*), while the sixth, eighth, ninth, and tenth were the "lower-four levels" (*xiasipai*). The word *pai* here was something of an equivalent to "master"—a term of exact status. They tabooed numbers four and seven, so these two levels were omitted. "Four" is pronounced "si," a homophone with the word for death; and "seven" is pronounced "qi," closely sounding with the word for rob, or catch (*qie*, or *jie*). The most powerful man in a branch was called "helmsman" (*duobazi*) or "dragon's head" (*longtou daye*). The number-two man had the name "sage second master" (*shengxian erye*); he was in charge of routine affairs and decision making. Number three was the "manager third master" (*dangjia sanye*), who controlled finance and revenue. In addition, the "red flag fifth master" (*hongqi wuye*) led communication and personnel and other planning, while the "black flag fifth master" (*heiqi wuye*) carried out actions and directed certain fights (for more details, see Appendix 1. Paoge Ranks).[45]

There was no one particular headquarters. All branches were relatively independent and did not belong to a center. But sometimes branches would unite as a federation to streamline leadership, while keeping intact their own structures and activities. Each branch of the Paoge had a different style of control and management, and although each followed the template found in *The Bottom of the Ocean*, it had many different versions. Such independence contributed to struggles between rival branches, and violence often occurred. Of course, cooperation was the more profitable mode between branches; the common goal as a secret society was to focus on a common enemy and common actions.

Some Paoge branches tended toward consolidation. On October 15, 1942, the Nationalist Party (Guomindang, GMD) provincial executive committee issued an official report on the Paoge in New Market (Xinchang), Weiyuan County.[46] Local military veteran Huang Chunian, "in order to increase power and to expand his organization," called for the Paoge branches in Neijiang, Renshou, Rongxian, and Zigong counties to unite into the Four-fold Union Renewal Society (Sihexing she). The report further said that in New Market four branches of the Paoge—Ren (benevolence), Yi (righteousness), Li (rites), and Zhi (wisdom)—which "except a few un-scrupulous elements, were otherwise law-abiding." Although the Paoge was prohibited, if they could be "law-abiding," the government would not interfere with their activities. The report indicated that their seeking to establish the united society was necessary under two scenarios: First, if the Japanese invaded Sichuan, all Paoge would unite and launch a guerrilla insurgency. Second, Sichuanese had to "unite to expel outsiders." Here the "outsiders" seems to have meant people from other provinces. After the outbreak of war a large number of refugees from coastal areas moved to Sichuan. It would seem that the Paoge desired to resist not only Japanese but also other Chinese.

Huang Chunian was "elected" as chairman. Based on the report, he was "the most active" in the organization. A former battalion commander under a regional warlord, Huang had developed ties with the Paoge everywhere. He was also involved in opium smuggling and attempted to expand that network. Although the report believed that his new organization had "no political agenda," it expressed concern that "if it was utilized by evil people, it could be harmful." During the Moon Festival, the Four-fold Union Renewal Society held a get-together and hired Sichuan opera troupes to perform for ten days. Such activities were similar to those held in the past by native-place associations, guilds, and deity associations. The Paoge was effectively replacing their roles in the local society.[47]

During this time, numerous Paoge members penetrated the military, and the government feared a joint force of secret society and army. In the case just mentioned, a veteran had become a Paoge leader, which confirmed the government's concern. Huang had the ability to bring Paoge branches from four counties together and round up two thousand people. The highest officials of the townships were also members. Huang had a solid financial base and garnered several thousand *yuan* to fund the organization. Each member also paid 10 *yuan* membership fee, which added many thousands more *yuan* to the coffers.

One of the reasons why the Paoge could continue to increase its power was local governments' permissive attitudes. Of course, the large expansion of the Paoge had a close correlation with the history of Republican Sichuan.[48] It was after 1935 that Sichuan really became incorporated under the jurisdiction of the national government. But it was earlier, during the warlord period, that the Paoge laid a solid foundation for their power. Sichuan lacked a strong unified government in the 1920s and 1930s, and as a consequence the Paoge filled local power vacuums, including participation in taxation and local security. Without the Paoge, daily life in the local Sichuan communities would have been difficult to keep in order. When the Nationalist government finally put Sichuan under its jurisdiction on the eve of the War of Resistance against Japan, the Paoge had developed to such a level that the government could not effectively control them.

Most members at the time were not orthodox elites and were mainly lower-class and marginalized people. Therefore, inevitably they were discriminated by orthodox elites. The Paoge's public activities and influence caused elites' anxiety. Although they expressed that they would not interfere with "any formal activities of the Paoge" because they "support freedom of association," elites worried that "gang activities have reached the highest point." Taking Chengdu as an example, the elites asked: "Can we find there is no headquarters of the Paoge in any street? Can we find in a teahouse there is no Paoge? Can we find the people who involve local self-government have no connection with the Paoge? Even in the government offices and consultative councils, there are many people who are the Paoge members." They pointed out that the reason why this gang was so active was because "politics is chaotic, laws are ineffective, and society is disorder." Therefore, the Paoge supported the government to reimplement the orders issued before and to strengthen the control. By this time, students joined the organization, and to deal with the situation, the elites asked the government to ban students' membership in the gang: any student who joined the gang should be expelled from school and the principal of said school should be subject to discipline for loss of control.[49] In fact, many school principals were also Paoge members, and local elites became concerned about the Paoge's control over educational resources.[50]

The Paoge's dramatic expansion in the first half of the twentieth century was closely linked with the formation of the modern state and the process of China's modernization. In traditional Sichuan there were various social organizations that played an important role in regional security, economy, and daily life, such as Qingming Society and the Deity Patron Association. But during the modernization in the late Qing and early Republic, traditional social organizations were gradually destroyed by the powerful state; the government was unable to fill the power vacuum, which created good conditions for the Paoge to expand its power into all levels of society. The Paoge accordingly extended their power into local government. He Song, who manipulated elections in the local government and consultative council, exemplifies this. Although the government criminalized the Paoge, Paoge members, to a considerable extent, served in the government, and many affairs in local places had to rely on their involvement (Chapter 6 details He Song becoming head of laborers for building an airport). Some Paoge masters turned into leaders of legitimate political parties or organizations; He Song became the chair of the Youth Party.[51]

During the War of Resistance against Japan there were numerous ways in which Paoge members could participate. Some joined armies, and others donated money. In 1942, to celebrate Chiang Kai-shek's fiftieth birthday, the Paoge in Sichuan motivated hundreds of thousands of its members to donate money to purchase an aircraft that was appropriately named Loyalty (Zhongyihao).[52] Although the Paoge was repeatedly banned, during the war they were an important force that aided the resistance, and thus the government hardly carried out its restrictions against them. The Paoge became a relatively more open organization and increasingly made collaborations with local governments. The Sichuan Army provides one example. An article pointed out that "the Sichuan Army has inferior weapons and training, but they are able to fight because the Paoge organization is their spiritual arm. In many of the troops in the Sichuan Army, officers were Paoge leaders, and had brotherlike relationships with their solders. If little brothers had troubles, big brothers would help to solve their problems. Therefore, when they engage in a battle, they fight without any fear."[53] After the Nationalist government finally controlled Sichuan, the GMD carried out elections at county and township levels, creating a good opportunity for the Paoge to enter local administrations.[54]

Shen Baoyuan noticed the Paoge's ability to manipulate the local community and was surprised to see "how powerful they are at social control." She wrote that "in Hope Township, the social organization (*shetuan*) is the center of the community.... The social organization takes responsibility for social sanctions by using their legal, political, religious, and ethical powers."[55] Shen's expressions provide important hints about her own orientation. In her thesis, references to the Paoge always used a certain newly important term being applied to local, self-aware groups throughout China—namely, "social organization." It was even in the phrase of her thesis title. Moreover, in phrases like this, Shen distinguished the social organization (*shetuan*) from the society (*shehui*) in which they operated. As a student of sociology, Shen chose terms with serious consideration. The word "Paoge," being a version of the name Gelaohui in Sichuan, was actually not the formal name of the organization. In fact, in their documents they often used "Gelaohui" or simply "the associates" (*huidang*), which is like saying "band of brothers." Because Shen Baoyuan studied them from an academic point of view, she adopted her "profession's" care to apply accurate names and categorizations; thus she believed *shetuan* was indeed accurate and neutral.

Another way by which the Paoge brothers could continue to manipulate and act as freely as possible in local affairs was to mirror and adopt the all-important local culture of cyclical rites, customs, and religious practices in which they lived and gave innate credence. The *shetuan* thus could fashion themselves as a "society" (*shehui*) within a larger society, by their use of well-known observances and their relatively secret argot and gestures. These activities are examined in the following chapters.

PART TWO

The Worlds of the Paoge

CHAPTER 3

Spirituality and Customs

THE PAOGE WERE NOT AN INVADING FORCE. On the contrary, they sprung up from within local places and local societies. The Paoge brothers and their ancillary members had originally energized their loose-knit organization to become nativist and Han ethnic defenders in the anti-Manchu revolution. One reason why they could and did act in this way was simply because they were innately embedded in Chinese society and rooted in the usual ways of life in the Chengdu Plain. Their attitudes and stances regarding popular customs, local rites, and the relatively broad landscape of religious practices linked to the annual calendar of ceremonies and festivals were those of the everyman—the people of any rural and urban locale in western, if not all of, China. Given this rootedness, the Paoge brothers took for themselves what was traditional and fashioned from it a variety of specialized rites and customs. In this chapter we turn to the unique observations of Shen Baoyuan, who was fascinated with what many in academe of her time thought of as arcane and superstitious ploys. As we examine the inner life, so to speak, of our band of populist brothers, we must keep in mind that over the past forty or so years, historians and students of Chinese society have taken a much-needed neutral, in some sense anthropological, stance toward China's broad landscape of rites, beliefs, and religious and ceremonial practices. We shall do the same, beginning with a short sketch of how traditional rites and beliefs were acted out in the Paoge's own local areas.

Rural people's lives were, and to some extent still are, linked to gods and sacrificial acts. There were the "stove gods" (*zaoshen*) inside the family's own space, "patron gods" (*shegong*, *tudi*, or *sheshen*) in community areas, and the "city god" (*chenghuang*). Other so-called gods existed for roads and mountains and waterways—for example, Shigandang, also called Taishan Shigandang, a stone sculpture placed at crossroads to suppress ghosts (Figure 3.1). Alongside the river that ran through Hope Township, there was a tortuous path lined with trees, and at the side of this road stood a Buddhist statue—a different order of god from those just mentioned. Shen Baoyuan's comments in her report are a good source of how local rites and festivals happened in Hope Township. But, as someone who had received a modern, Western education that valued science, she criticized popular religions as "representations of superstition." For villagers, however, worship and iconographic images were essential for spiritual sustenance. Shen herself actually stated that the Buddha statue by the road was "used particularly for saving dead souls, while also being an item at which to sacrifice for the suppression of evil."[1]

When Shen visited Lei Mingyuan's home, she felt that "superstition pervaded his house." In the main room a shrine was centrally located, where incense sticks burned, illustrating a "family belief in gods and superstition." Neighbors often circulated stories of supernatural power and ghosts. One summer, the rising river overflowed and washed away a temple statue, and villagers believed that this was a result of the patron god's quarrel with his wife, upon which the two deities had separated. The patron god's temple was probably the most common sort of temple in rural parts of the Chengdu Plain; it could be seen in almost every village, market town, township, and city. Some families also set up a patron-god shrine at home.[2] People believed that this deity was the god who protected the land, the closest most intimate force of public faith in people's lives.

Villagers believed in the efficacy of ceremonies for driving out evil spirits and mitigating ill fortune. Woman Lei told Shen that when her daughter Shuying once became seriously ill and lost consciousness, she sought out a woman who had "the same nature" (*tongshuxing*) as Shuying to be a sort of godmother. Here "same nature" meant the same birthday, horoscope, zodiac sign, general luck, and so forth. The rituals for the godmother had prescribed acts: first, one would bring to the godmother a large piece of pork, dozens of eggs, a pair of socks, a pair of red candles, and a bunch of incense sticks. Woman Lei physically supported the sick daughter as she walked to the godmother's home, and after lighting the candles and incense sticks, the daughter kowtowed to the godmother. The godmother accepted the gifts and gave the goddaughter 1,100 yuan. After the ceremony Shuying quickly recovered, so Woman Lei thus believed in the ritual's efficacy beyond any shadow of a doubt.[3]

The welcoming of the Spirit-Official (*jie lingguan*) was another activity for the driving out of evil spirits. In this rite, costumed actors performed a ritual before an image of this deity and had a conversation with it. Another

FIGURE 3.1 Taishan shigandang, a stone sculpture placed at a crossroads to suppress ghosts. *Source*: Photograph by Sidney D. Gamble, ca. 1917–1919. Reproduced courtesy of Sidney D. Gamble Photographs, David M. Rubenstein Rare Book & Manuscript Library, Duke University.

act involving evil spirits, known as "catching the *hanlin*" (*zhuo hanlin*, a legendary perpetrator), had a similar function. Whenever a plague or grave illness struck, people would hire a beggar to pretend to be a *hanlin* and hide in the graveyard. After catching the *hanlin*, they put him in a cage. There was also "snatching the ghost" (*shougui*). When a family member was seriously ill, the family would hire a shaman to identify the culprit as a ghost; the sick person would recover after said ghost was caught. Then the "ghost" was stuffed into a small crock and buried underground, or hung in a temple, or placed on stone gateways (*shi paifang*). Because of this custom, one could see many small crocks set on stone gates by the roads.[4] In Shen Baoyuan's view, all these activities were "superstitious" ones. Fu Chongju's *Investigation of Chengdu*, written in 1909–10, categorized these activities under the title "Superstition in Chengdu."[5] In the first half of the twentieth century, along with the process of modernization and Westernization, elites frequently used the word *superstition* to describe the rituals and customs of the working, farming, and generally "lower" classes. Even today, many urban, educated Chinese maintain this attitude.

Almost all local gazetteers that covered life in the Chengdu Plain recorded rural celebrations, and these records have become an important source for our knowledge of local rites and festivals. In peasant homes in the Chengdu Plain, people set up altars for heaven, earth, sages, ancestors, and various masters (*tian di jun qin shi*) as well as for their own deceased parents. Many of the objects of rites and sacrifices were attached to mundane effects, like those mentioned above, yet others were Buddhist in origin—for example, Avalokitesvara (Guanyin) and Maitreya (Mile). There were temples and/or shrines in every village, most of them dedicated to Guanyin, or to the non-Buddhist Guandi, or to the God of Wealth. Much of this worship was seasonal and fixed to the god's birthday (Figure 3.2). Seasonal customs were the most common pattern in local cultures. In the never-ending agricultural cycles and during major life events, people recognized the close relationship between seasons and production from the land, and between seasons and the cycle of death and birth (see Appendix 3. Selected Ritual/ Festival Events).

By characterizing traditional Chinese religious practices a bit crudely here for purposes of discussion, the aim is to show that at the heart of festivals and cyclic rites was a core of beliefs surrounding the powers of ancestors, ghosts and spirits, politico-historical legends, and astral regularities. Such beliefs should not be defined as either religion or superstition, but as fitting into a conglomeration that had its own regularities in the form of festivals, the calendar, and liturgies. For example, as the Chinese New Year approached on the twenty-fourth day of the twelfth lunar month, the people of Chengdu worshiped the kitchen god, who was said to ascend back to

FIGURE 3.2 A rural temple. *Source*: Photograph taken by Joseph Needham, ca. 1943–46. Reproduced courtesy of the Needham Research Institute, Cambridge University.

Heaven to kowtow before the Emperor of Heaven. Then it would return on the eve of the Chinese New Year, when people stayed up all night. This scenario can be thought of as a simple sketch of astral configurations at the Winter Solstice (the return to Day One, the return of expected asterisms, and the role of the polar asterism Beidou as emperor). People would open their doors early in the morning to "welcome the happy god (*xishen*) coming from the East." Shops would replace their older images of the door gods with new ones, and households offered wine and chickens at their altars, to worship the patron deity and bow before the god of wealth (Figure 3.3). Throughout this ritual process "people speak only lucky words, and it is taboo to say any unlucky ones."[6]

The preceding brief sketch of Chengdu Plain society permits us to see the rootedness and nativist leanings of the Paoge. The Paoge came from this mundane world of devotions, beliefs, and special rites and practices. In this chapter, as we lean in further to observe the processes and forms of the Paoge's inner world, we must hold close at hand the background upon which Paoge rituals, appurtenances, and codes were fashioned. Beliefs and rituals were naturally only one part of the way that ad hoc bands, families, and societies maintained themselves and their traditions. Future chapters

永鎮家垞

FIGURE 3.3 An example of the door god. *Source*: The image is a contemporary rendering purchased in Chengdu in 1997 by the author, which is very similar to those printed in the late Qing and early Republican periods.

examine the Paoge's rules and processes of membership as well as their use of argot and gesture, all of which allowed for the forming of a variety of controls.

★   ★   ★

Paoge members, coming from the broad swath of local culture, tended naturally to build upon that culture. For the local Paoge, as Shen Baoyuan noted, the thirteenth day of the fifth lunar month was associated with their Single Broadsword Festival (*dandao hui*). This was an important day for the Paoge in Hope Township and was held in the Patron Deity Temple. The day was meant for people everywhere to attend a Guandi Temple to celebrate the birthday of that great historical figure Guan Yu (or Guandi; d. 220 AD). For many centuries Guan Yu was a politico-historical hero and a part of the rhythm of local rites; he was regarded by locals as their protector as well as a wealth god.

Following the seasonal schedule, during their Paoge Broadsword Festival, Paoge members disciplined whatever brothers had done as offenses or errors; they also awarded merits and held introductory ceremonies for new members (the processes of selection, membership, and punishments associated with this special ceremony are discussed in finer detail in Chapter 5). The Single Broadsword Festival was named after a narrative moment in the legend of Guan Yu, a real personage who led his own loyal troops during the territorial and civil wars that occurred in the breakdown of the Eastern Han dynasty (25–220 CE). Guan Yu had carried a broadsword into his enemy's encampment for an invited banquet, in which a trap was designed to kill him but Guan came back successfully by using his talent and courage. This story was written by the famous playwright Guan Hanqing during the Yuan dynasty (1271–1368).[7]

In the Paoge ceremony a crescent broadsword was placed on a stand in the venue, surrounded by burning incense. The Hope Township helmsman, Tong Niansheng, was seated in the middle, and other Paoge leaders sat at both sides in their rank sequence. The ceremony would begin with the Paoge brothers welcoming Guandi, the apotheosized name of Guan Yu. They employed a stylized format, which we learn via Shen Baoyuan's invaluable report.

First called the Third Brother,
And the Third Brother responded, "Sage Guan has left the South Heavenly Gate."
Then called the Manager,
And the Manager answered, "Sage Guan is on his half way."
Next, the youngest brother claimed, "Sage Guan has arrived at the gate."

The First Master asked the Second Brother to welcome him and hung Guan's portrait; and all brothers worshiped him. After that, the Second Brother praised Guandi with poems:

Sage, Sage,
Who Swore in the Peach Garden.
He was loyal and courageous deep in his bowels,
And his story passes down forever.

Sage, Sage,
He has saved Jingzhou,
Got separated in Xuzhou,
But was reunited in the ancient city.[8]

The first verse is about another part of the Guan Yu legend, known as "Three Sworn Brothers of the Peach Garden" (*Taoyuan sanjieyi*). This seems to relate to the Paoge specifically, because it is about swearing brotherhood, and one of the most important procedures in the Single Broadsword Festival was the recruitment ceremony—taking the oath with a bloody fingerprint. The second verse recalls Guan Yu's experience as a hero and loyal warrior. "Saving Jingzhou" narrates the event of 214 CE, when Liu Bei, pretender to the Liu family's crumbling Han dynasty, led his troops into Sichuan, having tasked Guan Yu to guard Jingzhou, an important northwestern area within the Wu kingdom that was strategically situated on the Han River, above the waterways that fed into Sichuan.

"Separated in Xuzhou" is an earlier event of 200 CE, when the king of Wei state, Cao Cao, launched a military campaign from Xuzhou against Liu Bei. In this, Liu was defeated and his wife captured; in addition, Guan Yu was forced to surrender to Cao Cao. The fourth line refers to the following episode: Cao Cao admired Guan Yu's loyalty to Liu and his fighting skills and therefore appointed him as general. Guan Yu turned this down, however, supposedly with these thoughts: "Although Cao has treated me very well, I have sworn to Liu Bei to be together with him for life and never betray him." A saying states that Guan Yu's "body was in Cao's camp but his heart was still in Han" (*shenzai caoying xinzai han*, meaning "with the Han king, now represented by the pretender Liu"). This Chinese proverb is still in use. When Guan Yu discovered Liu Bei's location, he left Cao's camp by riding a horse and killing five major generals who tried to stop him. Finally, Guan Yu was reunited with Liu.

The Paoge turned to Guandi for a specific ceremony that marked loyalty. According to Shen Baoyuan's investigation, when new members were introduced by their sponsors (the "Obliging Brother," the "Leading-in Man," and "Guarantor"), they first worshiped at the statue of Guan Yu (Guandi), then kowtowed to the helmsman, and again kowtowed to his three supporters. They would present burned incense and sacrifices to the altar, culminating in the sacrifice of a rooster (Chapter 5 provides additional details about the sponsors and sacrifices).[9]

Roosters in this context remind us of the general shape of local rites and beliefs; in fact, rooster sacrifices show up in the long Daoist tradition of complex, formalized rites that were (and still are) held in local Daoist temples all over southern and southwestern China as well as in a variety of local rites throughout the Chengdu Plain. As far back as antiquity, roosters were linked with shamanistic practices conducted by Daoist priests and others; people believed that the rooster warded off evil. A general custom—often but not always done by shamans—was to kill a rooster and hang it, or to paste a painted rooster, on one's door. When people posted images of the door god, the patron deity, Guandi, or Buddha and the various bodhisattvas, they would first make the ritual of "opening the light" (*kaiguang*). For this, the shaman drew a magic symbol with blood from the crest of a rooster, accompanied by instrumental music and chanting, eventually pasting one or two feathers on the symbol. In this particular Paoge ritual for the new members, after killing the rooster, its blood was introduced into the wine used for drinking the oath.[10]

Offsetting this relatively messy aspect of rites, the Paoge were also known to adapt the abstract aspects of ancient Chinese thought that touched on metaphysics and had entered mainstream religions. The Paoge formalized verse (taken up in more detail in future chapters), occasionally melding metaphysics with the everyday belief in supernatural powers. In this way China's old, established religions could also play a role in Paoge rituals. Consider one of the Paoge's numerous teacup arrangement rituals that acted as a form of signal intelligence and gesture (a topic explored in some detail in Chapter 4). In this example we find mention of the Five Elements inside the accompanying verse:

Metal, wood, water, fire, earth—the Five Elements,
Five Elements are Rulai's (the Tathagata Buddha's) power.
If you understand the patterns in space,
You will be the wise man of the lakes and seas.[11]

The concept of the Five Elements was adopted from traditional Chinese thought; it occupied an early and chief place in important cosmological discussions. Later this concept formed a large part of Daoism. But Rulai refers to Sakyamuni, the founder of Buddhism. Basically, the Gowned Brothers tried to absorb useful ideas from many sources, including the great textual and liturgical religions.

★　★　★

For more than a thousand years the story of Guan Yu was expressed in written fiction, storytelling, and local operas, especially in the well-known novel *Romance of Three Kingdoms*. Some thought that the name "Paoge" originated in Guan Yu's legend. Cao Cao purportedly found out that Guan Yu always wore an old gown, although Cao had given Guan many good clothes. Cao asked why, and Guan replied that the gown was given by his oath brother Liu Bei. In modern times people built on this tale in calling the Sworn Brotherhood the "Gowned Brothers."[12]

The coopting of a legend that had already entered popular novels by Ming times, and entered folk etymology as well, was not just a surface fixation on the part of the Paoge. The politico-historical Guan Yu brought a deeper meaning, as found in the nativist and ethnic tensions that ran from the late Ming period to the end of the Manchu Qing. The Gowned Brothers regarded themselves as descendants of the Han dynasty (206 BCE–220 CE), which, coming after the commonly debunked Qin dynasty, stood out as the origin-point of ethnic Han empire-building. This sentiment lined up with the Paoge's loyalty to the native Ming dynasty, which had fallen to the Manchus. In fact, they believed themselves to be "survivors of the Han" (*hanliu*).[13] The Paoge regarded Liu Bei, Guan Yu, and Zhang Fei (another general in the camp of Liu Bei and one of Liu's sworn brothers) as their moral examples. Over the centuries Guan Yu was transformed into a god of war who had remarkable power. Because the Paoge's emergence had come about in the cause of "overthrowing the Qing and restoring the Ming" (*fan Qing fu Ming*), there was a natural belief system and political cohesion with Guandi, who represented "Han-ness." Although the Manchu dynasty indeed collapsed after the 1911 Revolution, anti-Manchu traditions and culture continued in many places in China.

Historian Prasenjit Duara has published an excellent study of Guandi worship in North China that examines the process of Guan Yu, from historical figure to god. He cites a certain story to clarify the origin of Guandi worship. A Buddhist monk in meditation under a huge tree heard a low voice: "Return me my head." The monk recognized the ghost of Guan Yu—spirit of the mountain. He reminded Guan Yu of those whom he had beheaded. Guan Yu consequently sought the monk's instruction and had a monastery built there, and he took up guardianship of the mountain. Later, people built a Guan Yu temple. Guan Yu gradually became the god of wealth, a protection god for temples, artists, secret societies, and various professions.

The oldest Guandi temple was Yuquan Temple in Dangyang County, Hubei (built in 713), where, it was said, Guan Yu was killed. Beginning in the 800s, monks there regarded him as a tutelary deity. In the Song dynasty, Buddhist priests regarded Guan Yu as their patron saint, and the state awarded Guan glorious titles. Later, under the Southern Song (1127–1279), the god's status was promoted from "duke" (*gong*) to "king" (*wang*), perhaps in reflection of the Han court's famous promotion of Cao Cao in 217 from duke to king, when most people thought this to be an invitation to Cao Cao to take the throne for himself. In the Yuan era (1271–1368), Guan Yu officially became the god of war, recognized as such by officialdom. In 1615 he was apotheosized under the title "Guandi." The Ming court adopted the White Horse Temple in Beijing as the highest-ranking official Guandi temple.[14]

For the Paoge, Guan Yu supplied cohesion and appeal. Such beliefs became an important pillar of the organization. In the Qing, Guan Yu beliefs were part of the basis for Chinese nationalism. After the 1911 Revolution, however, anti-Manchuism was no longer an agenda, thus this form of worship early in the revolution was later converted into an important basis for secret society identities. In the ceremony mentioned previously, by calling the name of Guan Yu, members imagined (or believed) that the ritual could invite their hero Guandi to join them in the present moment. The presence of the god gave the members power and legitimacy, and thus they felt a bond with the god. The various agendas in the meeting—beliefs, utterances, narrated hero-legend, and rituals—led to the sort of legitimacy and authority that created order within the Paoge's membership, but even more so, it helped the secret society apply certain kinds of order in the surrounding local society. The ultimate effects of Guandi worship among the Paoge could only have come about by means of the god's traditional, local roots.

CHAPTER 4

Secret Codes and Language

CHAPTER 3 EXPLORED the Paoge's creative use of the politico-historical legend of Guan Yu cum Guandi and how that "god" found an anti-Manchu resonance as early as in popular pre-Qing novels like *Romance of the Three Kingdoms*. Another aspect of Chinese novels and secret societies was noticed by British historian Eric J. Hobsbawm, who studied the political impact of "bandits." He pointed out that many were like the heroes in another famous Ming-era novel titled *All Men Are Brothers* (Shuihu). These antiheroes, as it were, were located at the edge of agricultural society; they lacked education and economic skills but formed unique groups and developed their own language, which we might call an argot (or cant).[1] This was as common among secret societies in China as in the West. Argots not only protected secrets but also became a tool of identification and tactical intelligence. In Shen Baoyuan's investigation, she found unique words used by Paoge members in everyday life, rituals, and communication. Often referred to as "black words" (*heihua*) or "hidden lingo" (*yinyu*), some secret words (the name of the Paoge itself) originated from an emotion and agenda of "national spirit" and "revolutionary ideas as a way to refer to the anti-Manchu revolution. Shen listed four such words the Paoge often used—namely, Paoge, Hanliu, *guanggun*, and *paopinao*—and provided explanations, many of which are discussed in this chapter.[2]

To study technologically and economically marginalized people, we have to face the issue of how to find their voices. The study of Chinese secret societies has depended heavily on archival sources, especially reports by local officials—from governors to magistrates—and on prisoners' confessions under torture. In such sources, however, the voices of secret society members are inevitably distorted. *The Bottom of the Ocean* (Haidi)—the canon of the Gowned Brothers—is filled with examples of Paoge secret language. The special language echoes the members' and leaders' political thought, identity, and behavior, particularly when in the late nineteenth century the organization faced government pressure and attacks, when it also experienced unprecedented expansion. The secret language and the canon of the Paoge developed out of a distinctive subculture in Qing China, which offers insights into the social and political structures that shaped that subculture.[3] By looking at the canon and the Paoge's special language and symbols, we are better able to understand not only their thought (meaning systematic beliefs and/or epistemology) and behavior; we can also approach aspects of their organization, regulations, membership, internal dynamics, and their effecting of order both within their ranks and throughout the surrounding locale and state.

Linguists define *argot* as dialect "used by certain professions and secret societies"; an argot is "not supposed to be understood by outsiders" and thereby "can be distinguished from 'private' languages, jargons and 'slang,'" which are not formulated in the mold of secrecy and can be understood, to some degree, more generally. Therefore, argots come from "a particular subculture that is marginalized in society" and "represent its [that subculture's] main means of communication and survival." The use of argots was meant to protect the group at large, to hide it from the public, and to stabilize its membership. Argots tend to be less stable than standard languages because if they become publicly known, they would have to be replaced by a new argot.[4] The situation of the Paoge has basic similarities with the description just given, especially in its early years, but after the anti-Qing revolution the society was out in the open and their argot became more symbolic than practical. Since the Paoge was widespread and decentralized, some of their old words remained in use even after many did in fact become known publicly. But it may be that those Paoge words that stuck in the general pool of idioms were not those more difficult ones that formed particular syntactical patterns in the members' obscure canonical books and ceremonies. Moreover, along with the expansion of the secret society's membership, new words were constantly being created. The Paoge's argot paradoxically came to outlive the organization, showing up in common daily usage.

A secret language has a variety of social functions; these preserve secrecy within the inner community, provide "an expressive instrument where special needs can be fulfilled," and stabilize "membership in a limited group and control information flow and exchange."[5] The development of the Paoge's secret language was based on two important factors: their organizational acumen and the social and political environment that facilitated their increased visibility and political involvement. The argot and secret signs helped create a common identity for members and established a boundary between members and all other people, underscoring both the value and distinction of the in-group. Paoge argot became part of popular culture in the Chengdu Plain, and eventually, as the Paoge grew ever more powerful, it impacted society as a whole in Sichuan. The argot and secret signs provide a window through which we can understand social environments at that time in Sichuan, and we can trace the ways in which a social group succeeded in its various struggles with the government, while building a solid foundation among local people and creating a subculture. Paoge members, significantly, could share a common language regardless of individual social status. The structure and form of the organization contributed to its success, and their special modes of communication played a crucial role.

The Paoge's secret language was called by a range of names, often related either to the secret society's fundamental text or to some aspect of their underground practices. Because the fundamental text was titled *Bottom of the Ocean*, speakers of the argot were said to "catechize *The Bottom of the Ocean (pan* Haidi)," or more informally, they "showed the *Bottom*" (*liangdi*).[6] Speakers of the argot were said to "play with words" (*tuan tiaozi*). Or, in reference to the secretive nature of the organization, they spoke the language of "internal investigation" (*neipanhua*), or used the "cutting edge" (*qiekou*), or "the point of springtime" (*chundian*), or spoke a language that "had the same surname as Heaven" (*yu tian tongxing*). The argot was so important to the Gowned Brotherhood that the group had a saying: "I would rather pay ten strings of cash than reveal our secrets; I would rather pay an ingot of gold than explain the meaning of a word of our argot."[7] Paoge argot had branched out into the physical dimension by the use of a system of signals known as "arranging teacup formations" (*bai chawan zhen*). The teacups could be replaced with wine cups if a conversation were taking place in a wine shop, or with rice bowls if in a restaurant.

In the nineteenth century, when the bulk of the Paoge's secret language took form, the languages of secret societies in China were usually called "black words," as mentioned above. In Chinese dictionaries *heihua* is defined as "a secret language used by such groups as gangsters, rogues, and bandits." Such argots have a long history in China: secretive languages were used for various professions as early as the Tang dynasty (618–907). In the era of the Song dynasty (960–1279) and the Yuan (1279–1368), members of the lower classes—such as prostitutes, gamblers, bandits, robbers, and thieves—spoke secret languages and used hand signs. In the early Qing period, coded languages took on increasingly political meanings when used by anti-Manchu secret societies, including the Triads (Sandianhui), the Heaven and Earth Society (Tiandihui), the Elder Brothers Society (Gelaohui), and the Hong Society (Hongmen). During this era of underground resistance movements, secret languages were formalized through printing, with the publication of *Vital Knowledge of the River and Lake People* (Jianghu qieyao). This dictionary of argots included thirty-four categories and about sixteen hundred words. In the 1880s Zhuo Tingzi recompiled, expanded, and retitled the dictionary *New Edition of Vital Knowledge of the River and Lake People* (Xinke jianghu qieyao).[8] In this context "rivers and lakes" (*jianghu* or *pao jianghu*) referred to itinerants who traveled around plying various skills, such as fortune-telling, medicine, astrology, and Buddhist and Daoist services, each of which had its own specialized jargon. These jargons influenced the argot of the Paoge.

Fu Chongju's *Investigation of Chengdu* in the early twentieth century contained a note under the entry for "The Language of the Gowned Brothers in Chengdu" (*Chengdu zhi Paoge hua*); it claimed that this was "the same as the language of the itinerant peoples of the rivers and lakes."[9] It suggests that although the Paoge had their own argot, they often shared words with the "river and lake runners." Their language thus should be considered a typical argot, following the standard linguistic definition. An argot developed "not only from borrowing from dominant standard languages, but also from other argots characteristic of outsider groups in other social settings and situations."[10] It is noteworthy, however, that when Fu Chongju compiled his book, activities and membership in the Gowned Brothers was illegal; its activities were forbidden by government regulations. As a member of the reformist elite, Fu may have been politically motivated to categorize the secret societies' argot together with the languages of thieves and "river and lake runners." By implying that the Paoge were in the category of thieves and criminals, Fu participated in an official discourse about the Paoge. He could not have imagined that just a few years after he finished his book, the Paoge would become a driving force in the overthrow of the Qing dynasty and would act openly during the revolutionary era.

★　★　★

The Paoge's terminology often expressed their political orientation. The organization was explicitly political in its consistent objective of overthrowing the Qing. This goal was clearly stated in its canonical text, *The Bottom of the Ocean*, which recorded the history, principles, membership, and beliefs of the Paoge. The organization and its members were also called Hanliu, a strong expression of anti-Manchu sentiment. Here *han* refers to the Han people, as distinct from the Manchus. The *liu* could be written with three different Chinese characters of the same pronunciation. The first *liu* means "remain, stay in," or more acutely in this case, "survive." Smoothing out the implications of the two-word combination, we get "Han people survive," referring to the Han survivors of the fallen Ming dynasty, who in their martyrological and military actions created the seeds of an anti-Manchu movement. The second possible *liu* is a character that, in an adjectival sense used in descriptions, policy statements, and other verbiage for centuries, referred to people who broke away from or were outside of the state's census or registration. They were wanderers, migrants—by the later time an obvious reference to the Paoge.

The third *liu* is the character for the surname of the family who had ruled the Han dynasty, bringing to mind Liu Bei, the king of the State of Shu (Sichuan) during the Three Kingdoms period (220–265). He was described in Chapter 3, concerning the deification of Guan Yu and the impact on the Paoge of the ancient story of Liu Bei's Peach Garden oath of brotherhood with Guan Yu and Zhang Fei. This, plus Liu Bei's local Sichuan roots, served as a model for the Paoge and indeed for other male sodalities. This poem lauds these "three immortals" of the Paoge:

Three immortals came from noble families,
Heroes everywhere they loved to wander.
In the Peach Garden the three swore an oath long ago,
Sacrificing a black cow and a white horse to earth and heaven.[11]

The name Hanliu, with its rich field of associations, connects the Paoge with ancient heroes, sworn sodality, anti-Manchu politics, and Sichuan. However, even though *A Complete History of the Survivors of the Han* (another book of Paoge origins) states that the "rise of the Hanliu [as an organization] started from Zheng Chenggong's Golden Terrace Mountain," we still do not know exactly when the term Hanliu came into use.[12]

The putative Han and Ming roots of the Paoge often became an important content of their secret language. When "catechizing *The Bottom of the Ocean*," the Paoge brothers often revealed their political origins through highly allusive conversations. From Liu Shiliang's *Complete History of the Hanliu*, here is a typical conversation:

Q: What is the meaning of Hanliu?
A: The survivors of the Han people;

Q: Who was the first to create the idea of Hanliu and who put the idea into practice?
A: Wang Chuanshan created the idea but Zheng Chenggong built the Hanliu;

Q: When and where did Zheng Chenggong accomplish this?
A: The eighteenth year of Shunzhi regime (1661) in Taiwan;

Q: Wang Chuanshan was the creator of the Hanliu, but why did the Hanliu worship Zheng Chenggong, not Wang Chuanshan?
A: Because the Hanliu emphasize practice, not ideas.[13]

These identifying dialogues could continue at great length and incorporate references to all aspects of Paoge history, national history, legends, religion, and cultural practices. A member thus had to be familiar with all sorts of information about the organization to respond correctly and establish his status as an insider.

The argot was a powerful tool that could separate secret society members from other people. It thus helped create a common identity for the Paoge. Any member who arrived within the territory of another lodge had to pay a formal visit to the masters of that local lodge. In the late nineteenth century, British officer William Stanton recorded his investigation of the manner in which different secret societies communicated: "Sometimes the question and answer consists of rhymed stanzas, which however are not always given in full, as a word or two is generally sufficient for the initiated." Stanton also described various ways of testing visitors such as "arranging and handling teacups, tobacco-pipes, opium-pipes and other articles, and noticing the manner in which they are received."[14] If a gowned brother met his local host in a teahouse, for example, after entering, he would sit at the right side of an empty table. When provided a cup of tea, he would not drink it but would leave the lid on the saucer and sit quietly to signal that he was look-ing for fellows. The waiter would immediately understood this signal and might casually inquire: "From far away?" The visitor would reply with his name and his lodge's name. The teahouse keeper "who is familiar with this ceremony" would report immediately to the controller of the local lodge, who would appear and ask "a series of questions to the refugee, who must reply in appropriate, extremely technical terms. If the refugee proves to be an offender against government (i.e., not against Ko Lao Hui [Gelaohui]) laws, the controller will offer him shelter, or sufficient funds, clothes, and the like to enable him to reach another destination of his choice."[15] As the anti-Manchu movement gained momentum, it created opportunities for the Paoge to expand their influence. In the process it also increased traffic between lodges. The use of specialized communication techniques, which acted as security and intelligence gathering, became one mark of participa-tion in the brotherhood and its antigovernment activities.

Members of the Paoge used their familiarity with *The Bottom of the Ocean* and the specialized spoken language used by the organization to prove their membership and also their experience and ability. For example, a visitor might introduce himself using a set framework as follows: "A dragon should have a dragon's place and a tiger should have a tiger's space. I might have seen some of you before but some I have never met. For those I have seen before, let me salute you again; for those I have never met, let me say hello to you. Let me introduce myself." Then he would say his name, which lodge he belonged to, his position in the lodge, and so forth. All the people around the table would do the same. Such treatment of visitors reflected the commonly held notion that Paoge brothers would always look out for oth-ers, even in a world where this kind of respect was otherwise hard to come by.[16] One Paoge lodge might host visitors from other lodges for all sorts of purposes—leisure or business travel, passing through the territory on an errand, seeking help in a fight, or escaping from law enforcement. Fugitives who committed homicide were usually given money to cover their travel expenses and sent away. Thus a Paoge brother could find a place to stay when he was on a trip or get financial assistance or protection when he needed it. This custom became a useful tool that bound members together, a powerful attraction that brought many people into the organization.

Some early accounts recorded concrete examples of how the Paoge brothers tested prospective members. For example, the question-answer interview might take this form:

Q: Where do you come from?
A: From the Kunlun (that is, Mount Kunlun).

Q: Where are you going?
A: To the City of Willows (Muyang cheng).

Q: How many streets and alleys are there in the city?
A: There are thirty-six large streets and seventy-two small alleys.

Q: "How many attractions are there in the city?
A: There are three stoves and eighteen pans in the East City Gate and three pans and eighteen stoves in the West City Gate.

Such dialogues make frequent mention of "the City of Willows." The term is argot for "headquarters" and another name for a lodge or, as it was sometimes called, "Mountain Hall" (Figure 4.1).

In his 1900 book, Stanton also recorded some more common Paoge questions and answers indicating membership. These include:

Q: Why is your hair so unkempt?
A: I was born under a peach tree.

Q: Why is your hair so ruffled?
A: I have been to extinguish a fire.

Q: Why is your hair so wet?
A: I have not long been born.

Q: Why has your hair got so many cobwebs in it?
A: They are not cobwebs, but five-colored silk.

Sometimes, a member would deliberately bump into an outsider on the street. If the outsider was a Paoge brother, he would say, "Are you blind?" The member would reply, "I'm not blind, my eyes are bigger than yours."[17]

Shen Baoyuan's report contains another aspect of secret language—that is, the more structured speech patterns that were uttered in high ceremonial contexts. She wrote about these under the heading "Examples of Paoge

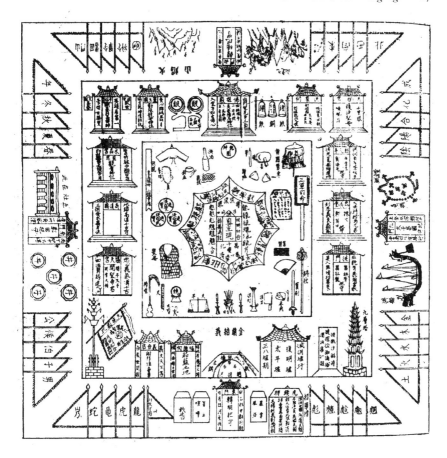

FIGURE 4.1 The floorplan of the meeting hall in a Paoge headquarter. Note the flags, slogans, terms, codes, tablets, and so forth. *Source*: Li Zifeng 1940: 101.

Collected Orders [i.e, Rites and Phrases]" (*Paoge lingji juli*), which quoted certain words or verses used in the procedures of Paoge meetings. Some examples are "initiation ceremony" (*kaitang*), "in praise of joss sticks and candles" (*zan xiangzhu*), "welcoming sages" (*yingsheng*), "greeting guests" (*jieke*), and "killing sacrifices" (*caisheng*). More specifically, the "Verse of the Initiation Ceremony," also known as "Opening the Dragon Gate" (*kai long-men*), announced by any Paoge member, was as follows:

Opening a lucky day in Heaven,
Where the Dragon Gate is highly auspicious.
Heroes gather together,
Meeting at the Loyal Hall.[18]

Then the First Brother (the helmsman) announced the "Verse for Seating" (*anweiling*):

Opening day is highly auspicious,
When heroes have a meeting at the Loyal Hall.
Have responsibilities as our ancestors,
And everyone finds his seat in order.[19]

Then the Fifth Brother (the manager) called out the "Verse of Han Survivors" (*Hanliu ling*):

All Paoge brothers are like a family,
And the meaning of Hanliu is significant.
The day we swear our brotherhood—different surnames become one belly,
Like begonia blossom in spring wind.[20]

In addition, there are some Paoge verses in a 1934 work titled *The Bottom of the Ocean in the Chengdu River and Lake* (Chengdu jianghu haidi). This is from the "Verse of Killing Sacrifice":

We are so happy in the Loyal Hall,
Where the First Brother places a phoenix.
Phoenix, Phoenix,
We will imitate Liu, Guan, and Zhang in the Peach Orchard.
Our brothers swear the oath,
Placing dragon and phoenix to show luck.
Happy in the Loyal Hall,
Younger brother comes to place the phoenix.
Since a table has four corners,
I place the phoenix at the center.[21]

Here the word *phoenix* means the sacrificial rooster in the Paoge's argot (Chapter 3 detailed the rooster sacrifice). Newcomers became new members after taking the oath and needed a long time "to learn rules." The helmsman taught the newcomers the Paoge's regulations, customs, and unwritten laws, including ten principals and ten preventative measures. Shen Baoyuan tried to explain this procedure from sociological theory: "this type of teaching actually contained inspirational" and "artificial control" aspects. In using the method, "the instructor uses his greater prestige to shape newcomers' faith in order to effectively control them." After the instructions the newcomers would memorize and recite those regulations, rules, history, and argots, all of which came from *The Bottom of Ocean*—"real teaching materials" and the "theoretical foundation" of the Paoge. All branches adopted the book as the basis of verifying the identity of a visitor or a newcomer.[22]

Generally, branches of the Paoge always helped each other and regarded helping and hosting the Paoge members as their own obligation. An official document said, "A member of Gelaohui or a criminal would carry an identity card." Wherever he arrived in a place, he presented the card to the local manager. When a Paoge member arrived in a new place, he first had to visit the headquarters of the local branch and to meet the helmsman and other brothers. This procedure was called "worshiping at the harbor" (*bai matou*).[23] The manager would arrange a lodge for the visitor, offer daily spending money, and protect his life. If one was involved a large criminal case, the manager would appoint a few brothers to travel with him and send him to a safe place. Therefore, "a refugee could always find his place to hide."[24] The Paoge brothers thus formed a tight network of self-protection. According to one member's memoir, a Paoge brother would be treated to food and drink wherever he went. A common phrase was, "If you expect a room [with the Paoge], then you will eat" (*wangwu chifan*).[25]

Before visiting a local branch of the Paoge, the traveler had to first present his identity card, called "personal card with cursive characters" (*caozi danpian*) as the initial introduction. If this newcomer was hunted by officials, a corner of his card would be torn off—a sign of the refugee, sometimes referred to as a "beach runner" (*paotanzhe*). Generally, the visitor had to recite the "text for worship at the Harbor" (*bai matou shu*), in which we do not get pure incomprehensible argot but merely several lexical substitutions, such as the use of "planting peach and plum," "dragons and tigers," and "precious harbor". For example, from Shen Baoyuan's report:

My coming is brash,
Hoping for the brothers' support.
I have long heard of our brothers' kindness,
Strong-willed and benevolent.
You have established headquarters here,
Gathering heroes from all over places.
Plant peach and plum trees,
Guaranteeing red fruit for ten thousand years.
I would like to obey your orders,
Although just arrived at your honored place, your precious harbor,
I present my identity card,
I pay respects at your precious camp, brother dragons and tigers.

The manager would answer:

I didn't know that elder brother comes this way,
So I did not prepare for ahead for your arrival.
Please do not blame me that I did not welcome you.
Elder brother is kind, righteous, succeeding in the Peach Garden Oath.[26]

Everyone who joined the Paoge would participate in a ritual that followed the model of the Peach Garden Oath, which became a symbol of the Paoge.

After the polite opening, they would begin a conversation using their argots. The visitor had to answer questions accurately; otherwise he could be considered a spy and might be executed:

Q: Did elder brother come via water or land route?
A: I came from both water and land.

Q: How many mountains from land and how many beaches from water did you travel?
A: I saw neither mountains due to heavy fog nor beaches due to vastness of the river.

Q: How could you prove it?
A: I have evidence.[27]

This last example may seem like words in normal conversational Chinese, but we might term them argot, as they functioned as semisecret codes and had to be used accurately.

Gowned Brothers frequently called themselves *guanggun* (literally, "bare sticks"), in which *guang* meant clean ("without any dust and bright") and *gun* meant straight ("without any bend"). They considered themselves the bright and righteous people, just the opposite of Fu Chongju's comments earlier in the chapter. This is possibly a subversive reinterpretation of the everyday vocabulary indicating undesirables and rogues. Generally speaking, a *guanggun* is an unattached male ("bare/naked sticks"); it could also mean a "hooligan" or a man without followers and friends. But in the argot of the Gowned Brothers, *guanggun* seems to have implied a certain fearlessness. The brothers simply could rework the vocabulary and argue that instead of bare sticks, they are unsullied and firm—that is, heroes and not villains.[28] The identity served the members well, since it was important to create a boundary that set apart their inner workings and solidarity from outsiders. A man who tried to approach the organization but without good knowledge of *The Bottom of the Ocean* could be regarded as a man who was trying to sneak in. He might be called "no basis man" (*kongzi*), who could be considered a spy of the government or of a rival group, and he might suffer punishment.

Besides the arranging of teacups and reciting of poems, the Paoge often used complex gestures and hand signs that underwent "endless changes." Without a word, they were able to communicate with each other, part of their "body language." Take the example of how Paoge verbiage and body language expressed the ancient metaphysical concept of the Five Elements (discussed in Chapter 3). A member clasped both hands together on the top of his head, representing the character "metal." He extended his hands across his belly, meaning "wood." He stood with his legs wide apart and placed his hands on his hips, indicating "water." He stood in the same

FIGURE 4.2   Paoge body signs of the Five Elements. From left, gold, wood, earth, fire, and water. *Source*: Li Zifeng 1940: 269.

position as above but raised his arms to either side of his head, as high as his ears, with his palms up, indicating "fire." He sat down on the ground and placed both hands on his knees, which meant "earth" (Figure 4.2).[29] One might say that these gestures were a kind of body-writing, since the body tried to articulate the shape of a Chinese character. While argots were influenced by the standard language and professional jargon, body language was solely created by the secret societies themselves, reflecting their ability to adopt many methods of communication for survival and for taking action.

★   ★   ★

Lineages, native associations, and professional guilds played an important role in traditional communities all over China, but marginalized groups usually did not have an establishment to protect their interests. Secret societies provided them with an alternative. The specialized language of the Paoge reflects its function as an effective network for the marginalized. A peasant or an itinerant peddler joining the Gowned Brothers entered the so-called garden (*yuan*, that is, the Peach Garden), gained a piece of "skin" (*pi*), and became a "stick" (*guanggun*). Hence he had a network for his protection. As one saying stated, "A stick will get ten people's help" (*yige guanggun, shijia bangmang*). Without the "skin" he would be regarded as a "no basis man": "Gowned Brothers are raised up by three steps; no basis men are pushed down three steps" (*hangjia tai sanfen, kongzi ya sanfen*). Upon joining the Paoge, the member might also be called a "man in the ocean" (*hailiao*) or a "man in the circle" (*quanzi*). His name would be passed around to let all members of the lodge know of his initiation; the process was known as "moving with the red sheet" (*zou hongdan*). In cities the Paoge often dominated streets or neighborhoods, and this phenomenon was called "skin rules the street" (*piguanjie*). As Zhou Xun, a magistrate in the late Qing, said, all of the heads of the streets in Chengdu "were members of the Paoge."[30]

According to linguist Wolf Leslau, argots generally have three forms: (1) using the "roots of the standard language" but "transforming them through various phonetic and morphological procedures"; (2) keeping the roots of the standard language "without transforming them but giving them special meaning"; and (3) borrowings.[31] All three types are in evidence in the specialized language of the Paoge. In the first case, the Paoge made up specialized characters to protect their secrecy. They did this using various methods. In some cases they omitted character components or invented weird characters, while in others they borrowed characters with the same pronunciation or blended a few characters into one character, or divided a character into a sentence, and so on. Therefore, even if a written letter fell into the hands of others, the secret would remain intact. New characters were called "hidden characters" (*yinzi*). For example, *Shun tian zhuan ming* ("Turning to the Ming by following the will of the Heaven") could be written *chuan da che ri* ("river, big, cart, sun"), taking a piece from each character in the phrase. This sort of word play was a subtle kind of onomancy, with roots in ancient occult arts and even used by political oracles. A volatile anti-Manchu political slogan thus could have a protective gloss or lexical code that obscured the real message to the uninitiated (Figure 4.3).

Such changed characters often appeared in the "cards for distribution" (*chuantie*) of the Gowned Brothers, which were of two types. One was in the form of a bamboo strip to be used on occasions of calling for a mustering; on the slip was written the time and place of the gathering and a warning of punishment for absence without cause. The second type used miscellaneous forms and carried a wide variety of messages, such as asking for help in a fight or for a place to stay.[32] Much of the specialized language used by the Paoge falls into the second category in Leslau's model. The brothers invested new meanings into words in the standard language without changing the words themselves. The manner in which new meanings were given varied. Often, simply toying with imagery gained a new meaning; for instance, a counselor or strategist of the Paoge was called the "hand-warmer holder" (*ti honglong*) (such warmers were common in winter, made of plaited bamboo set in an earthenware dish that held charcoal or wood embers). One can only wonder: maybe these counselors were thought of as the soft brains of the operation, requiring protection from the cold.

A Paoge master controlled a lodge, so he was usually the helmsman (*duobazi*). This argot term symbolizes the man's power, as he decided the direction of the organization just like a captain holds the handle of the rudder. Probably because the Paoge were always connected with "river and lake

FIGURE 4.3 Examples of "hidden characters." At top right, the words indicate *zhong xin yi qi* ("loyal heart and righteous force"). At bottom right, these four characters are combined together into a hidden character. In the middle, the words indicate *fan Qing* ("overthrow the Qing"); at bottom middle, these two characters combine together into a hidden character. At top left, the words indicate *fu Ming* ("restore the Ming"); at bottom left, these two characters combine together into a hidden character. *Source*: Li Zifeng 1940: 267–68.

runners," many of their argot expressions were related to water: their headquarters were called "harbor"; newcomers visiting local masters were said to "worship at the harbor." The Paoge itinerant lifestyle was compared to "running on the beach" (*paotan*); members being chased by the government referred to themselves as facing "rising waters" (*shuizhangle*); "water flowing rapidly" (*shuijindehen*) meant that the situation was dangerous; to say that the "water was leaking" (*zoushuile*) meant that a plot had been revealed.[33] However, there were many other borrowed words and phrases that did not follow any rules, used on a temporary basis to guard a secret.

The third type of borrowing existed as well, alongside the second. The Paoge appropriated local slang and professional jargon for their own use.

Gowned Brothers came from all kinds of backgrounds, which provided rich sources for their language, and they borrowed professional jargon, especially for argot words regarding criminal activities. For example, they avoided saying "kill" but replaced it with moderate words. Thus, to "feather someone" (*bata maole*) was to drown someone by throwing him into the water; "passing someone around" (*chuanliao*) meant to bury alive or assassinate him; "finishing him" (*zuole*) or "tearing him" (*caile*) also referred to killing. Many of these words and phrases were borrowed from the jargon of professions, including terms used by butchers, tailors, and craftsmen as well as by thieves and bandits with whom the Paoge shared certain affinities. If the brothers were planning a robbery, they would say "sneak into the village" (*mozhuang*) or "write on the counter" (*xietaikou*) or "see some happy money" (*kancaixi*). The ringleader was said to be the guy "carrying a roof beam" (*tailiangzi*).

To kidnap a child for ransom was called "carrying a boy" (*baotongzi*), but to kidnap a woman was to "welcome a Guanyin" (*jie Guanyin*) and to kidnap a rich man was to "pull a fat pig" (*lafeizhu*). After a successful robbery or kidnapping, they would divide the loot, termed "items displayed on the ground" (*baidiba*). If a member got a few ingots of silver, he would say he had a few "fat hens" (*feimuji*). For this reason Fu Chongju pointed out that the argot of the Paoge "also includes the language of thieves and bandits, which people have to fully realize. When one finds men speaking this language, he should stay away from them to avoid being hurt. They have many special words, and there is no way to give a complete list."[34] By listing these terms, critics of the organization (such as Fu Chongju) indicated that the Paoge was violent and committed all sorts of crimes. Their misconduct gave law enforcement a good excuse to pursue them. However, the Qing government sought to suppress the organization largely due to its anti-Manchu political agenda.

We do not have the kind of detailed information that would allow us to trace the processes through which this secret society's argot took shape over time. However, judging from when *The Bottom of the Ocean* and *The Language of the Itinerant Peoples of the Rivers and Lakes* were printed, we have reason to believe that the nineteenth century was a transformative period in the history of the secret language of the Paoge. During this time social and political challenges infused the organization and its language with new and more intensely politicized meanings. Hand gestures and teacup formations signaled anti-Manchu sentiment, even as the Paoge's use of politico-historical legend did make it seem in some sense like an innocuous local Sichuan worship association. By digging into the argot, we come to know the expressions used by an antigovernment counterculture that increasingly influenced, and was influenced by, popular sentiments.

The Bottom of the Ocean is a deliberately mysterious text whose purported origins and recovery bind it tightly to the earlier anti-Manchu politics. Through this canonical text the Paoge highlighted their organization's real or imagined roots in a lineage of anti-Manchu movements and identified themselves as proud members of an illicit group. Using the text and the gestures it encoded, strangers could create a connection to a larger community. By moving teacups, reciting poems, and participating in call-and-response dialogues, members from all walks of life could engage in political activities and legitimize illegal actions. In their own language the Paoge became righteous warriors who were trying to overthrow Manchu rule. In the government's words, they were a criminal gang of rebels and ruffians—an organization to be marginalized, suppressed, or exterminated. The general populace, however, had more complex feelings about the Paoge, depending on individual experiences.

Given that the members could and did commit relatively serious crimes, many of their illegal behaviors and acts were exaggerated by elites and officials, who had political power and cultural hegemony and whose discourse about the Paoge and how to handle them to some extent influences our views today. There was always an excuse to suppress "dangerous" people. The organization surely wanted their anti-Manchu ideology spread, so from this perspective a broader dissemination of secret language, codes, and gestures also helped disseminate its name and agenda. Because of this, the argot came out into the open; it became audible (and visible) in such public contexts as teahouses and streets. Through an open communication—and strategic alliances with such political figures as Sun Yatsen—the political thought of the organization spread and enhanced the group's antidynastic image. At the same time, it is also true that many of those without education, without political intentions, joined the organization chiefly to enhance their livelihoods or personal security.

Secret society argot and gestures like those of the Paoge were not unique to Sichuan, of course. We find similar phenomena in other regions. The Paoge had connections with other secret societies, and its origins can even be traced back to the Triads, the Heaven and Earth, and the Hong organizations. The Paoge canon—*The Bottom of the Ocean*—was also used by those societies. Therefore, it is not surprising that they all shared features of the broader manner of communication. In fact, the argot was not as secret as members might have thought. When the Paoge brothers spoke argot, engaged in "teacup formations," or recited poems in public, outsiders might have identified them easily because of such purposefully opaque techniques. When a member met a man who spoke the same language, he would regard the man as his own kind and naturally trust him. He was expected to offer help whether or not they had met each other before. All of these protocols reflected a political culture that developed inside a special niche of society.

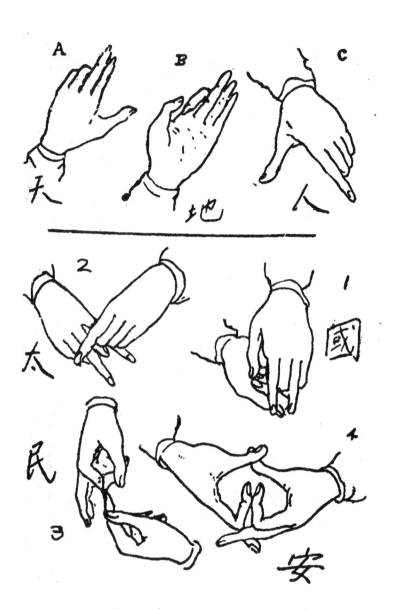

FIGURE 4.4 Hand signs of some important concepts of the secret society. From top left to right, the three signs indicate "Heaven," "earth," and "man." From middle right to left and from bottom left to right, the four signs indicate "country," "prosperity," "people," and "peace." *Source:* Li Zifeng 1940: 270.

The casual observer would feel that he was watching a unique performance when two Paoge brothers performed rituals. The behaviors per se separated members from other citizens and piqued the curiosity of ordinary people— the outsiders. Furthermore, their puzzling manner itself was a means of survival as well as a challenge to local power. At times, it seems the format of rituals became more important than communication itself because they were so proud of their identity and their knowledge of *The Bottom of the Ocean* that they became as actors who perform onstage, playing a role in a broad social drama (Figure 4.4).

CHAPTER 5

Disciplines and Dominance

PREVIOUS CHAPTERS have taken up the Paoge's Guandi rites, allowing us to bring the broader, social drama indoors, into the Paoge's own venues. Yet there was nothing truly secret or obscure about Guandi, at least in the eyes of the commoner of the Chengdu Plain as well as those living in Hope Township and other small towns. We also considered argot, formalized speech, and cloaked, tactical communication (the subject of Chapter 4). The Paoge could nurture an inner identity that demanded role-playing—as abiders in brotherhood, talkers of insider speech, performers of tactics—as a way to stay whole under pressure from governments and from interlopers. They were acting these roles openly but as secretive, self-controlled men. The group could thus refine and deploy their political potential. In this chapter the Paoge's methods of selecting members, keeping them in line, scrutinizing "others," and applying violence come into play. I contend that these increasingly outer processes (going from membership control and internal punishments, to the Paoge's larger profile in the local community) allowed them to fit into a relatively mundane yet important political role, much like that of traditional magistrates. We see this in particular in the practice of "negotiation tea"—the aim of which was to settle local affairs.

We start with rules. As a secret society, rules were essential in ways perhaps more critical than in open societies and groups. The reason the Paoge could survive for nearly three hundred years under constant attack from the state was to rely on strict, internal rules that called for utter obedience. These rules became a foundation for the Paoge's internal stability. The organization was so powerful that it attracted relatively powerless people to join and to take advantage of a clear-cut, rule-bound group that offered protection. Paoge regulations carried quite tough consequences for those who did not observe them properly. Any member who violated them would be punished accordingly, so they had a saying in their argot: "Six holes with three stabs, you yourself find the right places on your body" (*sandao liugeyan, ziji zhao diandian*). This of course referred to committing suicide: "six holes with three stabs" is three stabs from one side of the body through to another side.[1] A foreigner once investigated such punishments and wrote about two examples. One was called "falling on the knife" (*puqiandao*) in which the offender knelt before the tablets of the gods and applied a dagger to his thigh until the blood flowed freely. The other, "rolling on the nail board" (*gun dingban*), involved placing a board of nails on the ground with points projecting and then rolling the offender on this spiked board until his body was covered with blood.[2]

In the section of Shen Baoyuan's report called "Ten Restrictions and Three Taboos of Internal Rules of the Paoge," we see that all Paoge members had to follow certain ethical disciplines, otherwise there would be severe punishment. These include:

1. Fulfill filial duty for parents.
2. Respect elders.
3. No bullying of the weak.
4. Be friendly among brothers.
5. Keep a harmonious relation with neighbors.
6. Behave modestly and courteously.
7. Be loyal.
8. Be benevolent.
9. Understand one's own position and duty.
10. Speak and act cautiously.

In addition, there were three taboos toward women. The key was to avoid "lasciviousness." These rules included:

1. When you meet your sister-in-law, bow your head and do not stare at her.
2. When you see a woman, do not flirt with her; treat her just like your sister.
3. When you meet a widow or a nun, never have an obscene thought.[3]

Shen Baoyuan described the ritual of granting awards, exacting punishments, and taking oaths of membership—all of which took place in the Paoge's Single Broadsword Festival on the thirteenth day of the fifth lunar month (this was part of a wider celebration of the apotheosized Guan Yu, or Guandi). The Paoge manager (*guanshi*) presided over the procedures. During punishment discussions, all Paoge brothers "waited to see if something would inexplicably implicate them," which reflected the fact that punishment for offenses was based on "secret investigations without announcement in advance." Most of the lower-level brothers were "fearful with a guilty conscience," afraid that their names might be mentioned. If one was indeed named, he first defended himself or admitted the allegations, then he chose to take a voluntary form of punishment. Felony crimes such as adultery—including the relatively outrageous one of sexual relations with, or molestation of, a Paoge brother's wife—"could result in ordered suicide." In other cases, the criminal could be assassinated. Less severe violations might call for a downgrading of a member, terminating membership, or the delivery of corporal punishment. There was also a procedure of rewards, for those who had made contributions to the Paoge in some specific period of time.[4]

Potential new members had to attend a ceremony and take the oath. Prior to the formal ceremony, the candidate had to go through a procedure: he was scrutinized for his family background, often to find out if he or any of his family had ever been a bandit or a barber or a pedicurist. Pedicure service was considered a "lower-class profession" (*jianye*), specifically not allowed in a Paoge candidate. The Paoge banned barbers because of a political factor. It was said that there were no professional barbers in China before the Qing dynasty and that barbering as an occupation emerged only after the Qing government forced ethnic Han men to have their hair cut and wear the queue style. Barbers were thus known as *daizhao* (edict carriers), because they hung the imperial edict concerning this tonsorial imposition on their wooden boards wherever they set up practice. They were therefore regarded by the anti-Manchu Paoge as servants of the Qing. Barbers were called *daizhao* even in novels, such as those by Li Jieren.[5]

According to Shen Baoyuan's investigation, new members had to be supported by several active Paoge members. First, he was introduced by an "obliging brother" (*enxiong*); then he would be recommended by the "leading-in man" (*yinjin*); finally, he would be guaranteed by his "guarantor" (*baoju*), who would bear responsibility for the newcomer. When the ceremony was held, the newcomers first worshiped at the statue of Guan Yu, then he kowtowed to the helmsman and again to his three supporters. Next, they would present burning incense and sacrifices to the altar. After the ritual was completed, the Third Brother explained the structure and rules of the organization, and then the manager expressed his blessing. Finally, the oath would be carried out and a rooster killed as sacrifice. A poem in praise of the rooster was recited:

The rooster is more beautiful than a phoenix,
When it was born wearing five-color cloth.
As soon as civil officials hear its crowing,
Fingering the court tablets, they enter the court hall.
As soon as military officers hear its crowing,
They assemble men and horses and arrive at the drill ground.
As soon as we hear its crowing,
We arrange clothes and hats to go to the meeting hall.

According to Shen Baoyuan's report, when the rooster was killed, a song would be sung:

Rooster, rooster,
It is not me who wants to kill you today,
Because brothers would like to use you for luck.
Happy for you;
Congratulations for you.
Take off your jacket and wear a cloth gown.[6]

★   ★   ★

We turn now to a fascinating procedure called "arranging teacup formations" (*bai chawan zhen*), one that Shen Baoyuan did not document.[7] The procedure occupies the border between inner and outer actions of the Paoge. On the one hand, it uses a rather secretive code meant only for insiders; on the other, it addresses the wider world of intergroup intelligence gathering—that is, a desire for knowledge that could lead to territorial control. The mode of communication itself, very popular among the Paoge brothers, formed another sort of argot and ritual. The term "formation" is a clear reference to tactics on a battlefield, adopted from ancient military manuals. "Formation" indicated that a tea table could be considered a model "battlefield," where various forces challenged each other. Poems contain references to such "tea-table battles" and could often express anti-Qing sentiment and the hidden ideology of "overthrowing the Qing and restoring the Ming behind the movement of tableware."[8] This type of secret society activity existed widely throughout the long period from the early Qing to 1911. There were many specific teacup formations, and most were used to test a visitor's status and his knowledge of the wider organization. A host arranged the teacups into many formations, so the visitor had to have the ability to track quickly the changes of formation and to recite appropriate poems.

Engaging in so-called teacup formations involved a common set of circumstances. When any member entered a teahouse, the waiter would immediately recognize his identity from his gestures and the way he carried and set down his teacup.[9] When a local head of a lodge went out to meet the newcomer, he would place teacups in a certain pattern—a signal of the beginning of their dialogue. If the host first wanted to check the visitor's membership, he would make a "willow formation" (*muyang zhen*), in which one cup was in the saucer and the other to the side of it (Figure 5.1). The visitor would take the outside cup, place it in the saucer, drink from it, and then recite the poem:

The City of Willows is our whole world,
The sworn brothers can rely fully [on me]—just one spot of Hong.

Today my brother comes to make inquiries,
Please do not treat me like a stranger.[10]

Or the host arranged the "two-dragon formation" (*shuanglong zhen*), in which he put his teacup directly opposite to that of the visitor, who would recite the poem:

Two dragons are playing in the water happily,
Like Han Xin visiting Zhang Liang.
Today brothers meet here,
Drinking tea before discussing business.[11]

If a member went to another lodge to ask for help, he would set up a "single-whip formation" (*danbian zhen*), a teacup facing the mouth of a small teapot. If the host did not wish help, he would spill the tea on the ground. If he agreed, he would drink the cup of tea, then pour new tea into the cup, drink, and recite the poem:

The Single Broadsword rides a horse alone to the horizon,
Taking dust and more dust, to arrive at this place.
The transforming golden dragon: he meets with fortune,
And helps our lord mount the throne.[12]

The arranging of teacup formations and reciting of relevant poems expressed the thoughts, beliefs, morals, history, and culture of the Paoge. Many of their ideas came from popular novels, local operas, and legends. The "two-dragon formation," for example, represented Han Xin and Zhang Liang, the generals who helped Liu Bang establish the Han dynasty.[13] There are quite a few of these formations related to dragons. The Paoge used dragons to express strength and political ambition, which reflected their bond with the traditions of the Han people who regarded themselves as descendants of the dragon.[14] The Paoge also imagined themselves as survivors of the Han (discussed in Chapter 4), so they naturally had a bond with the dragon. In China the dragon represented the enormous political power to be found in an outstanding leader; he could dominate the world by enhancing goodness and suppressing evil, which fitted the ideology of the Paoge and legitimated their anti-Manchu agenda. The highest position in a Paoge lodge was often called the "dragon head" (*longtou*)—synonymous with the helmsman. He was the one who made final decisions.[15]

Indirectly related to the political power of the "dragon," the Paoge valued violence and regarded it as the best solution for problems in the outside world as well as within their own world.[16] For instance, the "treasure-sword formation" (*baojian zhen*) stated:

Placing the seven-star treasure sword in the center,
With iron mien and devoid of sentiment, the heroes emerge.

FIGURE 5.1 Examples of teacup formations. The diagrams indicate (1) "willow formation"; (2) "two-dragon formation"; (3) "single-whip formation"; (4) "treasure-sword formation"; (5) "loyal heart and righteous force"; (6) "five heroes tea formation"; (7) "turning the Qing to the Ming"; and (8) "one dragon formation." *Source*: Li Zifeng 1940: 210, 213, 218, 227, and 230.

Tens of thousands of heroes killed,
Without our Hong family's suffering a scratch.[17]

Many of the teacup formation poems expressed the ideology of "over-throwing the Qing and restoring the Ming" (*fan Qing fu Ming*). In a teacup formation called "loyal heart and righteous force" (*zhongxin yiqi cha*) three cups—one full, one half, and one empty—were lined up on the table. A member of the Paoge would drink the half-full cup and recite:

Neither do I care for the dry bowl
Nor do I like the full.
The Han are in my heart
So, I drink at last.[18]

The term "full" (*man*) in the second line has a double meaning; while seeming to be about the tea water in the cup, it actually indicates the "Manchus" (Man).

The poem for the "five heroes tea" formation (*wukui cha*) expressed a similar sentiment:

We struggle [*fan*] to bring back our old rulers
Because the Qing occupy our capital.
Restore [*fu*] earth and heaven to our masters
Bright [Ming] moon inspires us rebel.[19]

The first character of each line, together taken as a sentence, form the slogan "Overthrow the Qing and restore the Ming" (*fan Qing fu Ming*), the long-standing goal of the Gowned Brothers. In the teacup formation "turning the Qing to the Ming" (*zhuan Qing Ming cha*), there were eight cups, and when a member drank one, he had to say, "Restore the Ming and destroy the Qing" (*fu Ming mie Qing*) and then recite the poem:

The country belongs to the Hong family
Who bring the whole territory together.
Killing all Manchu barbarians
Our brothers protect true dragons.[20]

The poem of the "one dragon formation" (*yilong zhen*) also contains this core idea:

A lotus flower floating in the water
Use it to clean my cutter.
Swallow the Qing empire into my stomach
And blow it out as a giant blue-green rainbow.[21]

Simultaneously, members established contact with each other in wine shops or restaurants by arranging wine cups or rice bowls and reciting poems. If a member saw a pair of chopsticks placed on a bowl, he would raise the chopsticks with three fingers and claim:

Carry a metal spear with one hand
And a pair of maces with the other.
Break your city's wall and moat,
To save our true lord.[22]

If he saw five bowls on the table, with one at the center and four around it but only the central one covered, an insider was supposed to recite the poem:

All territory in the four directions belongs to the Ming
Only at the center is the Qing not yet destroyed.
The loyal and righteous do not yet share the territories
Brothers of the same heart fight the Qing to the end.[23]

★　★　★

In Hope Township, when a visitor passed tests like these, the helmsman would accept and treat him to meals every day for "ten days or even half a year, no complaints." If the problem confronting the visitor was not very serious, he might stay until the crisis ended; if it was a major case, the helmsman would examine the situation, estimate the risk, and then decide his fate. If the helmsman decided not to keep the visitor around, he could give him a sum of money and quickly send him out. In most instances, as long as the situation permitted, the local Paoge would shelter visitors, because the reputation of "chivalry" was crucial for the Paoge. Shen Baoyuan commented on this in her report: "The central idea of Gelaohui is mainly to train heroes to fulfill righteousness." In theory, she wrote, "to undertake benevolence and righteousness is their main doctrine." This attitude meshed with a certain type of traditional Chinese ethics. The Paoge could insinuate themselves increasingly in the processes of social control and build bridges between different classes of society. The Paoge with resources thus were seen from various points of view as relieving the poor. Unemployed people could depend on the Paoge to find work, while in the meantime being helped by the brothers. Even the "righteous river and lake runners," strangers who were criminals, received long-term assistance from the Paoge in some cases.

In Hope Township, and in many other places, all of this was not so utterly righteous. So-called local heroes set about "to seize their own power-area by using violence." Disputes between branches of the Paoge often took place, even resulting in deaths. Of course, using violence was essential for their survival. They solved problems that representatives of the government could not. Sometimes, according to Shen Baoyuan, "their power is beyond the government's domination over the place." In fact, the Paoge and local governments often became one. As mentioned previously, leaders of the Paoge often served as heads of township and ran the *baojia* system. Shen found that the leaders of the Paoge in Hope Township "have actually mixed together with the ruling class in the local place."[24] Often, local projects could be accomplished only after receiving Paoge support. The Paoge and state power in some local places were thus interdependent.

Of course, there were other social organizations in Hope Township, such as native place, charitable, and religious groups. Each played a role within its own area respectively, while functioning together. Most people in Hope Township were members of one or more of such organizations and, to varying degrees, were "manipulated by a secret society." At some point, this impact by the Paoge began to diverge from the relatively innocent affairs of native place, charity, and religion. In Shen's words, the Paoge in Hope Township had gradually moved away from the standard of "kindheartedness and justice" and "gallantry," from once challenging established powers to working simply to increase their interests "at the expense of the masses." They even degenerated into "accomplices of feudal remnants of the old regime." Shen felt that "it was quite a pity."[25]

Although this may not have been a completely accurate description of the Paoge in Hope Township, one can understand why Shen would make such harsh criticism. The tragic story recounted in Chapter 1—Lei Mingyuan's murder of his daughter—showed Lei's stubbornness, foolishness, and cold-blooded character, and these would likely have deeply colored Shen's feelings about the Paoge. But she also observed that "social control is rooted in the general social behavior, in the rules and institutions in a society, which had the power to constrain people's behaviors." For some reason, perhaps purely academic ones, Shen wanted to emphasize that the Paoge were restricted by rules and institutions. She even suggested that "this result can be explained through functional relationships (*hanshu guanxi*)."[26] This sociological theory of the time (espoused in universities worldwide) was discussed in the book's Introduction. Yet nowhere did the youthful student attempt to use the theory to reconcile bad and criminal behavior with the social constraints that she saw operating everywhere.

Shen also saw that "there are many different systems and many different forces" at work simultaneously in a community, sometimes intertwining and creating mutual impacts. However, in many complex systems, there is often one system, or one strand, that is particularly strong: "It can even form a central strength in the whole community, making other systems in the community automatically fit the track of the superior system." She concluded that "the Paoge in Hope Township had gained such a superior position" that its influence "matched or even surpassed that of the local administration." As a result, the Paoge played a role in "balancing various powers at the local level."[27] Shen did not go further into defining *system* and *power*. In my opinion the *system* and *power* of a local society are multidimensional and can contain politics (policies, institutions), kinship (family, clan), territory (national, local), economy, culture (customs, habits), ethics, law, classes, and groups. But in Hope Township the Paoge sat like a spider on its web, immediately responding to an emergent motion.

By examining the Paoge, Shen Baoyuan was very impressed by its "great power of social control." Here she brought attention to the English term *social control*, suggesting that the meaning was in terms of Western sociology. In that context it meant the balance between various social forces. At this time, academics and students generally knew of the works of Wu Zelin, a PhD in sociology from Ohio Sate University and a professor of sociology at the Great China University (Daxia daxue).[28] Wu divided social control into two senses: narrow (top-down control in an organization) and broad (mutual, without hierarchy and class)—also between control that was "forced" (*wulide*) and control that was "agreed upon" (*huiyide*).[29] What Shen used in her report was greatly derived from "organizations of social control" as expressed in Wu's book, including applications to family, school, government, church, and other establishments. However, because there are also unspecific controls—including public opinion, customs, beliefs, and so on—as Shen surveyed Hope Township, she thought to round out Wu's sharp distinctions.[30] She apparently felt that the power of social control, as she observed it, was comprehensive. It could be narrow or broad, it could be forced or agreed upon, and it could be applied directly or indirectly. Actually, the "social constraints" in her view might have been more like "social norms," in which people are used to acting and responding automatically in certain ways.[31]

Rural social control in traditional China generally depended relatively more on human feelings and morals taken into mutual consideration than on government controls. In the past, rural areas practiced a system of "village conventions (or compacts)" (*xiangyue zhidu*), which relied on "neighborhoods and village associations" (*linli xiangdang*). Studies of these conventions describe them as promoting the following sorts of community interaction: "promoting moral enterprises" (*deye xiangquan*), "regulating behavior" (*guoshi xianggui*), "interacting with rites and customs" (*lisu xiangjiao*), and "relief in adversity" (*huannan xiangxu*). Traditional Chinese society had three areas of mutual work in which such conventions took form: village schools (*shexue*), the *baojia*, and the community granaries (*shecang*). In the process of modernization, however, such structures broke down, and central officials, as well as heads of township and market towns, replaced them.[32]

The social control exerted by the Paoge seems to have been close to the Chinese traditional way but with a darker edge. In the Paoge system, people used their own private punishments, rules of the brotherhood, and their own likes and dislikes to replace laws. Shen Baoyuan used the theories and knowledge of sociology to observe Hope Township and found some issues that few scholars today have considered. For instance, she saw that "a lot of conscious or unconscious or automatic social controls" constituted "a social order" and influenced all aspects of society. In light of this, she felt that all power is "concentrated in the hands of the Paoge, who even have more power than the local administration and play the role of balancing local powers."[33]

The Paoge could contribute to local stability, but the organization could also cause chaos. One example was that of He Song, mentioned previously in Chapter 2. He was involved in numerous crimes, from illegally obtaining funds from municipal treasuries to bullying villagers and smuggling opium and ammunitions. He even used the national government's funds to draft young men into the military (during the War of Resistance in the late 1930s and early 1940s) in order to line his pockets, while supplying only a weak and unwilling body of new recruits. He's public identity was that of head of the township, but actually he had become a "bandit leader" who controlled the "two ways of black and white," which meant that he acted both within the secret society and without it, in his official duty. He Song offered favors to followers so that they would do anything for him. If anyone disobeyed his order, that person would suffer harsh punishment, from torture to execution. He brought dysfunction and suspicion into the workings of his own lodge as well as into local government. By the end of 1944, two branches of the Paoge in his area held a meeting to select a new leader. He Song wanted to exert choice of his own successor, but this was rejected by rival Zheng Guoshan. Just a few weeks later, Zheng was assassinated in an opium den. People knew that He was behind the murder, but nobody dared to say anything.[34] The Paoge members who bullied, corrupted, and killed could often avoid legal investigation and punishment. Lei Mingyuan's murder of his daughter, described in Chapter 1, was therefore not an isolated incident.

★　★　★

The Paoge, especially the helmsman, played an important role in settling disputes in local places. Shen Baoyuan found that the secret society had a power of "social sanction" (*shehui zhicai*) whose range was very broad, covering legal, political, religious, and ethical aspects.[35] This "social sanction" might be seen as connected to traditional "clan sanctions" that functioned in the past, but the Paoge's power was quite different from that of the clan.

FIGURE 5.2 A rural teahouse and its patrons. *Source*: Photograph by Sidney D. Gamble, ca. 1917–1919. Reproduced courtesy of Sidney D. Gamble Photographs, David M. Rubenstein Rare Book & Manuscript Library, Duke University.

"Drinking negotiation tea" (*chijiangcha*), or "talking through differences in the teahouse" (*chaguan jiangli*), provides an important view into the way in which the Paoge used and stabilized social control (Figure 5.2).

Paoge leaders used this type of outer social control for the solution of a great range of civil disputes, which was of great significance to the entire operation. Although Shen Baoyuan's report did not directly mention whether Lei Mingyuan joined such activities, she repeatedly noted that he spent almost every day in the teahouse. Up to now, there has been almost no research or scholarly investigation of "drinking negotiation tea," so we turn to other sources such as newspapers that contain many mentions of it but with little detail.[36] The detail comes from fiction rather than scholarly literature. Let us imagine Lei's "negotiations" in his favorite teahouses by following a well-crafted depiction of this very real phenomenon that is part of the 1940 novel *In the Fragrant Chamber Teahouse* by Sha Ting, a Sichuan native and famous writer.

As a secret society, one might think that the Paoge members would choose relatively secret places for their activities, but actually it was the opposite, especially after the 1911 Revolution, when the Paoge's activities emerged and remained more open. Most of their headquarters were in crowded teahouses, many of which were run by the Paoge, who considered teahouses ideal places for their work. People noticed signs or lanterns on which "such and so society" or "such and so public port" was written, which clearly indicated Paoge headquarters. In establishing headquarters in teahouses and elsewhere, each branch could firm up its power base and take responsibility for security, the resolution of conflicts, and protection of theirs and others' economic interests.

To drink tea while engaging in a negotiation was a popular way for all sorts of people to resolve disputes. People generally did not want to go to the government court but instead went to the teahouse for mediation. The typical procedure was that a prestigious man, usually a leader of the Paoge, would be invited to mediate between two parties. Both sides stated their reasoning, then the mediator would make a judgment. Although "drinking negotiation tea" was a widely accepted custom, it could not settle all disputes. There was always the possibility of violence occurring and of reactions to an unjust verdict, due to a mediator's prejudice and partiality. These reflected the limitations of the practice. It is no surprise that because the Paoge did not have a centralized hierarchy of power there arose disputes between branches. Lodges competed for local power and were always expanding their power areas and seeking economic interests—all of which could lead to violent disputes. The public negotiation was a means to resolve conflicts, and for the Paoge, this was not simply an internal ceremony of gesture and argot; rather it was external to the extent that the activities of the disputing parties connected to the wider society.

This brings us to Sha Ting's novel. The story *In the Fragrant Chamber Teahouse* describes a power struggle in a small market town in wartime Sichuan.[37] In the relevant scene, the major characters are the director of mutual security, Fang Zhiguo, and a local powerful gentry named Yao Chaochao.[38] When Fang hears that the new magistrate would rectify wrongdoings in the military draft, he writes a secret letter to the county authority informing them that Yao's son should have been drafted, but because of Yao's influence, the son was deferred four times. As a result, the son was caught by the county draft office. Yao believed that Fang had damaged his interests and had humiliated him, so he mustered his followers to drink negotiation tea in the Fragrant Chamber Teahouse with Fang. A certain Master Xin is invited by Yao to be mediator. Xin seems to be a relatively obscure figure. The reader does not quite understand how he came to be brought into the affair, but he did have some role in balancing power in the local place. To some extent, this shows the significant roles and statuses of retired Paoge leaders. Certainly Master Xin had such a local reputation.

When Xin shows up in the teahouse, the author describes him as follows: "Master Xin earned his *xiucai* [the lowest of three levels] degree in the last civil service examination. He was in the position of the head of local militia for ten years and the head of the Paoge for ten years. Although he retired eight years ago and has not been involved in affairs in the market town, his opinions are still effective, as he was the head of the militia."[39] This passage demonstrates that Xin had various identities and his degree was still useful. As a local elite, he had been a leader in the *baojia* system, especially in local security. Actually, here his most prominent position was "head of the Paoge," the last position before he retired and also the most important leverage of his authority. Some Paoge brothers ran rampant through force, but others were highly respected because of their reputations. In Sha Ting's novel, Master Xin clearly belongs to the latter. Eight years after he retired, he was still invited as a mediator to settle disputes.

As soon as Xin appears in the teahouse, he becomes the center of the action. Everyone "called for tea money" (*han chaqian*) to win his attention: "Calls come from every corner of the teahouse. Some of them are still seated, but some stood up while shouting and waving bills in their hands. Everyone raises his voice high and is afraid that Master Xin doesn't hear him. One patron even becomes angry and shouts: 'Don't take others' money! Hey, son of a bitch, did you hear me?...' He immediately ran to the waiter and put a bill in his hands."[40] In situations like this, as descriptions in various records, a newcomer might offer to pay for his friends' tea. However, the friends usually replied, smiling, "Huangguo" (literally, "replaced"), which meant, "Okay, I will ask for a new bowl of tea that you will pay for" (although it was seldom taken literally). Sometimes, if the recipient did not want a new bowl or had to leave, he would uncover the bowl and take a single sip to show his politeness—namely, *jie gaizi* (uncovering the lid).[41] People's eagerness to buy tea for others was part of an important social custom in Sichuan. Certain men needed to make a gesture of hosting friends or acquaintances, even though the host might not really have wanted to do it. A man who failed to make the gesture would "lose face." Whose money paid for what was taken seriously. Moreover, a waiter could easily offend a patron if he did not handle the matter tactfully and could even drive patrons away or lose his job if his boss received complaints. Some people, according to some cultural observers, liked "pretending" to be wealthy or generous, which made it difficult for a waiter to read intentions.[42]

Sha Ting's novel reveals that a general practice in the market town was that usually "people do everything according to the rules, but important people did not have to follow the rules." Master Xin was one who did not play by the rules. For example, when some activities such as a "rite for departed souls" (*da qingjiao*) were conducted, people would pay their share, but Master Xin would not, because his participation and appearance would bring the activity glory, which he and others considered to be his contribution.[43] Otherwise, as Sha points out, if he contributed money, people would be surprised and think that Master Xin had lost face, just like an ordinary man. "Face was essential in this market town," wrote Sha. Powerful men like Yao Chaochao had to pay respect to Master Xin. Yao complained to Xin of being bullied by Fang, but Xin did not believe it. Yao's response was interesting: "Really, otherwise, I would not dare to bother you!" In the novel Yao was described as an evil and powerful gentry, but Master Xin was important enough to Yao to get the latter's great respect (another indication of Xin's status). Meanwhile, Fang Zhiguo pinned his hope as well on Master Xin. One of Fang's followers suggested that he first meet Xin privately. But Fang analyzed all the incidents in the past in which he had dealt with Xin and felt unsure about his position; he thought he may have offended Xin on some occasion. Therefore, he was not confident about this specific negotiation at the teahouse.

The negotiation in fact did not go smoothly. Master Xin wanted Fang to find a man as a replacement for Yao's drafted son, but Fang was not in favor, for fear that the new magistrate might found out. His attitude peeved Xin. Although Xin had handled things properly, Fang refused to follow the instruction and repeatedly stressed that he "cannot bear the responsibility." Yao could not hold his anger anymore and grabbed Fang; the two fight. When separated by Xin, their heads are bleeding. Master Xin's suggestion to us is intriguing for what it reveals about inside secrets of local power. As a respected local, he actually recommended that a local official conduct an illegal action. In a local place, when local officials dealt with instructions from above, they could easily collude and work together tacitly to deceive the upper level of administration. It is easy to assume that in cases like this, as described in the novel, upper officials were not so quickly fooled. But as long as the thing could get done, they turned a blind eye to the means employed.

★   ★   ★

The practice of "drinking negotiation tea" reflected the relatively autonomous field of control in rural society; people tried to resolve conflicts without official involvement and followed extant norms and power structures outside the state. These structures were authorized through the social reputation of mediators, who were elites and often Paoge leaders or heads of the *baojia* or militia. An article published in 1942 in a local newspaper said that the teahouse was "the most democratic court." Those who fell into a dispute would say, "Let's have tea at the corner." This meant that they went to the teahouse at the street corner to drink negotiation tea. Generally, the loser would be "sincerely convinced," pay for the tea, and apologize to the counterpart. "Sincerely convinced" might be an exaggeration, but mediators still showed considerable authority. Even if some people did not feel justified, they still had to obey the verdicts. The conclusion of the article was that the phrase "Let's have tea at the street corner" was therefore the "most democratic expression."[44] The author repeatedly emphasized the word *democracy*, reflecting people's general conviction that local negotiation was fairer than that presided over by officials and court rulings, although the author might not really have understood accurately the situation of functioning democracies.

That residents preferred the verdicts of mediators to those of officials not only suggests that they did not trust "muddled officials"; it also shows the expansion of nonofficial sources of local power. Several scholars of Chinese history, such as Mary Rankin and William Rowe, have emphasized the dramatic development of elite activism after the mid-nineteenth century—disaster relief, granaries, charity, civil construction—and its profound impact on society. Still, they did not include the teahouse in their analyses.[45] I suggest that the participation of Paoge luminaries in the activity of "drinking negotiation tea," which was pictured in Sha Ting's fictional setting, indicates an extremely fine-grained field of social order in which elite activism handled conflicts among specific individuals and between such individuals and their surrounding society. This is a window through which to observe how the community maintained as much as possible a certain social stability and how civil order existed outside the official justice system.

Of course, such mediating activities could be found elsewhere in premodern and modern China and had become an important part of social self-control. The absence of government authority in many areas left a large power vacuum that attracted the Paoge members, whose activities became a foundation of community stability. The reason that teahouse negotiation became popular was because most people preferred to conduct mediation in a public place so that it would appear to be as "equal" as possible under the watchful eye of the public; otherwise, public opinion might go against the reputation of the mediator. People could successfully defend their own interests by using teahouses as "civil courts." This is how the phrase "drinking negotiation tea" became a synonym for mediation. In addition, violence was much less likely to occur there if a mediation was not successful.

What the practice represents extends far beyond the activity itself; it reveals that in Chinese society a nonofficial force always existed and played a crucial role in everyday life. It is true that this type of mediation was very limited, nor was it a force that ensured utter impartiality. In the face of state power, such social agency seems fragile, so that we often are skeptical and underestimate the full spectrum of nonstate power. When we carefully examine it, we marvel at the deep soil and tough conditions in which it grew. For example, a problem occurring in a teahouse negotiation often was magnified by government so that the phenomenon could be suppressed. In this way, many aspects of self-governance and protection in local society disappeared one by one in the political and economic changes caused by attacks of the state and the impacts of their ideological and cultural waves, but drinking negotiation tea survived. It is just one of several ways that local societies in modern China have confronted attempts to diminish their range of interest and agency.

PART THREE

The Rise and Fall of the Lei Family

CHAPTER 6

A Tenant Farmer and Paoge Master

SHEN BAOYUAN POINTED OUT in her 1946 report that "the Paoge are the center of Hope Township," which means that these sworn brothers were at the center of politics and power in the village. The man who controlled a Paoge branch was usually called the "helmsman" (among one or two alternative names; see Appendix 1. "Paoge Ranks" for a detailed list of the group's hierarchy), and he typically directed the immediate group. Supporting Shen's point, the township head and vice head, as well as its chief of security and the heads of the *baojia* (local security system), were also members of the Paoge. This phenomenon was not only apparent in Hope Township but in the entire Chengdu Plain as well as throughout Sichuan.

A researcher in the 1940s, Wu Cang, wrote that "the Paoge and Green and Red Gangs in Sichuan" were very strong in wartime Sichuan. Local officials had to depend on the Paoge if they wanted to exert their policies. Otherwise, affairs "would inevitably lead to nothing."[1] This phenomenon is also reflected in the archival data. In the summer of 1942, army veteran Huang Chunian organized the Four-fold Union Renewal Society, which had five departments. It is worth noting that the director and deputy director of its Department of General Affairs were the head and vice head of Xinyi Township. The Guomindang (GMD) Executive Committee was very upset about the way that local government dealt with the Paoge, and it seems clear that part of this was because the Renewal Society's links with government boosted Paoge local power.[2]

When Bai Jinjuan, Shen Baoyuan's classmate (whose enjoyable descriptions of nearby farm families were explored in Chapter 1), investigated rural education in Jiuliqiao, a market town close to Hope Township (see Map 2), she noted that the Paoge "have absolute powers in public and private life."

The society was "a common phenomenon in the rural areas of Sichuan." In Jiuliqiao, in fact, "the organization is not a secret any more," and "it has long controlled all social activities." There, "the highest official of the township is the helmsman of the Paoge." Two kinds of people held local power—local officials and Paoge. Bai pointed out that "real power is in the hand of the helmsman. All the other managers, those who issued political commands, collected fees, carried out penalties, and smuggled opium, were under his control. The Paoge also were concerned with maintaining order. Without Paoge agreement, the government cannot carry out any policies."[3] Bai's work sheds light on the finer details of the extent of Paoge local control: top down, it spread out into rural Sichuan.

The helmsman was selected through an extended negotiation among the Paoge brothers. He enjoyed authority and possessed money and power by means of all the connections with government and ordinary folk. The helmsman's authority extended to internal secret-society matters as well as day-to-day external (social or town) responsibilities. A deputy helmsman helped the helmsman. Below them came "third brother," "fifth brother," and so on. The terms *brother* (*ge*) and *master* (*ye*) were functionally equivalent, and these names were used to refer to specific persons by their status. The term *row* (*pai*) was an abstraction of rank, not used as a status title by which to refer to someone. All these terms were ranked one (the high end) through ten (the low end), but without using four and seven because of their ominous homophonic meanings. Newcomers would start at the lowest abstract row-status—for example, either the ninth row (*jiupai*) or tenth row (*shipai*). They would take an oath before portraits of the ancient legendary heroes Liu Bei, Guan Yu, and Zhang Fei. After making his own contributions to the Paoge, a new member gradually rose to the level of sixth or fifth brother, all the while learning how to handle routine affairs. It was more difficult to continue to move up from this rank. Before being promoted to second brother, for instance, a member had to have three top brothers' support as a "grateful brother" (*enxiong*), a "brought-in brother" (*yinjin*), as well as being "recommended as guaranteed" (*baoju*). Rising from the second brother (or second master) to the first master (the more glamorous helmsman) was a great step, as one had reached the top of the organization. This saying referred to the various statuses: "The first master is the dragon head, the second master is sage, the third master is the decision maker, and the fifth master is the manager."[4]

Paoge rules were very strict. If a brother did not obey an upper master or violated a rule, he would be reported by the manager (fifth master) to the helmsman and his membership would be removed, called "putting up a black plaque" (*guaheipai*). If the wrongdoing was serious, he would face trial at a members' meeting. Some violators would even secretly be executed. If a brother had a conflict with another social group or another Paoge branch, or if a certain conflict of this type caused serious harm or death, the helmsman would become involved in finding a solution.[5] Lei Mingyuan was the deputy helmsman of the Paoge in Hope Township. Shen Baoyuan had never observed such a person so closely. She found that when she chatted with Lei, he repeatedly told the story of his catching bandits twenty years ago (implying that the scene was in the mid-1920s). Every time Lei recounted this tale, he became "passionate" and "vivid and dramatic." As Shen noted, Lei often used "purely heroic gestures" to describe his past "heroic deeds." Especially startling was one episode when, as Lei told it, he was surrounded as a local security chief by kidnappers. He described the details of the bandits—their behavior, dress, and depredations—with great verisimilitude.[6]

In 1937, when war broke out with the invasion of China by Japan, middle-aged Lei Mingyuan was still quite energetic. In his mind he wanted to be "heroic" again and so surrounded himself with a group of loyal brothers. At the time, his economic situation was very good, so his band of young brothers often lounged at his house and were treated to meals. Lei often made trouble on the outside, however, and once he killed a "stick man" (a "bad" or "muddy-water" Paoge). This caused the stick man's own band to seek revenge. Conflict between different branches of the Paoge were often violent. One time, when Lei was alone in a teahouse, nearly twenty armed men approached and shot at him. He jumped up and quickly ran out, going up a hill while shooting skyward three times to give off an alarm. Lei jumped over a ten-foot-wide ditch, leaving the enemy behind. His Paoge brothers rushed to the site, and a bloody battle took place. Lei and his followers killed several fierce fighters. In the end, Lei escaped harm. Even a few years later, villagers relished the telling of such thrills. That particular battle strengthened Lei's position in the Paoge, and since then, the stick men did not dare to challenge his power.[7]

According to Shen Baoyuan's report, the head of the township, the Paoge helmsman, controlled thirteen counties around Chengdu. Lei Mingyuan was the former vice head of the township as well as the current deputy helmsman of the Paoge in Hope. Despite the leadership ranks, when Shen asked Lei how he handled local administration, he often said that "he is merely a character of the local community." In this way he subtly stressed his Paoge identity more than anything else. She mentioned that the Paoge in Hope often associated with Guomindang (GMD) secret agents and that they "violated people's interests" and "opposed democracy." One feels, almost instinctively, that we are looking at a youthful but strong leftist political persuasion shared by other youth and by academics all over China. The township office employed high-pressure policies and imposed stiff taxes; it registered sons of ordinary families as soldiers, trafficked in opium, and "prohibited people's thought, speech, association, and even freedom to read newspapers, using the dual identities of local administrators and leaders of the Paoge."[8] Here Shen reveals the Paoge's collusion with the GMD. Thus, when we understand Shen's leftist notions, we should not be surprised if we find criticisms of the Paoge.

★ ★ ★

The following accounts are from two different kinds of source material: the first is a Paoge helmsman's memoir originally written in the 1980s, after which we turn to a product of a type of local historiography. According to the memoir of Cai Xinghua, a helmsman in Linjiangsi, Kaixian, there were four branches of the Paoge, each with a named identity: Benevolence, Righteousness, Ritual, and Wisdom.[9] On the surface the branches regarded each other as brothers, but each used its strength to establish a sphere of power. The Benevolence Branch and the Righteousness Branch were locally called the "officialdom Paoge" (*guanchang Paoge*), since their members were relatively rich and powerful. It also implied that they had close contacts with government officials. Those who participated in the Ritual Branch and the Wisdom Branch were called the "buttock Paoge" (*dingzi Paoge*), as they were mainly from society's lower echelons. In Cai's description this form of deprecation was somewhat enjoyable for the Paoge, even though these so-called buttocks members were looked down on as "deadenders" (*wuke naihe*) by the more well-off and powerful Paoge in their area. Cai implied a certain dark humor when he called participation in Paoge activities "playing at Paoge" (*wan Paoge*), indicating the fun that could occur in the organization although much of the participation requirements was a serious matter.

During the Qing period, the Paoge's mission was to overthrow Manchu rule; with this clear political purpose, participation in the Paoge was dangerous. After 1911 the mission changed, however, and the Paoge chiefly aimed at a local political agenda of order and self-protection. Cai pointed out that during 1927 and 1928, because of conflicts among branches, some Paoge members became bandits; they "robbed, raped, and committed all sorts of crime under a trademark of robbing the rich to help the poor." They actually caused disasters for ordinary people. The period Cai mentioned was the most chaotic in Sichuan. After the War of National Protection (1916), Sichuan fell into turmoil, and Sichuan, Yunnan, and Guizhou armies fought for power. After the GMD's unification of China in 1928, Sichuan was still very much controlled by area warlords; the situation maintained itself through the eve of the War of Resistance against Japan—that is, up until 1935 and 1936.[10]

Cai Xinghua claimed that he became a Paoge member in childhood.

If this is true, it is easy to assume that he was influenced by his family and that his father or another male relative might have also been a member. In 1932, Cai became the first master of the Ritual Branch, but his memoir does not reveal his early activities, so we do not know what made him that kind of leader. He recalled incidents involving his revitalization of the branch. During this time, struggles among branches were common, and the Ritual Branch was in decline. Upon Cai's inauguration as first master, he reorganized the branch by soliciting support from local powerful people and by focusing on personnel, especially some of the major positions, such as "red flag manager" (*hongqi daguansu*, a fifth master), who controlled personnel, dealt with communication with other branches, and took charge of ceremonies. This manager acted like a speaker for the organization, so he needed to have the ability to "express his ideas clearly." Otherwise, he could poorly affect the reputation of the branch. Cai paid close attention to building up the membership, especially bringing in lower-class workers like boatmen, peddlers, street performers, artisans, sedan-chair carriers, seasonal workers, Buddhist monks, and beggars. Its membership soon reached nearly a thousand.

According to Cai's account, the first master of the Benevolence Branch was a "loyal running dog of GMD rightists, who was believed to have had strong back support, thus he could do all kinds of evil things." If this first master's followers assaulted Cai's people, Cai indicated that he would lead a few dozen or even hundred for revenge, especially the boatman brothers, who "took paddles and rods, viciously rushing to opponents' places, and these rivals became so scared." Even their first master could not stop them. Cai also announced that if any of his brothers robbed from the people or wounded anyone, he would personally go to the victim's place to apologize and return any property as compensation. "Until today," Cai recalled, "the story is still circulating in the local place how the buttock Paoge took revenge." With this interbranch struggle, we see how a master like Cai Xinghua could legitimize himself through both populist ideals (protecting the folk) and national political agendas of both sides (Communists versus GMD) during the civil war.

In his memoir Cai specially emphasized his support and help for "progressive people" (*jinbu renshi*). Here the so-called progressive people, although Cai did not specify their identity, would have referred to Chinese Communist Party (CCP) members. He later revealed his secret connection with "communists," leading to his house arrest for a month. Cai gave several examples of his support for CCP. The first was to help "progressive people" join the Paoge, and some Communists did join his organization. The Ritual Branch helped Cai, who had a dual identity as both CCP and Paoge member. He also provided means of communication through the Paoge's "secret

letters" (*toupian*) meant for "progressive people," whose activities were protected by the Paoge. Once, when GMD secret agents planned to arrest
"progressive people," Cai sent someone to notify them; despite the warning,
some were caught and executed by the GMD.[11]

★ ★ ★

The other type of writing examined in this chapter is China's much-utilized
genre of local historiography—a genre with a very long tradition. We look
at several stories told about He Song (first introduced in Chapters 2 and
5). Compiled in 1990 by local historians Wang Shiliang and Diao Chunjin,
these stories can be characterized as amateur local history.[12] He Song was
born in 1910 in the small town of Zhugao, not very far from Hope Township, in the northeast suburbs of Chengdu. His father was a helmsman of
the local branch of the Paoge known as Lords of Benevolence and Forgive-
ness (Renshugong). There were ten sons, of whom He was the oldest as
well as his father's favorite. The Wang and Diao collection describes He
as possessing a "tyrannical, arbitrary, cruel, and cunning personality" from
childhood. After entering politics, he learned "intrigue, [to] use hidden
tricks, and abuse power," and he "did a lot of harm to his homeland based
on his evil deeds."

He Song taught primary and secondary school students and may have
been considered locally as some sort of literati. In these early years he was
a "humble and polite" man, taking teaching work "quite seriously," elicit-
ing good impressions. In 1938, through his father's connections, he was
appointed director of "united security" (*lianbao zhuren*)—a title that later
switched to that of "head" of the township. As soon as he held power, He
Song began to show his "tyrannical, dictatorial style" and saw to all decisions. He dismissed all former employees in the township office and hired
his own people. He embezzled public funds and tried to collect additional
taxes. Not even a year in office had passed when "his evil side was fully explored"; he frequently cursed and struck people, and often delayed paying
employees their salaries. Because his behavior caused outrage, in the winter
of 1939 he was removed from the position.

In early 1940, Yang Xiushi became the township head, which He Song
resented. He believed that his downfall had been orchestrated by Yang.
When Yang was on his way home, a dozen bandits mustered by He attacked
him, but Yang escaped. Yang recognized the danger if he continued in his
position and therefore resigned. After Yang's resignation, He thought that
the position would be returned to him, but in early 1941 the county magistrate appointed Lei Lie as the township head. He Song was furious and
sought ways to force Lei's resignation. At this time, bandits were rampant;

they robbed during the day and ransacked at night, and as a result daily life and business were seriously interrupted. People who suffered from banditry often went to the office of the township to complain, but the head did not have any means to suppress the banditry. He Song thought that this was a good opportunity to force Lei Lie to step down. To worsen the situation, He pushed his followers to rob in the area, frightening the locals. Lei Lie could not stabilize the situation and ultimately had to resign.

Following Wang and Diao's narrative, early in 1942 He Song got what he wished for: he was made head of the township once again. As soon as he came to power, he hosted a big feast, with invitations going out to local gentry, the Paoge masters, and his trusted subordinates "to win over people and to strengthen his reputation." He used "feudal reactionary forces" (*fengjian fandong shili*)—a term often used by local Communist historians, referring to the Paoge and the Youth Party in Jintang County (Jintang xian qingnian dang)—to cultivate his personal power, to set up the town of Zhugao as his center, and to conduct "criminal activities." From the narrative we learn that He "widely recruited bandits" and other local toughs to stabilize his power base. During that time there were nine branches of the Paoge, each of which dominated a certain area. But after He rose to power, he consolidated them under his leadership as chairman of the Paoge Nine-Mountain United Association of the Zhugao Area (Zhugao diqu Paoge jiushan lianhe zongshe).

He Song operated in a typically corrupt way, once he became a Paoge linked to local affairs and local finances. In 1944 the government began construction on a military airport in Guanghan County (Guanghan xian), which should have taken three months. He was appointed as the captain of rural laborers to supervise work, but he went to the site for only a short visit, being "unwilling to endure hardship at the site"; he returned home without taking care of construction matters. He illegally took over the funds collected from local sources that were meant to help pay for the airport. Because a large part of these monies were now gone, labor deteriorated, with many workers sneaking off. Ultimately, the project was far behind schedule. The magistrate decided to go after He and arrested him in June 1944. But during He's escorted return to the county seat, two hundred or three hundred of his Paoge brothers rescued him. He took refuge, so to speak, within an army troop but continued to conduct illegal activities such as smuggling opium. At some point later on, He tried to get the case dropped, during which he resided again in Zhugao.

In 1946, He Song "dominated" the election for county council (*xian canyihui*), winning easily. The local historians characterized this turn in He's life: "He made a comeback and continued to manipulate local affairs in whatever way he wanted." In April 1948 the Youth Party in Jintang County held a representative assembly, which raised up He as their chairman. He often attended various county meetings under this title and would make clear his intent to, as worded by the CCP writers quoted in Wang and Diao's narrative, "follow the GMD reactionaries who were carrying out criminal activities against the people and communists." From the perspective of this later writer, who made it a point to refer to the GMD as "reactionaries," He Song had become a "heinous villain." However, we must view that judgment with caution and skepticism when using this kind of source material (for discussion of this and other sources, see Appendix 5. "Brief Comments on Texts, Myth, and History"). For our purposes now, the judgment is unimportant, for we merely wish to acquire a snapshot of another Paoge master, a man who was a somewhat narcissistic striver, like Lei Mingyuan and many hundreds of others in the Chengdu Plain. Let us see how that might stack up against Lei, who operated out of Hope Township, only a few miles away.

We should not assume that Lei Mingyuan was as rich and powerful as He Song. In fact, he was only a tenant farmer. Lei's story shows that there were many types of Paoge leader, and we should expect to learn about such differences, once we are outside of the context of histories written by local communist historians. Such historians published what were called "local historical materials" (*difang wenshi ziliao*). Many of them worked in government offices, schools, or other organizations.[13] Even among Paoge helmsmen per se, the gap between these two men of the 1930s and 1940s was very large. Shen Baoyuan herself knew that the various leaders of Paoge groups in Hope Township were of two kinds: one was "the rich and powerful, who have land" and the other "won status and reputation through fighting." Obviously, Lei belonged to the latter. He had no land of his own, but rented 40 *mu* (6 *mu* equaled 1 acre) of paddy field from a landlord named You, who lived in Chengdu like many other landlords in the Chengdu Plain. For example, Wu Yu, a leading anti-Confucian scholar, recorded in his diary his contacts with tenants and how he would go to Dragon Bridge (Longqiao), in Xinfan County (Xinfan xian), to look over his 103 *mu* of land (see Map 2).[14] Dragon Bridge was very close to Hope Township, halfway between it and Chengdu.

Lei Mingyuan, however, had to support his whole family as a tenant; according to Shen Baoyuan, he idled around as a master of the Paoge in Dianshang. Why did Shen mention "Dianshang"? She did not explain it, but the cite is likely another name for the Yaodianzi. There one would find a few shops, such as a grocery, teahouse, opium den, or restaurant (Figure 6.1). It was a place for villagers to kill time and socialize. Although Lei was a tenant, he did not work in the field, so he had time to be idle.[15] Lei did not drink much, which can be considered unique among the Paoge

FIGURE 6.1   A street and shops in today's Chongyiqiao (Hope Township). *Source:* Photograph by the author, 2014.

brothers, but he was a heavy smoker. He often stayed for the whole day in the teahouse with his Paoge brothers, playing cards or mahjong, talking in their secret language (discussed in Chapter 4), covering such topics as business, recent adventures, and general secret-society intelligence. Waiters and other patrons did not dare to treat them lightly.[16]

In the past, scholars generally believed that a tenant belonged to the economic class of poor peasants. But Lei Mingyuan, as a real tenant farmer, did not actually do fieldwork. Rather, he hired a long-term laborer who was paid annually two *dan* of rice, plus 20,000 yuan. He often hired four short-term laborers, paid on a daily basis. To have a clear concept of their wages, we can compare with other available information. There are no data on rice prices for Hope Township, thus I have taken available data for Pi County (Pixian, see Map 2), 25 kilometers from Hope Township (Chongyiqiao) and almost the same distance from Chengdu. In July 1945, when Shen Baoyuan was in Hope, the price of rice in Pi County was 18,633 yuan per *dan*.[17] The price of rice was sold as a unit of *dan*, but it was confusing as to how many kilograms made up a *dan*, because there was no national standard. In

Jiangnan, for example, a *dan* of rice was about 140 to 160 *jin* (1 *jin* is 0.5 kilogram), while in Hubei and Hunan a *dan* was heavier. However, a *dan* in Sichuan was heavier than that in Hubei and Hunan. In late Qing Chengdu, a *dan* was about 280 to 300 *jin*; but in the 1940s it was no more than about 280 *jin*.[18] Therefore, the long-term laborers earned and purchased a total of about 860 *jin* of rice.[19] In Sichuan, to survive with even the minimum of food, a peasant needed at least 730 *jin* of cereal or grain, and a family of five thus needed 3,650 *jin*.[20] Without other incomes, the long-term laborer and his family would encounter difficulty.

In the Chengdu Plain the amount of land rented out was very high. According to a survey, land farmed by owners accounted for only 19.28 percent of the total in service, while 80.72 percent was for rent.[21] It was the same in Hope Township, where, in Shen's words, "real landowners are almost invisible, but big tenants (*da dianhu*) can often be seen."[22] Shen did not articulate what or who exactly were these "big tenants," but most likely this referred to a sort of tenant farmer in the Chengdu Plain. Large land-owners generally lived in Chengdu or county seats. If they leased land to a number of smaller tenancies, one by one, it would have been inconvenient because of the time needed for management, lease procedures, and collec-tions. Therefore, they tended to let relatively large parcels to merely a few "big tenants," who then divided the parcels up into smaller pieces and sublet them to the smaller tenants. The tenancy relationships became complicated, with landlords, big tenants, and small tenants. Obviously, in comparison to the small tenants, the "bigger tenants had stable incomes and lives."[23] This being the case, Lei was able to host Paoge brothers for meals and present himself in public as a sort of "big man." However, he was not a "big tenant" in a strict sense, because he was not subletting to other tenants. His hiring of farm labor was simply part of a profit-line calculation of overhead and hours; doing so, it seems, simply maximized Lei's hours and energies.

Shen Baoyuan's work describes the relationship between the Lei family and their hired laborers, as well as how 40 *mu* of land were managed. In late spring, when it was the planting season, farmers set out seedlings in the paddies. For this seasonal work the use of independent laborers was popular. Shen states that farmers "struggled to find skilled laborers to help for a few days." Perhaps because of this short supply, hired hands were usually well treated. There was a custom followed in some places in the Chengdu Plain called "the planting wine" (*chayang jiu*), in which hired laborers would have five meals per day—three formal meals (including a large lunch spread) and two snacks. Shen described it as "an employer's way to thank his hired la-borers' work." Of course, in the 1940s labor was very cheap, only 300 yuan per day, and a *dan* of rice was sold for 18,000 yuan; this meant that a laborer working steadily for three months could probably buy less than two *dan* of rice. For comparison: a cup of tea in Chengdu at this time was about 12 yuan.[24]

Lei Mingyuan had an advantage as a Paoge leader: his Paoge brothers on various occasions came to help, which no doubt sprang from an obligation for all the Lei family meals they were served during the year. It was a time to make a contribution to their leader. This was the busiest time in the countryside; people worked in the field under the warm spring sunshine and breathed fresh air. Anyone observing the scene might notice how the paddies changed from soil-black to plant-life green. Even if one had grown up far from such scenes, he or she might have gazed without end, in appreciation of harvest time and the future in general. Shen was this kind of young adult. As a student from the city, the scenes of Hope cultivated her good mood: "Seedlings are neatly in the field, touched by soft spring breezes; water is slowly irrigating between fields, truly interesting."[25]

★　★　★

Mere decades ago, under stern, Communist revolutionary discourse, there was a serious misunderstanding of landlords; they were flatly regarded as enemies of the revolution and their image was greatly distorted. While some landlords were undeniably tyrannical, perhaps even evil, the majority simply relied on hard work, good management, and frugality to accrue some profit. Many experienced generations of hard work just to accumulate some land, and they carried on good, or at least peaceful, relationships with villagers. Shen Baoyuan, as a leftist, would not have thought to purposefully exaggerate landlords' good treatment of hired labor. What she did was merely to describe as accurately as she could the financial and economic aspects of farming and employers' treatment of hired laborers in a rural society.

We are gaining a rough picture of how rents and commoditized labor worked in the Chengdu Plain in the prerevolution years. Tenants could pay in products for their rent fees (*shiwu dizu*), the dominant method. There was also the approach of tenants' using labor itself as rent payment; finally, cash was used.[26] However, many tenants paid rents the older way—that is, by an agreed ratio of the harvest, a method called sharecropping (*fencheng zhi*). The ratios (for example, 5:5, 4:6, 3:7) were set based on such factors as the amount of cattle, seeds, and tools provided by the landlord. In the prefect of Chongqing most of ratios were 5:5.[27] Earlier, during the Qianlong period (1736–1795), sharecropping had gradually been replaced by a system of fixed rents; this turned out to be the main form of rents in Sichuan. With this economic development, peasants' financial positions were strengthened, along with their increasing independence. Because the amount was fixed, not made as a ratio, the tenant's share was not affected by the actual size of the harvest, thus giving them more freedom of production. Tenants could keep the profits from improvement of their technology or through increased labor efficiency and working hours. This form of rents, as well as the fact that fixed rents were in some cases flexible and could be renegotiated, stimulated local economies.

Because of this weakening of the dependency on landlords, the landlords attempted to use economic means to ensure their interests. One way was to take rent deposits (*yazu*). In this system tenants had to pay a deposit up front for their land rental. The landlord possessed this payment as a buffer against any failure to pay (because of increasing population density and shortages of arable land, tenants were "begging landlords to rent a piece of land," and landlords took such opportunities to extort tenants). Sichuan was one of the most developed regions in this system of rental deposits, which generally amounted to not just the entire year's rents, but 150 percent of it; this overage was settled only after the harvest was made. The system thus favored the landlord and could be abused. There was another form of rents that coexisted with the rent deposit: prepaid rent (*yuzu*). The prepaid rental was a fixed sum determined and paid at the beginning of the season, not after harvest. As commercialization and monetization increased, there was also a trend toward cash payments. Cash payments for land rents prevailed in the Chengdu Plain, which meant that tenants could convert their products into money as payment of rents and therefore the tenants would sell rice—a higher-value product—for cash to pay the rent. In general, cash payment was more popular in the cash-crop areas. In the Chengdu Plain rice was the most important agricultural product and became a main object of calculations of rents.[28]

According to Shen Baoyuan's investigation, 90 percent of the harvest from fields, including rice and vegetables, "belong to the landlord." She wrote: "At the harvest time, tenants sent their products to the landlord who lived in the city." Such a heavy "squeeze" was the "greatest burden" for tenants. Shen's statements here may be misleading, however. She mentions only rice and vegetables, but tenants kept higher portions of other products, especially coarse cereals. Tenants in the Chengdu Plain paid rents mainly in rice, so they could only keep a very small portion of their rice. For example, if 2 *dan* of rice was the yield per *mu*, then the 1.6 *dan* (80 percent) paid to the landlord seems very high. One must take into account all the produce (vegetables, wheat, seed, beans, and so on) and the multiple harvest seasons. In the North China Plain there was only one crop per year, so the rates there turn out to be lower than those in the Chengdu Plain, which was far more conducive to wet and dry plantings throughout the year. Factoring these advantages, the rent rates in the Chengdu Plain should be about 50 percent.[29] If there was a natural disaster (drought, locusts, or flood), tenants had to pay rents in full. They could only keep their coarse cereals and wheat "to feed their families with insufficient amounts of food." Although the Paoge were powerful, they still had to follow these rules in rural areas. As Shen pointed out: "Even the Paoge and their families cannot escape landlords' exploitation."[30]

This last observation by Shen points to something that cuts through the usual interpretations of rural society in the Republican period. Scholars often seem to encounter the notion that local powerful men did not tolerate being exploited and would force landlords, sometimes violently, to make concessions. But with all that has been argued, we can now understand that in this part of China most followed the social and economic practices and unwritten rules. Was compliance with contracts seen as a necessary condition for the maintenance of order and stability? It is hard to say. The Chengdu Plain did not play any important role in the Communist movement, while elsewhere there were peasant movements from the 1920s on in Hubei, Hunan, Guangdong, Guangxi, Jiangxi, and other provinces. Throughout the whole of Chinese history, we hardly find any peasant uprisings in this area. Two important reasons probably caused this quiescence: First, inhabitants in the Chengdu Plain enjoyed a relatively stable life because of the ecological and natural environments that provided a consistent even if sometimes poor living. This led to the second reason—namely, that the rural people recognized this fortunate situation and, to prevent disruption, followed their established systems of social organization and order. Essentially, there was not much soil in which social unrest could be successfully planted.

★   ★   ★

Lei Mingyuan's family had five members, and rented 40 *mu*, which could produce sufficient products to allow them not to worry about food and clothing, yet these statistics did not place them in the category of wealthy. Generally speaking, what amount of land did a tenant need to lease to support his family? This would be determined by their productivity, on the method and timing of rent payment, and whether the luck of weather and rental agreements yielded enough grain both to eat and to reseed. A tenant tried not to lease a parcel larger than he could handle. Of course, if he was by some definition a "big tenant," the situation would be different. He could sublet surplus land to others. Based on these factors, we can estimate a data-based answer for at least the Qing period in Sichuan. A peasant needed at least 730 *jin* grain and 3,650 *jin* for a five-person family for food and other expenditures.[31] But if Lei was able to lease more than the theoretic minimum, he might have been able to keep some surplus. Operating in this way allowed tenant farmers eventually to accumulate their own properties. All in all, during the Republican era an intensification of agricultural production in the Chengdu Plain did not improve overall yields, and things remained as they had been in late Qing. For Lei, careful planning and budgeting of his potential income would have provided some ability to save or at least to have money for further necessities, but his Paoge status made this habit hard to instill. (Chapters 8 and 9 reveal the deep crisis that he faced in this regard).

Lei Mingyuan's relative status in his locale challenges the conventional understanding of the rural class stratification during these decades. According to the social systematization arrived at later on by the CCP during the Land Revolution of the early 1950s, there were five categories: landlords, rich peasants, middle peasants, poor peasants, and hired hands. Tenants were generally classified as poor peasants. However, in this scheme what was Lei's place? The first three categories were those who held land ownership, so they are out of the running. However, he cannot fall into the latter two categories. Although Lei did not have any land, he employed a long-term and four short-term laborers, which became one of the criteria of identifying landlords and rich peasants. He was more like a farm operator who manages the operation, rather than one who runs the farm per se. The challenge for Lei was chiefly how and whether to run a business properly. If done well, incomes would be sufficient to support his family and help his Paoge brothers. Otherwise, he might face bankruptcy.

CHAPTER 7

Entering the Paoge

THIS MICROHISTORY OF A YOUNG WOMAN, an academic profession, and a patriarchal monster has its own framework—a double-trunked story that twines together the "sociology family" and the "Paoge family named Lei." But we should not overlook the tree trunk itself. It is a place, a platform that hosts thriving activity and various convolutions of social energy, albeit some of it disturbing. The trunk is broad at the base, near the ground, and puts its old roots down far and wide. What we are talking about, ultimately, is the small place of Hope Township. It grows on the fine branch tips—the larger, twined trunk of Chengdu, rooted in the ancient western plain of Sichuan. This is the framework of place, the hosting ecology where the young student Shen Baoyuan entered the Lei family and soon sensed dilemmas and frights emerging from the very ground and the embedded society.

In Shen Baoyuan's eyes, Hope Township was by 1945 still a pleasant place, a typical, small market town in the Chengdu Plain. Close to Chengdu, it was entirely rural in atmosphere. Residents easily ventured into the large city for certain errands and returned the same day. On festival days, people traveled to Chengdu to watch street ceremonies and attend temple fairs. Thus Hope was convenient for engaging in a small trade or for looking for work. The rural dirt road in and out was good mostly for "poultry wheelbarrows" (*jigongche*).[1] When Shen arrived in Hope Township, it was the height of summer, seedlings were lush and the rice fields were verdant. People raised a variety of vegetables, rice crops had started to bear ears, and water ran through the fields. The fall harvest was a little ways off.[2] Farm residences were not far from the fields so that field maintenance was an accessible task. For nightly cooking, farmers went out to their vegetable garden to pick produce. Like most farmers in the Chengdu Plain, in Hope one could typically see a black water buffalo bathing in the ditch or wallowing in mud to withstand the summer sun; small and large waterwheels carried water up to the field from the ditch day and night (Figure 7.1).

Very different from urban life, the countryside was quiet. On summer nights a variety of insects sang, especially the frogs who cried in the rice paddies. Fresh air blew into the houses, creating a sleeping environment that city people could never experience. At dawn, roosters crowed one after another, calling people to rise early. Summers on the Chengdu Plain were not the busy season: the rice had not yet ripened and farmers could take care of paddy fields at a leisurely pace or work on the vegetable gardens. In the morning a farmer might slowly walk on the ridge with a hoe on his shoulder, looking at the endless green paddy fields slowly turning yellow, sensing the presence of irrigation water that came from Dujiangyan. The water carried the snowmelt from the mountains in the upper Min River (Minjiang) valley (see Map 1). The idyllic setting makes it easy to imagine tranquility.

But this area of the Chengdu Plain was not a Shangri-La. The fate of the country was closely tied with cities like Chengdu and even small towns like Hope. Only a couple of generations earlier, during the 1911 Revolution, Qing troops had looted Chengdu. Mutinous soldiers transported booty out of the city, but residents guarded city's the four gates to stop them. The Paoge had undertaken self-defense action: they formed militias, raised funds, and stood neighborhood watch.[3] After the Revolution, because of the frequent power shifts, especially in the warlord period (1916–1927 nationwide, 1916–1935 in Sichuan), the provincial capital itself became a battlefield, and the countryside and the little towns were the most vulnerable of all. In the 1920s, banditry was rampant; and the Paoge's role in local order took shape specifically in 1926, nearly twenty years before Shen Baoyuan came to Hope Township. When bandits wantonly harassed local places, the Paoge quelled them, thus many Paoge became "local heroic figures." The victors in the battles against banditry became leaders of the secret society in Hope Township: one of them was Lei Mingyuan.[4]

Shen Baoyuan described her first impression of Lei: "In the summer, even if it was a cloudy day without sun, he worn sunglasses. With a folding fan in his hand, wearing a black silk shirt and black pants, and a straw hat behind his back, he was hastily walking to his shop." When Shen came to Hope Township in 1945, Lei's power had been in decline. Every day he had to take care of his shop. On another occasion Shen described Lei as possessing a "dark brown face, with long permed hair down to his shoulder, and his jacket unbuttoned."[5] In that era, in the countryside a man with permed hair man was extremely rare; and this revealed, perhaps, a uniqueness about Lei. Shen realized that to understand the Paoge, she had to know

FIGURE 7.1 A large waterwheel in the Chengdu Plain. *Source*: Photograph by Joseph Needham, ca. 1943–46. Reproduced courtesy of the Needham Research Institute, Cambridge University.

this legendary man, although in his case "legend" came with a dose of infamy. The timing was right for her to get to know Lei. If he had been at the height of his power, he would probably have disdained a female college student and not spent his time with her. But now that he had been become idle, his power diminished, Lei had time to sit with Shen and recall past deeds. He played the role of the elder, recollecting past glories and sharing them with pliable youth.

After Shen had been in Hope Township for a week, she got the chance to meet Lei Mingyuan. He had gone to the Yenching University office in the township to enroll his stepdaughter in summer classes, but he left quickly. Because of his stepdaughter's enrollment, Shen had many opportunities to meet the Leis and soon became familiar with the wider family. Shen recorded her first visit to Lei's house, which was near the Yenching office. Entering their cottage, there was an ox pen to the left and a loom room at the right; the front of the house was the central room. There, Shen saw a typical setting in houses like this on the Chengdu Plain: it revealed that the Lei family were Buddhist believers. A matched couplet was pasted on the wall, and a spirit tablet for ancestors was in the middle. A wooden birthday placard hung from the ceiling, surrounded by five flags that were meant to suppress devils. There were bedrooms at the left and right sides of the central room, in which all the furniture was an old style. When Shen arrived at the house, her hosts let her sit in the central room, where tea was served. If the guest had been a man, a water pipe with tobacco would have been offered. They talked and laughed; Shen enjoyed the Lei family's rural, earthy quality. Even as "a strange guest," Shen felt a "sense of both complete ease and her hosts' cordiality."[6]

At first, Shen did not feel confident about what she thought were the results of this first meeting. As a young, socially inexperienced, female college student, she had been talking to "a special character," but she did not know what information she could get. As a leader of the local Paoge, Lei Mingyuan had experienced ups and downs and seen all kinds of people. During their first conversation, he was very friendly, but Shen noted (to what extent a reflective marker of what she only later found out, we cannot know) that she had an uncontrollable "apprehension." Later, with further exchanges and approvals of mutual understanding, she "gradually felt at ease."[7] In her investigation and writings, Shen rarely used the name "Lei Mingyuan"; instead, she used "Lei Daye," which I assume she was following how his family and villagers referred to him. There are probably two meanings of *daye* in this sense. In rural Sichuan, an older man would usually be called *daye*, meaning "elder uncle" or "grandpa"; it was a respectful name. The leaders of the Paoge were also called *daye*, meaning "master" (but only one of several terms for them). I think that Shen's use of *daye* might have carried both meanings or either one, depending on the situation.

According to Shen's observations, although Lei was a Paoge leader, he was not omnipotent; rather, he was imperceptibly influenced by social constraints. He had to support his family and fulfill family obligations (for the Lei family tree, see Appendix 2). He had moved to Hope Township only nine years earlier, coming from Quandian, a market town near Hope. Lei's mother had died three years before. He had two younger brothers; one had died and another was a farmer. Woman Huang was Lei Mingyuan's first wife, now forty years old: she had given birth to their two sons and two daughters. The elder son, Julong, was sixteen; and the second son, Jiewa, was ten. The younger daughter, Xiaoyu, was only eight when Shen Baoyuan came to know the family. The fate of the elder daughter, Shuqing, had already been sealed by the time of Shen's appearance.

Woman Lei was the second wife. First wife Woman Huang had had a serious conflict with Woman Lei; Lei Mingyuan's father had sided with Huang, but Lei supported Woman Lei. As a result, Lei moved his family to Hope Township, leaving Huang and his own father at their old home. After that, Huang no longer lived with her husband and their children.[8] Julong was grown up: he did not like school and preferred to help in the field.

Withdrawn and quiet, he was not talkative with strangers. Shen said that he was a "small adult with problems." According to her, Julong's relationship with his birth mother, Huang, was "very indifferent." Although the distance was not far, he seldom went back home to see her and his grandfather. Julong's father Lei, was an important figure in their new township and constantly entertained guests. Lei would sometimes ask Julong to take leftover food back to the old home, for grandfather and Woman Huang. When Julong went there, he tried to avoid meeting people, which made Huang sad. Shen captured how Huang might have felt about the arrangement, quoting Huang as saying: "Now my children have been given to others, so I'll let it pass."[9]

Shen seemed to get along well with Woman Lei, which allowed her to hear many stories and details about the family. Woman Lei had received a primary school education. Although most of her current children were not her own, they were in fact now all living together. Shen thought that if these stepchildren eventually had a good future, Woman Lei could benefit from having "raised the children." Huang was a "typical farm woman" and kept to the traditional moral codes for women, thus she graciously served her husband's father. The long separation from Lei did not change her personality. As for Woman Lei, Shen described her as completely different from Huang. Woman Lei was not very competent in housework, she was "shrewish and dissolute," with a toughness that made her suitable to be a Paoge's wife. Shen guessed that this personality was perhaps not Woman's Lei's true nature but was caused by the pressures of the social environment she faced.[10]

Woman Lei's unfortunate childhood had been filled with "sorrow and pain." Her father was a blacksmith, whose business was not good, and her parents did not take care of her well. She rarely mentioned her early life. Although she received little formal education, she was proud of what she did get, and later in life she used it to some benefit. For example, she liked to read novels and often discussed the stories with Shen; Shen herself said that she actually had "little knowledge of them."[11] Woman Lei preferred old classic novels, such as *Dream of Red Mansions* and *Water Margin*. As for modern novels, she would read only those written by the popular novelist Zhang Henshui of the Mandarin Ducks and Butterflies School.[12] Interestingly, Shen defined Zhang as a "boring literati," and it seems that, to Shen, Woman Lei was equally boring for having read Zhang's novels. Zhang was disliked by Shen and other left-wing intellectuals. This attitude might have reflected elite intellectual bias against the crude aspects of popular culture. These intellectuals never expected that in the late twentieth century, Zhang's novels would be revived and become very popular. Today, Zhang's works are read with an eye behind the love stories that were the grand narrative of a nation's destiny.

Lei Mingyuan was not Woman Lei's first husband. Sixteen years prior, she had married a tailor from Chengdu but was abandoned by him after having two daughters. The elder one died of illness at a young age. Shen Baoyuan did not specifically describe that bleak situation but only said that Woman Lei had been "tossed into the marketplace" and "fell into the trap of hell on earth," to live a "shameful life." Shen pointed out that there were "two green stigma in her hand, a proof of her reduced life."[13] We must look closely at Shen's words here, since they suggest that this woman was more than merely poor. Being abandoned in Chengdu—"tossed into the marketplace"—may imply human trafficking (*renshi*) in Chengdu. The *renshi* in Chengdu was not literal human trafficking but instead a labor market that included buying and selling women's services as maid servants, wet nurses, concubines, and so forth. The boundaries, however, are not too clear.[14] As a young woman, Woman Lei may have been sold into sexual slavery because she had the two stigmas. That would explain why Shen used phrases such as "fall into," "hell on earth," "trap," and "nonhuman life." Shen did not mention details, perhaps out of sympathies with the woman's experiences as a young woman, but it seems clear that her previous life was sad. As for how Lei Mingyuan's eventual new wife met her husband, Shen's report did not mention that either; Woman Lei might not have wanted to disclose this to anyone, or Shen did not disclose to protect Woman Lei's privacy. Shen only said: "Since she met Lei Mingyuan, she became his second wife, and her surviving daughter, renamed Shuying, became another Lei family child."[15]

Here, Shen Baoyuan used sociological language to explain the marriage of Lei Mingyuan and Woman Lei, whose former family life had achieved a "balanced state" (*junheng zhuangtai*). After the young woman had been abandoned by the tailor, "her life's balance was disturbed," and her entire world collapsed. But the subsequent marriage with Lei produced "a new kind of interactive relationship and established a new equilibrium" (*pingheng*). Meanwhile, Lei experienced "a process of balance reconstruction"—namely, his separation from the first wife and the move to Hope Township.[16] These terms, plus others, like "function" (*gongneng*) and "functional method" (*gongneng fangfa*), may be seen as derived, or obliquely borrowed, from the theory of structural functionalism (*jiegou gongneng*) as mentioned in the Introduction. However, Shen's report never used the latter term explicitly.

The tough environment had created Woman Lei's "paper tiger," her shrewish character. Shen guessed that her experiences urged her into acting, at least on the surface, as if she were not a "coward." This turned Woman Lei toward being relatively "violent" and even "close to viciousness," as Shen reported. She had a bad temper and a loud voice. Several years before Shen's stay in Hope, Woman Lei's momentum "could overwhelm her husband" and even manipulate her husband's Paoge brothers. She behaved like "somewhat of a bitch" and "could roll on the ground" when fighting with someone. The Paoge brothers called her the "crazy woman," but she did not care about the nickname. She was quite proud that those who were "threatened by her temper ultimately had to obey."[17] Woman Lei indeed had a close relationship with Lei Mingyuan's Paoge brothers. Although she sometimes brought trouble, "such a wife, like an assistant," advanced Lei's position among the Paoge.[18]

Seven years earlier, Woman Lei had fought with her neighbor, a Paoge brother, over the selling of rice straw (a small-level commodity). She slapped the man twice on the face and the two wrestled. Together, they fell into the river and continued fighting in the water: the scene was spectacular. In describing that event now, it is a bitter coincidence, when we consider that since there seems to be only one river in Chongyiqiao (Hope Township), it was probably the same river in which Lei shot his daughter and pushed her under. To solve Woman Lei's dispute, the Paoge had called a "great hall meeting" (*dachuantang*), in which the helmsman mediated based on a type of trial. Lei Mingyuan kept his head down, uttering not a single word—letting his wife argue and bicker. Under Chinese traditional ethics, especially in the conservative countryside, this was indeed strange, bolstering the image of Woman Lei as a "shrew" with a bold personality. After all, Lei Mingyuan was the vice helmsman, and the leaders had to consider how to save face for Lei. The Paoge did not carry out "excessive punishment" against her. No one "dared to ridicule Lei behind his back."[19]

Although in traditional society, the so-called shrew was not typical, this archetype was not unheard of, especially in women of poor families, who in a certain sense had fewer scruples about Confucian family ethics and rituals. The poor in general were less constrained by traditional principles concerning female attitudes and responsibilities. In Chengdu some women from underclass families were less restricted on the streets by traditional "woman's virtues" and were known to fight with men in public. As the writer Fu Chongju mentioned in his investigation of Chengdu in the early twentieth century, "incorrigible wives from poor families (*pinjia efu*) often fight in the streets and shout abuse in the lanes (*dajie maxiang*)"; their typical gesture was called "the teapot" (*chahu shi*), with one hand pointed out and the other planted on the waist. Educated people considered poor women to be "unpracticed in the womanly virtues" (*fude buxiu*).

We have other examples of this evocative shrew archetype. Local newspapers often reported their public behavior. A man who was addicted to gambling was intimidated by his wife, an "extraordinary shrew." One day, after he lost his clothing in a bet, he snuck back home to take a quilt as barter for his next wager but was caught by his wife. She promptly dragged him into the street, "abusing him in every possible way," threatening to send him to the police despite his pleas for mercy. She quit only after the street headman intervened and made her husband apologize. Another case is even more dramatic: when a rickshaw puller with a passenger accidentally knocked down a certain boy, his mother, the wife of a petty peddler, jumped into the street and punched the puller in the face. The blow was so strong that it punctured his left eyeball, covering his face with blood, and he lost consciousness.[20] These stories reveal that the commonplace perception of the family male as dominant and intolerant of assertive women was not quite universal and accurate. So-called shrews displayed a hidden side of women's behavior, much different from the stereotype of submissive Chinese women (Chapter 9 includes a discussion about the intolerance and discriminatory attitudes toward women in China at the time).[21]

Shen Baoyuan explained that because the Paoge "focused more on the interests of their group, they strictly enforced "social constraints" (*shehui zhiyue*). Here, "social constraints" means using the group's rules to restrict members' behavior, such as the resolution of the dispute between Woman Lei and her Paoge neighbor, which could only be settled by the helmsman and his "persuasion." Of course, this sort of constraint was multifaceted. Resolutions were also influenced by, as Shen noted, "other aspects such as laws, religions, education, customs, social and public opinions." The final resolution of Woman Lei's fight was also a result of "public opinion."[22]

⋆   ⋆   ⋆

Shrewish Woman Lei played an important role in Lei Mingyuan's life. Her image was very much like that of Aunt Cai in Li Jieren's novel *Stagnant Water Ripples* (Sishui weilan), a popular novel published in the 1930s, although we don't know if Woman Lei read it. The fictional character lived in Shibantan, a small market town in the Chengdu suburbs (see Map 2). A shop owner, she had an affair with a Paoge named Luo. Cai was charming and sultry, and men in the town were crazy about her, but they could not make any play for her because of Luo's power and money, as well as his large band of Paoge brothers. Cai did not like her husband; she became smitten with Luo's boldness and enthusiasm, which was a real shock in her small town in the late nineteenth century.[23] We can compare Aunt Cai's Paoge lover with Lei Mingyuan and consider the men's reactions to the conduct of women in general. Our hearts leap toward the tragedy of Lei's murdered daughter, Shuqing. The fictional Cai seems lucky to have had a Paoge lover who was not threatened by a woman's strong sexual and social roles. Could Shuqing have escaped her father's severity, and taken charge of her self-made world, like Aunt Cai? Probably not: she was too young to have developed a modern sort of boldness.

CHAPTER 8

The Decline of Power

WHEN SHEN BAOYUAN CAME to Hope Township (Chongyiqiao) in 1945, Lei Mingyuan was a strangely stylish man with swagger. He wore flashy clothes and was known to own and use a handgun, not an uncommon possession in Republican-era Sichuan. Lei's economic level was barely located among the ranks of land-managing farmers and householders. He employed people and entertained his male underlings with food and drink, for they were usually junior-ranked Paoge brothers. Lei was someone who was owed respect and consideration by the Paoge headman, especially when the matter concerned any trouble he might have got into. Along with this sort of local power came his outbursts of violence, usually directed at women whose assertiveness about their rights and views, and their actions as sexual beings, might cost him much "face." Lei's attitudes thus compelled him to mount a forceful resistance.

Lei's economic situation could not remain strong. As we recall his apparent lifestyle and role in society from about 1939 to 1945, it seems he was incapable of maintaining them. He experienced severe financial and leadership problems, which he covered up. When Lei spilled forth his stories to Shen, he never mentioned his mundane "family responsibilities and burdens." Shen learned from others that over the past two years Lei had become "very impoverished." His Paoge activities were no longer delivering financial benefits. In the local branch of the Paoge, manager Liu (manager actually being third rank in status; see Appendix 1) benefited most, and helmsman (the top man) Tong Niansheng gained the next amount; Lei basically "failed to gain financial benefit," so he could only be considered as a "thin Paoge" (*shou Paoge*). As someone in the leadership ranks, however, he considered his "face" most important and thus never mentioned his family's difficulties to Shen. Just the opposite, Lei boasted about his wealth. When he met an unfamiliar guest, he always invited him to the market town for tea and wine and a meal. If the guest did not accept his invitation, Lei would be very unhappy and thought of how he had lost face. Because of his diminution in status, the family finances deteriorated day by day. Yet Lei felt compelled to spend more and more money on sustaining an entourage; he perceived himself as a leader who had to exert a look of power.[1]

The heads of the Paoge often had to travel around to other Paoge territories to establish a relationship and a power network. In the spring of 1943, Lei traveled in a large circle, going to Mianzhu, Dazu, and other places (Map 4), spending generously, "looking like a rich man," and being quite satisfied with himself. Money brought him reputation in the wider circle of the Paoge, which made him friends here and there, a worthwhile result. At this point, however, because the traveling created even larger deficits, Lei had to sell grain to fill the gap.

To better picture how Lei Mingyuan, or in fact any Paoge brother, might have sought out new or increased revenue, we turn to He Song, a Paoge leader discussed in earlier chapters. He's life was the subject of modern, local historians. The heads of the Paoge were always seeking out legal, or corrupt, or bluntly illegal access to cash. The notorious He Song, to expand his turf, united several nearby branches and established a headquarters of the Common Benevolence (Tongrengong), thus becoming helmsman who controlled all activities and garnering many followers. He's family had only four members, but often there were more than twenty people daily for meals at his house; they were his talons and fangs—namely, his personal strike force. From there, He was able to siphon funds from government agencies and municipal government budgets, to smuggle opium, and to terrorize his way onto a seat on the local town council. He became so rich and powerful that his legions did his bidding like an army.[2]

Lei Mingyuan lived out his golden years, however brief, thanks to good harvests from the lands he rented and from his reputation in the Paoge.[3] But holding power was difficult. Although Lei tried his best to maintain influence, undeniably his position had gradually declined as he experienced challenges from others. Lei felt frustrated: the Paoge in Hope Township was still developing, but his own power was shrinking. He vented at home; he was "just like a devil at home and frequently cursed loudly." Only Woman Lei could deal with him, but their relationship was getting worse. Lei Mingyuan left home early mornings and often came back at midnight; his heart was not fixed on his family. Woman Lei maintained peace at home, but "the entire family was in a state of unrest."[4]

Lei Mingyuan watched his entourage gradually drop off: he was becoming "a master without any responsibility" (xian daye).[5] The primary reason

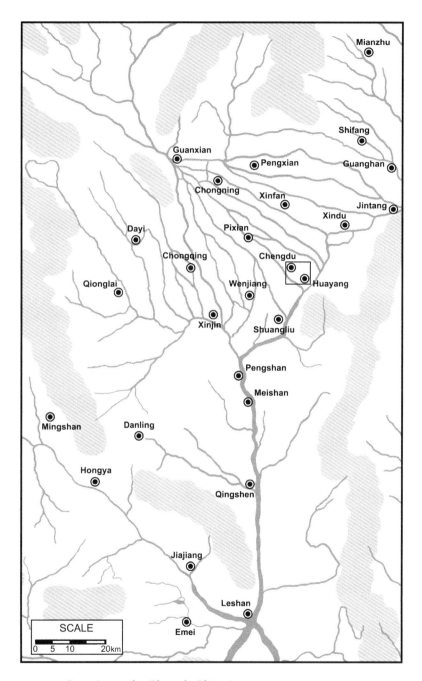

MAP 4. Counties on the Chengdu Plain circa 1945

that got him into this monetary situation was that he was unable to pay his land rent on time. It is perhaps hard for us to understand, but certainly not for those around him: here was a former deputy head of the township, former chief of security, and vice helmsman of the local Paoge who could not do anything to settle up with his landlord. The latter therefore took the 40 *mu* back and rented them out to a new tenant, the Cai family. In the last lunar month of 1945, the tenant arrived to take over the spread. The house in which the Lei family lived also belonged to the landlord, so Lei had to transfer the house to the Cais. A ceremony of transferring the rental was held, in which neighbors and the local Paoge members were invited. Cai gave Lei 50 *dan* of rice as a concession.[6] At the time, the custom was for the new tenant to give the previous one a large compensation. For a certain period, the old tenant would have a cushion on which to make a transition. The rice could help Lei's family for this transition. Later, however, we see that Lei used this rice to cover his daily expenses.

According to a superstition in the rural area, it was taboo to move one's household in the twelfth lunar month, but the new tenants—the Cai family—had to move in, so the Lei family had to relocate from the front rooms to temporarily stay in the side rooms. They had to transfer the large kitchen to the Cais. The Leis moved to a small kitchen, "which is really an omen indicating that a big family has gone into decline." As Shen detailed the scene, a piece of preserved meat given by the Cais hung on a beam, and Woman Lei sighed with emotion when she saw it; she always thought that her family was going to collapse, and she gave the piece of meat a fitting name: "the falling meat" (*kuagan rou*).[7] The new tenant valiantly tried to make up for the inconveniences suffered by the ex-tenants. Despite Lei's discontent about the whole situation, in dealing with a humble Cai, he hardly was able to place any anger toward the new tenants. Woman Lei kept her sense of humor, anything otherwise might be considered humiliating. For Woman Lei, it was not the end of the world: she had experienced much worse situations. To live in poverty again was not so formidable a bridge to cross.

★   ★   ★

The financial crisis inevitably affected the Lei children. Son Julong did not have much motivation for studies, so to Lei there was little sense in keeping him in school. Thus he quit and became an apprentice in automobile repair shop outside the West City Gate of Chengdu. He was introverted and conducted little emotional exchange with his parents. He did not come back home for two or three months after starting his apprenticeship; it might have been an excuse to escape the family or to escape study. Shen commented: "Apprenticeship was a most deforming, unreasonable, and exploit-ative system, in which capitalists use underage laborers." Many children like Julong, under the guise of learning skills, had to work all day "like a cow and horse to serve the owner and their family" without wages for three years.[8] Shen's criticism of the apprenticeship system, despite a full dose of Communist ideology, did contain some truth. It is easy to find examples of bosses or masters who used apprentices as cheap labor, where the ap-prentices were hardly given any real training by their masters. However, the problem was not as simple as that. Apprenticeships offered an opportunity for children of poor families. During their apprenticeship, although they did not receive wages, many starving children were provided accommodation and meals by the shops, thereby helping them to survive. Moreover, many occupations required a considerable period of time to nurture proper train-ing. If shops had to pay a wage to the apprentice for such long periods, they would consequently do better by hiring a skilled worker to simply get the work going right away. Therefore, owners of manufacture and service busi-nesses could save costs by training apprentices.

Shen's teacher Liao Taichu (Liao T'ai-ch'u) published an article in 1941 discussing the apprentice system. Liao pointed out that China's apprentice-ship system started in quite ancient times from family businesses that in-cluded farmers and artisans. After the Sui (581–618) and Tang (618–907) dynasties, more shops and guilds increasingly opened up in the commercial and cash society; this in turn increased the number of young men who sought opportunities to go out of the family circle and enter society on their own. Training periods took from nine months to four years. Since the Qing, because of commercial expansion, more regulations were made by guilds regarding the taking of apprentices, signing contracts, the training pe-riod, and so forth. At that time it was estimated that the number of Chinese apprentices was as high as thirty million, but Liao estimated the number around ten million to twenty million.[9]

Liao also stated that "those who really want to learn the skills of a profes-sion will find a livelihood for a lifetime." However, because of oversupply, it was not easy to find work in a shop, except by having a "rich and pow-erful man's introduction and guarantees." Apprentices were usually twelve or thirteen and older, but not beyond twenty years old. The items in the contract often stated "no liability if he was beaten to death" and "no liability if he were hanged, drowned, or had run away, etc." Indeed, some appren-tices lived in by the motto of the "three pots" (*sanhu zhuyi*): tea pot, wine pot (serving masters personally), and chamber pot (including the intimate and unsavory parts of domestic life). Therefore, "an ordinary apprentice is like a slave." But "after a hard life, industrious work, and harsh training, ap-prentices finally graduated and got rid of prison," one of the biggest possible turning points in their lives. Then apprentice thereafter regained the "freedom of the body and mind, and his attitude towards life has completely changed."[10] This was a far cry from the cant Shen expressed. One can only wonder about the disparity between Shen and her mentor and explain it as the unpredictable impact of certain ideas on young minds and the way such ideas push past relatively more empirical and well-metered analysis.

As a once influential local Paoge leader, for Lei Mingyuan to allow his son to become an apprentice was no doubt a further sign of decline in Lei's status. He and his wife knew that it was certainly not a bright future for apprentices, but they seemed to have no better choice. Woman Lei felt a bit relief, however, because Shuying still went to school every day—at least this daughter could nurture hope for herself. Lei Mingyuan acted as if there was no problem in Julong's apprenticeship and mocked himself by saying that he now planned to save a few million yuan in three years, and when Julong graduated, Lei could buy a truck for him, who might then make a living as a freight driver. If Julong could really achieve this goal, it would be a good outcome. Seen from the actual economic situation of the Lei family, however, the possibility of saving this amount and achieving such a goal was quite slim.[11]

The twelfth lunar month was difficult for the Lei family. Lei was now not returning home until midnight every day, while Woman Lei was often out doing things. This left Shuying, Old Zhou (a hired hand), and Junfang (the servant girl) at home, and they had to depend on pickles and rice for survival. Still living in smaller parts of their old house after the Cais moved in, they could hear the sound of Cai's looms nearby, making a picture of a busy and thriving scene; it formed a sharp contrast to the Lei family's quietness.[12] Shen's report did not provide much information about the Cai family, but we sense that they were relatively well-off, proven by the fact that Cai was able to give all that rice: a typical tenant could hardly have done so. In addition to managing the rice paddy, he also made handicrafts and seemed like a capable person who kept his family business running.

★   ★   ★

The Chinese New Year was approaching. On the twenty-eighth day of the twelfth lunar month, the Paoge in Hope Township, according to their habit, gathered in the Patron Deity Temple; they ate meat dishes, drank wine, played finger-guessing games, and gambled at poker. As usual, on day one of the Chinese New Year, the Paoge brothers spent their day at their own homes. Then began the visiting and offerings—important activities for keeping or establishing friendships, and for appreciation to flow up and down the ranks. On the second day, they all would pay the helmsman a New Year call with gifts, and the helmsman would treat them to a banquet. The third day was for the deputy helmsman; the fourth day, the third brother; and the fifth day, the fifth brothers (that is, the two managers; recall that there was no "fourth"). The event moved down a level of ranked brothers day by day, until the lowest of the brothers was reached. Therefore, the lower-level brothers, by the fifteenth day of the first lunar month, had attended banquets every day but also had to bring gifts to the host of each party, amounting to a large burden.[13] But on this Chinese New Year festival in 1946, the Lei family did not have the means to treat the brothers, and therefore deputy helmsman Lei Mingyuan spread the word that this year he would not hold a banquet. He had broken the longtime general practice. Lei effectively withdrew from the cycle of friendship, which no doubt spelled a fatal blow to his reputation and position in the organization.

The power and status of a Paoge member often linked with economic foundation. Paoge brother Cai Xinghua of Kaijiang County recalled that money was always a problem for him (his memoir was examined in Chapter 6). The revenues collected by the organization included a 3-5 yuan membership fee (but poorer members might be exempted), a "harbor fee" (that is, a headquarters fee), and donations, plus protection fees from shops. As a head of the Paoge, Cai had to donate more money to the organization; otherwise, he would be mocked as "a mean master." After he became the helmsman, he spent more but earned less. To solve this problem, he opened and operated a weaving room, a tung oil shop, a salt shop, a teahouse, a restaurant-inn, and so on. When he needed more hands, his Paoge brothers would come to help. Despite all this, Cai claimed, "although some small profit came in every day, I still failed to meet a variety of expenses."[14] It is noteworthy that he opened most of these shops after he became a Paoge helmsman: Paoge position brought prestige enough to further his income potential.

Cai mentioned other costs, such as financing visitors from other branches and sometimes even the brothers of his own branch. He had to treat local civil officials with banquets and money. Whenever there was a holiday, he had to make donations and gifts. He had to find sources for all this so that he could make cash offerings to brothers under the name of "New Year money" (*yasui qian*) and "wine money." In short, a helmsman had to not only manage all kinds of social relations and maintain his power, but those specific tasks required him to be "popular and generous."[15] Lower-level brothers were poorer in general, and they expected their usual feasts. When their leaders needed them, accordingly they would charge forward and even sacrifice their lives.

Lei Mingyuan had never been keen enough to develop the large variety of income streams that Cai Xinghua had. He had shown that he would be a

Paoge who led others by violence, having early on incited some interchapter warfare. That affair actually had raised Lei's aura, but then came his ugly action against his daughter, and the other misogynist outbursts, thus proving that he was not of the landed-elite type of Paoge leader but the low-class type. Lei's leadership character and potential were fixed into a rather low stratum. He began to falter in his own family's household operations and lost his crucial land lease. The 40 *mu* had been his own way to maintain pride as some kind of landed earner, even though he was just a struggling renter.

Lei became more and more slothful, and perhaps he thought of himself as too much of a manager. He spent days on end at the teahouses, strutting around. His smoking and drug consumption tore him down further. Perhaps Lei's opium den business had been intended to get him back financially, to make up for the damage losing the lease had caused. But it did not work. He became his own worst problem, and he sunk even lower when he took up the opium habit for the second time.[16] His economic situation was by this time beyond repair.

CHAPTER 9

A Family Crisis and a Rural Woman's Fate

BOTH THE DEVASTATION OF HIS MONEY SUPPLY and his diminished power hit Lei Mingyuan hard, and he became completely disoriented: he did not know how he would survive it. Lei went out in the morning and came back every night late—around midnight—when Woman Lei and her daughter were already sleeping. His excuse was some sort of business at the opium den. In September 1945 he had resumed his opium habit, and month by month he used increasingly more of it, finally up to 30,000 to 40,000 yuan worth each month, which became an enormous burden for the Lei family.[1] This was a twin downfall: not only was Lei's income dramatically reduced, but he was a real addict now. This created a deep crisis for his family, and the subsequent focus of judgment and reaction came from Woman Lei. Having no regular commitments or responsibilities, and absorbing the destructive opium, Lei's health grew worse than ever, and within a few months his appearance had changed greatly. He smoked opium for a whole day; therefore, he was unable to retain his solid reputation in the Paoge. He gradually moved away from close contact with other brothers. With "withered face and skinny body, he lost his burly physique and heroic spirit that he used to have, and did not have energy to manage the activities of the Paoge."[2]

On the eve of the Chinese New Year in 1946, Julong came back home after Woman Lei's repeated calls. On the day of the New Year (the first day of the first lunar month), Lei Mingyuan—very unusually—did not go out. In previous years, he always paid a New Year's call to the helmsman, but this year the practice was not kept. After rising in the morning, family members said auspicious words to one another; the children said "Happy New Year" to their parents, and the parents wished them well in return. In the past, a formal ceremony would have Julong wearing a long gown on behalf of the family, as the oldest son; he would kowtow to the gods and ancestors, then set off firecrackers outside the door. But this year things had become simplified, and the usual procedures were not apparent.[3]

Lei Mingyuan had brought his opium equipment home and smoked in bed. Shuying and Julong took this opportunity to persuade their father to quit using opium by talking about the drug's harm; they encouraged him to preserve the family business by closing off the opium den and operating a different kind of business. Shuying told her stepfather: "You see, your health has been damaged by opium. If you quit it, you can recover and have strength. Everyone would be happy. Why should you act as you do?" Probably because it was the Chinese New Year or the sense of Shuying's words, Lei Mingyuan smiled and responded with kindness: he promised to quit. Woman Lei was pleased to hear this, and the whole family had a happy dinner on the New Year's eve.[4] The custom was that on the third day of the New Year, the Paoge brothers went to pay a call on the Lei family, but since this year Lei himself had canceled the event, this day turned into a quiet one. Lei still fixed a table of dishes, but this was to treat his opium friends.

How quickly it was that Lei Mingyuan broke his promise to quit opium. After the fifth day, he resumed his routine and hung out at the opium den. He so totally forgot his promise that instead he smoked even more. After the fifteenth day, the family did not have money to buy vegetables, which finally caused a fight between the couple. Woman Lei was so angry that she cried aloud and smashed his opium equipment. The result of the fight was that Lei simply offered more money to go toward the family's daily costs.[5] The 50 *dan* of rice given by the Cai family when the rental had been transferred was probably the largest piece of Lei property, but Lei started to sell this, a few *dan* at a time. Soon only 30-plus *dan* of rice were left. There was no way that Woman Lei could stop him.[6]

However, Lei Mingyuan was not so quickly reduced to nothing. As a leader of the Paoge, he still had local connections and enjoyed some privileges. For example, he ran his opium den and sold opium without any trouble because he "colluded" with a secret agent to co-run the business; thus he did not have any problems from the authorities. There were two or three other opium dens in Hope Township, which operated in similar circumstances.[7]

★ ★ ★

Lei's business and his use of opium were connected to a veritable flood of opium in Sichuan. A steep growth in production occurred after about 1850, during the Qing dynasty. According to a report in 1869, Sichuan had the largest opium plantation in China.[8] By the end of the Guangxu reign (1875–1908), there were more than 140 counties that grew opium. In 1906 annual production was 238,000 *dan* in Sichuan. At this time, national production was about 584,800 *dan*, so Sichuan accounted for 40.7 percent. Opium became the largest export in late Qing Sichuan. According to Japanese scholar of economics Tadashi Negishi's estimate, in the late nineteenth and early twentieth centuries, the total value of Sichuan-produced exports was about thirty million taels, but opium reached twelve million, which was 40 percent of the total value.[9] It was not just production: Sichuan also was consuming the drug. In late Qing times the Governor-General Xi Liang established an agency to promote quitting, then banned planting, using, and the opium dens themselves. Thus, by the end of the Qing, growing and using opium were basically eliminated in Sichuan.[10] But in Sichuan's warlord period (1916–1935), spurred by steep land taxes imposed by certain warlords, the planting, sales, and use of opium in the province revived. In the 1920s and 1930s plantation expanded, so the price of dropped.[11] The dens became as popular as teahouses and wine shops. In 1934, Chengdu alone had nearly six hundred such establishments.[12]

How many opium users did Sichuan have? According to an account by the Office for Eliminating Opium in Sichuan, during the "defense area period" (*fangqu shiqi*, 1918–1935), there were 3.1 million opium users out of a 60 million population.[13] The massive consumption resulted in a high density of opium dens, found almost everywhere in the province. Some small places that had no restaurants or lodges would at least have an opium den.[14] As an estimate revealed, the number of opium dens reached to more than fifty thousand and supported over two hundred thousand livelihoods. When adding the number of people involved in making opium equipment at the time, the number probably would reach three hundred thousand.[15]

After Liu Xiang became the governor of Sichuan in 1934, he prohibited the military from involvement in the opium trade and issued policies for prohibiting planting, transporting, and use; his plan was to completely ban opium in six years. By 1940 the Sichuan Provincial Government announced that opium had been completely eradicated. In fact, although it was dramatically reduced, use of opium was still going strong in a number of local places. From 1940 to 1949 opium revived in Sichuan, which was in great part the result of a road that opened between Leshan and Xikang. The opium produced in Xikang could now be transported to Sichuan (see Map 1). Furthermore, previous agencies for handling the opium problem were abolished, and the overall goal devolved to local governments, which did not pay much attention to this matter. As a result, the opium den business flourished again.[16]

Bans on opium undoubtedly were a great blow to the Paoge's income, so the organization waged a tenacious resistance. The dens were becoming gathering places and centers that shuttled funds to the Paoge for their activities. Quite a few opium den owners joined the Paoge for protection, and some Paoge leaders were den owners. The Paoge strongly maintained the intertwined opium business, and even used their arms to transport opium and used opium revenue to buy more weapons. When the government forcibly closed dens down, they on occasion would face a military situation.[17] By 1945 such a small place as Hope Township had several opium dens, indicating a failure in the antiopium campaign. The campaign had seemed spectacular, but actually it did not touch many local places. Given these circumstances, we should not be surprised that Lei Mingyuan operated an opium business and himself used the drug. Opium caused an economic crisis in the Lei family to deteriorate further. But the Lei family's troubles were far from over. One after another, a series of events happened to the family, which made Lei Mingyuan's situation worse.

★   ★   ★

The Lei family had their unusually quiet Chinese New Year, but they could not avoid another complicating incident. On the nineteenth day of the first lunar month, the servant girl Junfang ran away at night with a certain man. It was another blow for Lei Mingyuan. According to Woman Lei, as told to Shen Baoyuan, Junfang stole Shuying's new cotton robe, blue cloth gown, fabric, short pants, socks, towels, and other items as well as a few hundred yuan.[18] For the Leis, who had already suffered financial crisis, this would further damage Lei Mingyuan's reputation. First, if he could not even control a little girl, how could he manage Paoge matters? Second, even a mere girl was ignoring his authority, thus how might the Paoge members respond to Lei's future orders? Third, the girl had run away in great part because Lei had treated her violently—a matter further described below. In rural society, abusing a servant girl gave one a bad reputation.

It was not just a matter of the Lei family; the event pointed to the good name and decency of the local Paoge more generally. Helmsman Tong Niansheng was very angry when he heard the news and felt it was not a small matter. His attitude fixed upon the potential of dishonor that might involve a local householder and Paoge leader. One answer to the problem was to think in terms of Lei Mingyuan merely having been robbed of his personnel. How dare someone take away a servant girl who belonged to his deputy! If news of the incident spread, what would brothers in other branches think of them in Hope Township? Tong commanded brothers to solve the case immediately and catch the girl. After all, the Paoge had a great ability in the collecting of intelligence: they had eyes and ears everywhere.

In just three days the report came back: Junfang was hiding in a mountainous area, about 150 miles from Hope. The man who had taken her was also a Paoge member: in fact, his older brother was a secret agent and a powerful man. When Tong heard these facts, he realized that handling this case would be more complex than anticipated.

Tong learned more about the ins and outs. Junfang's flight had occurred after being beaten badly by Lei. Shen in fact stated in her report that Junfang "escaped from a tiger's mouth with wounds all over her body."[19] It seemed to everyone that it had been a matter of self-defense. With this new layer, the complexity of a workable solution surprisingly became much easier to deal with. If they were to catch Junfang with force, it would inevitably make a bad confrontation with another Paoge branch. Tong knew about Lei Mingyuan's bad situation and thus felt it was not necessary to make an enormous sacrifice for a man like Lei—someone who was already so diminished. Tong stopped thinking of the matter as requiring serious and complex tactics in order to help Lei save face. It is easy to imagine that Tong was simply through with Lei, unwilling to help him further. Lei's status and reputation in the organization had become dramatically low by this point. From the other side, Lei recognized Tong's indifference and his own slide downward, and he did nothing about it. Even though he was a deputy helmsman, Lei did not have a close relationship with Tong. Several years earlier, the two had experienced their own power struggle in a certain matter. Junfang's case was thus ultimately given little notice, and Tong did not pursue it. Lei may have thought that he was merely unlucky to have fallen into a bad position among his society brothers, and that at present he simply had to show on the surface "a magnanimous and carefree attitude."[20] At least, this way of handling the whole business was the men's way.

★ ★ ★

We have explored how the male-dominated world judged and reacted to a scandalous incident of woman-bashing. Concerning argot, gestures, and the various ways of effecting and keeping order, the in-crowd of Paoge brothers and brothers from related chapters had a vast supply of roles to perform to protect and promote themselves. There were rules to enforce or ignore and personal reputations to hone. Shen Baoyuan is our only source of this incident, and she certainly could not cover all aspects of local affairs. But it is valid to deduce from what she wrote that Lei was let off easy. This happened probably from a combination of some obligations still owed him and Tong Niansheng's thinking that Lei should be written off as a viable "brother."

Let us turn to the women in this local society. We can safely make this generalization: women had a different set of resources and options than men. Despite nationwide attempts by the Nationalists at producing modern, Western-inspired legislation and institutions to ensure women's rights in a variety of contexts, women in 1940s rural China remained to a great degree under men's thumbs. Woman Lei was losing tolerance for her drug-addicted husband. Like thoughtful women in this society, she no doubt had the maintenance and protection of her family foremost in her thoughts. But she needed to come to a decision about the Junfang incident. How would she handle it from her side? How would she judge and react, as the local Paoge brothers did? Woman Lei did not care much about having Junfang back in the house—she knew it would not work. Even though the Leis were able to support the servant, nevertheless, after being caught, the Paoge would predictably hold their meeting to decide about punishment. It was inevitable that the crude morals of Lei Mingyuan would be revealed and thus taint the family with further embarrassment. Junfang was big and physically strong; the family could not lock her up, as more than likely she would run away again.[21]

One fascinating resource broadly used by women all over China was fortune-telling (not to say that it was exclusively a female activity). It could provide indications for determining hidden causalities (or even hidden things), how to judge people's inner motives, and how life spans and actions meshed with, or ran against, the larger forces of nature and the cosmos. Fortune-telling was a system of codes, links, and reliabilities that could suit those who had no special society of loyal sisters to protect them. Woman Lei thus told Junfang's fate via a curious fortune-telling book, pronouncing Junfang's experience as a "bitter life." We know from Shen Baoyuan's report that there was a book involved, but Shen did not name it. Yet, because Shen provided details about the technique, called "weighing bones," we can deduce that the book resembled, or actually was, the popular work *Telling Fortunes by the Weight of Bones* (Chenggu suanmingfa), written by Yuan Tiangang in the Tang era (618–907). The bone method was combined with the astral aspect of one's birthday (year, month, date, and time).[22] It is quite possible that Woman Lei had access to this work, because she determined that Lei Mingyuan's bones weighed 5 taels, and Junfang's only 1.2.[23] This interpretation made Junfang's life explainable as a "cheap life."

Woman Lei is not reported to have divined the fate of her husband, but in the Tang-era book there is a description of the kind of person who had "5-tael bones"; it includes phrases that Woman Lei might easily have analogized to Lei Mingyuan's life situation. We learn that the "5-tael" person will "not worry about clothes, etc. and will be rich, but he works hard for his profit and fame." The latter might have indicated for Woman Lei something about her husband's participation in Paoge activities. Furthermore, the

5-tael man will meet "troubles in his middle age" (perhaps pointing to Lei's loss of the lease on his land). Finally, in the book it is said that the "5-tael" man will be rich again when he is old. Woman Lei would not have been able to corroborate this.

Yuan Tiangang's text has commentary about the "5-tael man": "He has no property passed from ancestors and has to depend on himself." We do not know about any inheritable property, but we do know that Lei fended for himself quite well. "He starts from nothing and does not have many friends or relatives to support him; his brothers are weak but he can collect wealth from all over place." One of Lei's brothers died early. As head of the Paoge, Lei's occupation was to extract money from many places and activities. Let's look at one longer paragraph from the commentary: His hands can earn him money, but he cannot keep the money. He does not know how to take care of himself. He marries late and has children late. In his forties he suddenly has great luck—a new lease on life. Yet he will have a calamity at forty-nine. Then, after ten years, he will be lucky in money, accompanied by his wife and concubines. His two children will take care of him until his death at sixty-nine years old in the eleventh lunar month.[24] Lei could not keep his money, leading to the family's financial crisis. Next, although Shen Baoyuan did not state Lei's age, based on other details in her report, we can calculate that Woman Huang (Lei's first wife) bore their son Junlong when she was twenty-four; thus in 1945 Lei was between forty and fifty years old. If we say that marrying Woman Lei was his "great luck," it may have been Lei's "new lease on life." As for "he will have a calamity at forty-nine," does it refer to the loss of the lease? Woman Lei might have pondered this.

In divining Junfang's fortune, Woman Lei was reaching for something useful for her own mind and to her way of judging the circumstances. She found that the servant girl had light ("cheap") bones, thus by correlating with Yuan's book, the girl would "have a short life and her life would have all kinds of disasters. Unfortunate things come one after another, and she suffers her whole life." With Junfang's bones as they were, "her fate would be as a poor person, someone alone her whole life."[25] All of this might have been an excuse for the way Woman Lei comforted her own stark needs at that moment. It was not the poor way the family had treated the unfortunate girl, it was the girl's fate! Junfang could now be viewed as a causality, a vector of cosmic motive, relative to the family's horrible fall: "The bad luck of the Lei family in recent years are brought by Junfang, who possesses a bitter fate." As reported by Shen, she observes that since Junfang's arrival, chickens were eaten by yellow weasels, chicks died without a reason, and six sows died of swine fever; then the main door got out of shape and could not be shut; there were inexplicable sounds in the kitchen; the harvest declined; and now even the land lease was gone. The family could not live in the house any more and were driven to move quickly! Woman Lei felt that Junfang was a ghost that caused the fall of the Lei family. Now she was gone, perhaps signaling a good turn.[26]

Woman Lei was pained by the things Junfang had stolen: after all, the family was not as well off as they once had been. It would be good if the stolen property were recovered, but the Paoge brothers headed by Tong Niansheng did not want to spend the energy; they felt that since Lei Mingyuan never paid Junfang a salary, the stolen pieces could be considered compensation. Some neighbors advised Woman Lei by saying that the stolen clothes were too used, so why bother with them? Woman Lei gave up any further action for regaining the property.[27]

★   ★   ★

We should ask an expected yet difficult question: why were the women in Hope, on the Chengdu Plain, subject to such misery and penury, their options so limited and subservient? What was the social dynamic that called the women to offer their ceaseless, drudge labor, to show their support of shiftless, or just insensitive, husbands, and to become swept up in petty struggles over small relationships, status, and goods? These were enormous pressures to live under, but things do not get bad for women in a wide sector of a vast local society for no reason. Of course, quite a few people in this rural area of China were poor and struggling, especially from the 1920s through the 1940s. But there was one sector of humanity that was systematically pressed down even lower: women.

Women were the object of deep, enduring discrimination about their social status, their minds, and their bodies. In fact, one of the reasons why Lei Mingyuan had killed his daughter in 1939 was his prejudice about sexual status, something that sprang from a deeply fixed discrimination about women's bodies, all too common among the Paoge in Hope Township. The brothers required that women's behavior be in line with traditional standards, and they disliked women who were "free thinking"; they actually hated what they considered "frivolous women." These attitudes, traceable to at least the late Qing period, were rife throughout the general populace, and part of social engineering on the part of local elites.[28] By the 1930s women were restricted and scrutinized, especially rural women. Conversely, to a large extent, well-educated women could elicit respect in rural society: for example, Shen Baoyuan the college student, who arrived in the countryside. Lei had to be polite to her, while concurrently broadcasting disrespect to the rural women around him. Shen expressed her deep concern: "Such social control in the traditional habits and stale customs has a profound influence on the rural society. If anyone violated the old moral codes, she would get social disapproval and public opposition." Although it was Lei who killed his daughter, the society and the dark fate of women also contributed to her death.[29]

Lei and many elites in Hope Township carried with them old, conservative attitudes toward women. In the traditional society, women were considered men's appendages, without independent personality and economic status. Using a variety of local gazetteers, we can sketch a picture of society's moral requirements for women and the traditional forms of control. Local gazetteers often commended *lienü*, those women who were categorized as righteous (*jie*), filial (*xiao*), chaste (*zhen*), and spirited (*lie*) as good examples for women. These categories oppressed women and their bodies and minds through common exhortations such as "obeying her son after her husband's death" and "the mother enjoys glory because of her son's success."[30] To commend a woman's ethics and morality meant aiming a thick front of public opinion at her, thus creating significant psychological pressure.

In Sichuan, beginning in the early twentieth century, a new sort of public opinion began to emerge that favored women's so-called liberation. This was the advent of social modernity, caused by the many new schools, new ideas (many from the West and its spokespeople and actions), and the development of new media. Some activists vigorously advanced women's liberation: "I will use my hands to break the inequality between men and women. I will use my loud voice to promote the wave of woman's education."[31] These activists called for freedom of marriage and overall equality with men. The Chengdu Civilization Press (Chengdu wenming shuju) published a "Song of Free Marriage" (*ziyou jiehun ge*), openly demanding freedom of love and marriage and opposing arranged marriages and foot binding. When the Railroad Protection Movement emerged in 1911, women had reached the point of participating in political life; they set up their own political organization—the Railroad Protection Association for Women (Nüzi baolu tongzhi xiehui). They issued a public call for women in Sichuan to save the province from peril. They used this movement to struggle for their own rights and against discrimination and oppression. In the late Qing, Sichuan women announced a goal to "change useless women of the past four thousand years to be pillars of protecting the country and nation and to build happiness for our descendants."[32] However, when we see woman's social status in 1940s Hope Township, such a change obviously became stalled somewhere in the thicket of bamboo groves.

Shen Baoyuan's report provided examples of women's humble status in Hope Township. There were two military families—people who had seen the outside world. Their girls were different from others in the area, but locals felt that the girls were "frivolous" because they had male students as friends in middle school. Therefore, Shen explained, "many villagers were against them." Lei Mingyuan had "a stubborn mind" and was afraid of their "bad influence" on his daughter, so he forbade Shuying to play with them. Once, when Lei saw Shuying with them, he went on a rampage, "pushing her down to the river." Fortunately, Woman Lei came quickly to Shuying's rescue, so that another river tragedy was avoided.[33]

In this male-dominated world, young men and boys were given more chances. Lei Mingyuan had a positive attitude toward his elder son Julong, thinking that perhaps he could carry on the family line and eventually support the household. Lei was willing to pay for this son to go to school, and he prepared for this future investment when his son would have earning power. For Shuying's education, however, he was not forthcoming. Of course, this was also due to the fact that he was only her stepfather and he simply wished that she would marry. So he treated Shuying as less than. Woman Lei often argued with him about the unfair treatment, but she had no way to make him change his mind.

If Julong could not manage to get enrolled in school, Shuying had no chance at all, thus Woman Lei always tried to enroll Julong. As a stepmother, she tirelessly urged her stepson to study, and she knew it was a positive move that reflected well on her daughter's chances because she could likely tease out some money for Shuying from the fund for Julong. As a good mother, she even sold her jewelry to a pawn shop to pay for the daughter's tuition. But Julong ultimately had no interest in studying and often played truant, while Shuying was smart and studied hard. She often helped her brother with course work, and Woman Lei was happy and proud of her; she praised Shuying to neighbors. As a man who looked up to men and down on women, however, Lei Mingyuan was unhappy: it was a loss of face. He did not like Shuying's lively personality and believed that a girl should be quiet and well mannered. When the school held a party and Shuying performed on the stage, Woman Lei was talking and laughing happily, regarding the daughter's accomplishment as the mother's glory, as many women would do only for their sons.[34]

Lei Mingyuan's treatment of the servant girl Junfang also reflects his misogyny. Junfang was once a child-bride (*tongyangxi*) in Huang Village, a market town not far from Hope Township; she had run away two years earlier because of her mother-in-law's abuse.[35] For hundreds of years the child-bride was a common feature of Chinese rural society, something seen in both rich and poor families. Often a girl from a poor family was sent (often sold) to another family if the girl's parents could not feed everyone. But the child-bride would be only a nominal daughter-in-law, living with the new family, performing tasks, with the understanding that she would be a real wife of the intended groom in the years to come. Sometimes child-brides were purchased for unfit sons, who were outside the normal market for brides. These girl brides could serve as payments for loans, as seen in a well-known Yuan drama titled *Dou E's Injustice That Moved the World* (Gantian dongdi Dou E yuan).[36] Some relatively kind families treated child-brides well, as their own daughters. But others used them strictly as servants, with beatings and scoldings, such as happened with Junfang in the Lei family. Junfang had come to them through a middleman expressly to cook, launder, and sew. But, as Woman Lei shared with Shen, Junfang had a strong personality and was "stubborn." She felt her situation sharply and was unhappy about her bonded servitude; thus she "often resisted." She would try to get breaks or sleep longer, or get something to eat from the kitchen. As the anthropologist James Scott described, it was the "resistance of the weak."[37]

In the 1940s, Qin Mu described China's trade in servant girls, which was often consummated in the so-called "human markets" (*renshi*), a phenomenon that had touched the world of Woman Lei in particular (Chapter 7 recounted her story after she was abandoned by her first husband). Usually a matchmaker brought a "poor little girl" age eight to twelve to a family—old enough for work but not old enough to run away. The transaction was not conducted in the front hall, but only in a side room by the gate, handled by the woman of the house. The master came only to review the girl's appearance and to decide a proper price. If the girl's zodiac was a tiger (considered uncontrollable), or had light hair, or small eyes, or bad teeth, and so forth, the price would be haggled down. When the purchase was made, her name would be immediately changed, often employing names for seasons plus names of flowers, such as Chunmei (Spring Plum) or Xialian (Summer Lotus). The new servant then "began her long, dark night of a life." After she grew up, the owner married her to a peasant for a high price or sold her to an older rich man as a concubine. Girls on the "human market" were of humble, often desperate beginnings, and their stories were rarely recorded. Qin Mu, however, told two stories from his own experience from his youth. His family bought a servant girl, and she often stole rice out of hunger. The other story concerned a tragedy in the village. One night, several servant girls from rich families committed suicide by tying themselves together and jumping into a river. Such deaths were only those of servant girls, so "soon forgotten."[38]

In his autobiographical novel *Family* (set in Chengdu), Ba Jin described a servant girl named Mingfeng whose life was sad. The master forced her to become a concubine of an old man, but Mingfeng loved her young master Juehui and wished that he would save her. But at that moment Juehui was busy with a writing project, thus he paid no attention to her. Since Juehui was her lifeline, Mingfeng lost hope. She decided to kill herself, first recalling her suffering seventeen years of beatings, abuse, and grief. She swore to

Juehui: "I'll never go with the old man." That night, she threw herself into a pond. Juehui subsequently contemplated about this tragedy and stated: "It is not just me, but our whole family and the society are the murderers. But, in such an environment, how can I get married with her?... I am tired of this life."[39]

Of course, Junfang was not Mingfeng, who gave up her struggles. Junfang could not confront her master; she could not keep from being used, and with no one to save her, she acted out based on her faith in herself. Yet her resistance brought more disaster. Junfang's personality invited Lei Mingyuan's reprimands. When she rebutted with a few words, she was beaten badly—black and blue everywhere. Beating of course did not change her to Lei's liking; instead, she became more unbending, inviting even worse treatment.[40] As Shen reported, Junfang did find a bit of happiness when she was alone with friends, such as the other Lei family hired hands. One could indeed find her laughing, even a little manic. If anyone bullied her, she would "use the worst words in response." She often cursed Lei Mingyuan to die early. She represented the "noneducated, suppressed, and wild women." In these respects, Junfang was like Woman Lei, who had an even more miserable life. Marriage to Lei Mingyuan hardly brought about a happy life, but at least she escaped from a worse fate. Junfang, however, still wanted to struggle. Woman Lei, who sympathized with her, said: "Her fate is not good, so she can only be a servant girl." She reached this conclusion through her fortune-telling book.[41]

According to Shen Baoyuan, Lei Mingyuan possessed a "feudal mind" (*fengjian naojin*).[42] He was well-known for cruelty; he wanted to play a role in keeping order in his local place and severely scrutinized the women in his own family. Woman Lei had a childless older sister whose husband died early. After Woman Lei was abandoned by her first husband, she left her daughter Shuying with this sister. When Shuying was five, Lei Mingyuan brought Shuying to Hope Township and this widow also moved to Hope. She opened a teahouse for her livelihood. Shuying had a closer relationship with her aunt than with her mother, Woman Lei. In 1942 a rumor arose that one night a man spent the night in the widow's teahouse. When Lei Mingyuan heard the rumor, he was enraged and grabbed his pistol to kill her. Highly distressed, Woman Lei followed him to the teahouse. The widow had run away before Lei's arrival. Upon arriving, he smashed teacups, tables, and chairs. He swore he would kill her as soon as he found her. Afterward, the widow never dared to return to Hope Township and lived in Chengdu, working as a peddler.

Shen Baoyuan felt it was quite possible that the widow had been wrongly accused. If a sexual liaison had actually happened, in the end there would have been only gossip and public opinion. In normal circumstances, such a woman would not have been shamed publicly nor had her life threatened. However, the Chengdu Plain, in Shen's overview, was "a rural area enveloped by the old moral and ethic codes. As a Paoge head, Lei had to respond to rumors."[43] Lei did not use his power to track the origin of the rumor but instead turned to his misogynist tendency, to his typical discriminatory feelings about women's bodies and sexual status. He wanted only to punish the widow. Another brutal and arbitrary killing was in the making, like his murder of his own daughter; but this time it was not carried out.

In the view of the budding sociologist Shen Baoyuan, in addition to social controls, moral and religious ones were also needed, and "if they were used correctly, they might play a positive role in social reform." For Shen, social control was embedded in culture and tradition, but in the Chengdu Plain it made "little contribution to the improvement of society." Shen simply saw "old-fashion feudal habits," which "only harmed the weak." Therefore, it was all simply "a terrible control, and contrary to civilization."[44]

★ ★ ★

On February 17, 1946, Shuying had to register at school; tuition was over 60,000 yuan. How to get this amount? Woman Lei delicately made a proposal to Lei Mingyuan that they sell 2 *dan* of rice.[45] But Lei expressed neither agreement nor rejection, only ambiguity. Woman Lei then heard some bad news: Lei Mingyuan was setting things in motion to take a concubine, a woman who lived in Chengdu's western suburbs; she had once been married but now only tended to her mother. This woman owned 30 *mu* of paddy field and operated an opium den. It was said that she used to be a teacher in an elementary school; with her permed hair and blue gown, she was stylish. When Woman Lei became aware of Lei Mingyuan's plan, she kept quiet, limiting her confrontation to the matter of her daughter's tuition. But because Lei was unforthcoming, she went to see Liu Zixing, a Paoge manager (a fifth brother), directly and openly complaining about her difficulties. The manager gave her 70,000 yuan to pay Shuying's tuition.

On February 20, Woman Lei finally burst. She stated her desire to divorce Lei Mingyuan, and condemned the "bad woman" (Lei's planned concubine), swearing to kill her. Woman Lei had become disheveled; she told everyone of her bitter situation, how she had been supporting the family and had helped Lei gain a foothold in the Paoge society, and so on. As Shen reported, she used "the most obscene words" to describe her husband and the "bad woman." Lei Mingyuan avoided a direct confrontation, but when he could stand her abuse no longer, he finally left home. For Woman Lei, the idea of leaving the house was a complex and difficult one. For any woman in 1940s rural China, this was a relatively dangerous option.[46]

Woman Lei had no clear idea of what divorce meant for the future: how would she live? If she chose to stay with her man, however, she would be unable to stand the facts: living with an opium addict and his concubine. How could she face others' looks and their gossip? She decided to act on two fronts: she asked all kinds of people who had relations with Lei Mingyuan to persuade him to change; she was convinced she needed to act in a direct and logical way, so she hired a lawyer to present a lawsuit that would give her a chance to take Lei's opium equipment to the court. She went to Chengdu on her own and found Butcher Liu, who was the closest friend of the Lei family; she asked him to press Lei Mingyuan not to take the concubine. Upon her return to Hope Township, Woman Lei packed her clothing and was ready to leave the house at any time.[47]

Butcher Liu traveled to Hope Township to help ease the situation. Lei Mingyuan knew the man had been invited by his wife and kept silent; he ignored the visitor, as if at home nothing had happened. Liu sat for a while but did not find a chance to discuss the matter, so eventually he left. However, after the Paoge brothers in Hope Township heard the news, they came one after another to provide comfort and to mediate. As discussed in Chapter 5, the Paoge often involved themselves in local disputes; now they were mediators in an internal problem, since the brothers' families were part of larger Paoge affairs. The first one was Fifth Brother Liu Zixing, who persuaded Woman Lei not to take things too hard. He tried to inquire about Lei Mingyuan's general attitude. Lei ignored his guest, suggesting that people should not interfere with his family business. Liu Zixing was unhappy about Lei's attitude, so he informed the Paoge brothers and Woman Lei that since Lei Mingyuan did not care much for the brothers' friendship, the brothers would support Woman Lei in her suit against Lei Mingyuan.[48] From the way this mediation played out, the extent of decline in Lei's power is illuminated. Lei was the second brother, but here the fifth brother decided on behalf of other brothers to stand against Lei.

After Liu's decision became known, Lei softened his attitude somewhat. He knew that his own prestige in the Paoge was not as great as it had been in the past and that his brothers might not respect him as before. His golden age had passed, and he had to adjust to a kinder attitude toward his wife and his Paoge brothers. Therefore, to break the deadlock, he gave 3,000 yuan pocket money to Shuying and food money to Woman Lei. The house was due to be transferred to the Cai family, so he started to discuss moving somewhere with Woman Lei. He did not mention the concubine.

With no viable options, Woman Lei made peace with Lei Mingyuan. Later, they found a house and moved, becoming the neighbors of two cart pullers—that is, coolies.[49] Lei Mingyuan finally lost his power and prestige and thus began his ordinary life. He was actually a paper tiger: when he needed to be powerful, he acted that out with violence or bullying inside his family. Several cases of violence concerned those within his family circle. But now, when confronted with a man who swept up his servant girl, or with the new tenant Cai, or with the landlord who refused to grant a new lease, Lei seemed powerless. Physically weakened and damaged by opium, he became skinny. When he moved to the new place, he carried over the furniture with great effort, helped by Woman Lei. The place had two small, dark rooms. Lei brought his opium equipment there. He intended to continue his opium business, and he would lay on the bed all day smoking opium. Woman Lei did not have any idea how long Lei Mingyuan would live. Shen Baoyuan was not optimistic either; she reported that "he will not have much time left."[50]

PART FOUR

Picking up the Threads

CHAPTER 10

Fall of the Paoge

FOR CENTURIES the Paoge had had numerous experiences involving confrontation with government authorities. The result of this—the achievement of working fronts with governments—was their inevitable safeguard, allowing the Paoge to grow and develop. They never expected that, upon the advent of the Communist regime, their huge organization, their rich experience, as well as their weapons, could not save them. They were destroyed almost overnight. The commonplace members of the Paoge, the lower-ranked brothers, surrendered to the Chinese Communist Party (CCP) government, and they mostly were able to live normal lives. But the Paoge leaders who would not, or simply did not, create close relationships with Communist cadres bore a tragic fate.

Many Paoge leaders were executed; other members were subjected to various forms of punishment. Several categories defined survival for a Paoge member. First, the low-level members who had joined the secret society to enjoy a certain kind of protection belonged to what the CCP called "oppressed people." Second were those had a certain relationship with the CCP, who disliked the Guomindang (GMD) and its local governments and secretly sympathized and supported the activities of the Communist Party.[1] Third—the last category that defined the Paoge survivors after the Communist takeover—were those relatively moderate Paoge leaders who had handled local affairs without making political enemies and without blood on their hands.

Cai Xinghua, the Paoge member and memoirist, mentioned elsewhere in this book, was in the second category, so he lived rather normally after 1950 and thus had an opportunity to write about his Paoge experiences. Because Cai had had a close relationship with the CCP, he was even able to make it through the turbulent Suppression of Counterrevolutionaries, a top-down political scouring and winnowing during 1950 and 1951 that affected the whole nation. During this movement, all overt Paoge members were wiped away—either forced into passive relinquishment from pressure and fear or else killed. Many leaders were executed. The members of the Cai-led chapter of the Paoge, named the Ritual Branch, were lower-class people, so the CCP were not inclined to harass them. Cai said that his leadership position brought economic burden, so "to really lift away this kind of trouble could happen only by ending the Paoge organization."[2] We do not know whether this thought came from his heart and soul, that he actually regretted the loss of status as a Paoge master, but it is pretty clear that after 1950 that Cai would not have had a chance to state anything positive about the Paoge's role, under the political environment of the moment. Since he had a close connection with the CCP, we assume that Cai offered what was a sincere welcome toward the new regime, at least visibly so. Again, historians often lack surefooted access to what lies most deeply, and quietly, inside people in the form of their unstated beliefs and opinions.

Except for the Cai Xinghua type of Paoge—that is, those who were relatively friendly with Communist cadres and the party—after 1949 many Paoge leaders did not escape severe punishment. In writings compiled by local historians, sponsored by local governments over the past several decades, the Paoge are nearly all condemned. Recently, I read through nearly all of the historical data compiled by local historians at all levels (province, city, county, and district), and I developed a certain understanding of the historical writing on the Paoge. The work that focused on our infamous He Song—head of the Paoge in Jintang County, mentioned several times in this book—is a typical narrative made under the CCP; in it we have a title typical for such works: "Reactionary figure He Song, who combined multiple identities in the party, military, politics, banditry, and Gowned Brothers." This article was referred to earlier in the book. One does not have to read the contents to know it is a biography of a local "bad man." The purpose of writing is didactic: to display before the public the evil things done by evil people. In December 1949 the People's Liberation Army (PLA) entered Jintang County. To "prevent his demise, He Song madly struggled" and "organized revolts." In July 1950 he was sentenced to death and executed in public.[3] This happened only thirty to forty miles from Chongyiqiao (Shen's "Hope Township").

There is a tiny bit of information about the fall of the Paoge in Chongyiqiao, to which I will turn after we look at a rather detailed finding about the Paoge's last days in Xinfan County, only ten to fifteen miles from Chongyiqiao (see Map 2). Based on an unpublished official report titled "General Situation of the Paoge in Xinfan County," we know that at some time during the early Republic, five branches of the Paoge in Xinfan had organized a general society, called the Society for Good Times Together (Tongle she), whose headquarters was set up at a county site.[4] The motive had been "to reduce conflicts," a phrase that is ambiguous but probably a benign cover for strong-arm work. By 1942 a total of fourteen public societies of the Paoge "gradually began to collaborate." The leaders of branches tried hard to expand their power and secretly pushed their followers to "kill and rob." Therefore, "at the surface, most of them were pure-water [that is, the name made them seem like nonviolent, business-oriented Paoge], but in fact they were linked to banditry." They controlled all opium dens and gambling places.[5]

Still working with the same document about Xinfan County, we learn that "if commoners did not have a Paoge background, they lost all safeguards. Anyone who wanted to open a business had to get an approval from the Paoge and to share a part of profits so that the business would be protected by the Paoge. In local places, joining the Paoge often became a glorious event that was envied by others." As a result, there developed a sense locally that "it was shameful if one was not a member of the Paoge." As a result of this dynamic, "almost all local gentry and landlords joined the organization," some of whom held real power in the County Consultative Council (*xian canyihui*). They also often forced merchants to pay protection fees. Although bandits tyrannized the area, the magistrate failed several times to clean up the problem. He had to ask He Zaizhi, a head of the Paoge, for help. Within three days, all bandits and robbers were gone. Apparently, the capability of the magistrate could not match the head of the Paoge.

In May 1949 the Paoge in Xinfan held an assembly in a place outside the East City Gate to discuss how to deal with the coming CCP; they swore to "protect the homeland." The assembly required that all Paoge members unite and stop any internal fights. Three months before the PLA entered Sichuan, He Zaizhi and local leaders organized a guerrilla force to "keep local stability." After the PLA took over Xinfan in January 1950, "bandit revolts" broke out. The "bandit chieftains" (*feishou*, using the CCP's terminology) were "almost all Paoge members." After the new administration was established, according to the document, the Paoge members knew that their "feudal organization should not continue to exist." Hereafter, they "gradually disappeared" and "invisibly dissolved."

There is little direct information about the Paoge in Chongyiqiao after the PLA took control, but I stumbled on some relevant information. It seems that Chongyiqiao actually played a role in the peaceful takeover of its large urban neighbor, Chengdu. Deng Xihou (1889–1964), former Sichuan governor (1924–25, 1946–48) and one of the leaders of a "peaceful uprising" in western Sichuan, recalled that before the uprising, he and two other leaders of the Sichuan Army—Liu Wenhui (1895–1976) and Pan Wenhua (1886–1950)—felt a dilemma: They understood very well that the CCP's victory was inevitable, but they were not sure how the CCP would treat them, even though all of them had fought with the Red Army (the early name of the CCP's military force) before.[6]

In 1949, Sichuan governor Wang Lingji, who had close ties with Chiang Kai-shek, was determined to fight the Communists. On the one hand, Deng, Liu, and Pan, as leaders of the Sichuan Army, did not want the defeated Nationalist troops from other regions to enter Sichuan—something that easily might have caused chaos. On the other hand, Wang did not care much about Sichuan; he only wanted to show his loyalty to Chiang by preparing for a last defense under the GMD. Finally, to avoid active fighting and damaging the troops, Deng, Liu, and Pan made a secret agreement to guarantee a peaceful PLA takeover. Thus contact was made with the PLA. This process and outcome, in the CCP's historiography, is called a "peaceful uprising" (*heping qiyi*)—that is, they surrendered to the PLA without a fight.

On December 7, 1949, as the three military leaders met at Liu Wenhui's home, Chiang Kai-shek notified Liu to come see him. They worried Chiang might force Liu to fly to Taiwan (the Nationalist government had withdrawn from mainland China to Taiwan), and thus the three decided to escape from Chengdu. To keep it a secret, they did not take any luggage; they snuck out of Chengdu by making such excuses as going hunting or having a critical doctor's visit. Each man passed the Chengdu checkpoint at the North City Gate and arrived in Chongyiqiao; the next day they went on together to Dragon Bridge (Longqiao). On December 9, Liu, Deng, and Pan issued a "public call for all Sichuan people" (*Gao quan Chuan minzhong shu*), telling the populace that they should give up resistance against the PLA. "This was a public break with Chiang Kai-shek and was a stance on the people's side," Deng later said. "It was the beginning of accepting the leadership of the CCP and the beginning of a new life." Although Chiang Kai-shek ordered Hu Zongnan, one of his most trusted generals, to put on the pressure, the Sichuan Army ultimately dispatched a large contingent west to Chongyiqiao and maintained the force until the end of the month, when the PLA approached Chengdu.[7]

There was no major battle when the PLA took over Chengdu and surrounding areas on December 27, 1949; it was a "peaceful liberation" (*heping jiefang*). However, why did many insurrections—called "bandit insurrections" (*tufei baoluan*) by the new government—take place at the county level outside Chengdu, early in 1950? The Paoge should have known that their forces were unable to confront the PLA. So why did they go through with what would surely be a lost cause? The suppression of these "bandit insurrections" was certainly a serious blow to the Paoge, who disappeared soon after. What motivated the too-little-too-late local resistance after 1949? Plausible answers to these questions emerge as we examine specifications about tax impositions.

★ ★ ★

We have looked with some detail at how the PLA entered the large cities, but not yet at the situation in rural townships and market towns. Discussing the Paoge's fall in Xinfan County helps us in this regard. Various accounts of personal experiences (in the form of memoirs) published in the 1990s provide a better understanding of the process of the takeover. Like Chengdu, Xinfan County was peacefully taken over. The entire political structure and all personnel in Xinfan—including the GMD party, government, township administrations and markets, police, local armed forces, and *baojia*—were left untouched, awaiting the PLA's arrival. Although the GMD prepared for guerrilla war before the expected arrival, the lower-level officials, military officers, and the Paoge brothers did not carry out such a plan after they calculated the power balance and then received the announcement of support for the CCP by the major leaders of the Sichuan Army. They felt it would be meaningless to form any resistance.

Let us push further to try to understand the tactically unsound "bandit insurrections," remembering that "bandit" implied major help from the Paoge. The PLA entered Chengdu on December 27, 1949. A few days later, on January 2, 1950, a military representative and a team for carrying out grain levies (*zhengliang*) arrived in Xinfan and met with magistrate Zhang Xun. On January 4, Zhang held a meeting, at which all heads of townships and market towns attended. The military representative declared that they came to take over the county under the instructions of the CCP's West Sichuan Commission, and all major action and policies had to be approved by the military representative in the future. The key work at the moment was to carry out the grain levies "in order to ensure food supply for the PLA troops entering Sichuan." Various sources indicate that a primary cause of riots in general was the resistance to such levies.

Cao Yunsheng, head of the grain levy team, recalled later that the imposing of the grain levy represented a "political movement and a furious class struggle." Those objecting were "mostly landlords, despotic gentry, and rich peasants. It was very difficult because land taxes had been paid."[8] As I pointed out in Chapter 6, there were actually a small number of big landlords and local tyrants in the Chengdu Plain. In fact, small-holding peasants were the major targets as sources of grain.[9] Therefore, so-called riots were an instinctive resistance against losing one's critical output of grain. It is understandable why landlords and peasants, for their respective reasons,

FIGURE 10.1 Farmers threshing in the fall, Sichuan. *Source*: Photograph by Sidney D. Gamble, ca. 1917–1919. Reproduced courtesy of Sidney D. Gamble Photographs, David M. Rubenstein Rare Book & Manuscript Library, Duke University.

refused to pay land taxes because they had paid them under the GMD regime (Figure 10.1).

Another account by a local historian published in the 1990s has revealed that the granaries in local places were not refilled after the previous year's harvest. The Nationalist army and local powerful people sold much of the grain, and by this time the granaries were almost empty.[10] Food shortages were a serious problem in Chengdu, Xinfan, and other places. Profiteers took the opportunity to drive up grain prices, causing panic. Moreover, both PLA and GMD surrendered troops that had been operating in the area, numbering in the hundreds of thousands each. Therefore, the food supplies were hardly sufficient. The targets of the grain levy were mainly "heads of townships and *baojia* who had the privilege of paying less or not paying land taxes at all and landlords who had close relationships with officials and thus avoided taxes."[11] This was basically the CCP's accusation, which seems to have been partly true. But peasants too had to pay their land taxes. The so-called bandit riots would not have taken place if there had not been this new grain impost. In the beginning of the peaceful takeover, the policies and orders were temporarily carried out by the existing heads of townships and *baojia*, so that "there was no basic shakeup of the feudal powers in local places." The old local leaders could still work together with the new administration. However, for the authorities to take grain directly threatened their interests, so that "they overtly agreed but covertly opposed the levy and performed their duties in a perfunctory manner. They even colluded with evil people, spread rumors, and incited the mass to refuse to pay the land taxes."[12]

The same useful account reveals how a bandit-organized resistance opposed the grain levy. When the team held "a mass meeting to collect grain," a certain "chief of local bandits" (*tufei touzi*) named Second Brother Wang (Wang Erge) openly instigated that local people refuse; he encouraged them to leave the "grain-collection mass meeting." Apparently, this chief was a leader of the Paoge. His attitude reflected peasants' general resentment; therefore, as soon as someone stood up to lead, the villagers were happy to follow. The "bandit chief" was, in the words of the new government, not someone who robbed properties but who helped people instead to prevent giving up their grain to government agents. Later, this account categorized all men who participated in or organized riots as "bandits" and called the crackdown on the resistance a "suppression of bandits" (*jiaofei*). Second Brother Wang was arrested and ultimately executed because he had "participated in the bandit riot and killed members of the team that was imposing the grain levy."[13]

According to a study of Jiangjin County in East Sichuan, in late 1949 and early 1950 the new government enforced extra 80 percent grain levies for landlords and rich peasants. Some of them who were unable to pay the levies had to sell their lands for such payments. For those families, the more they paid for grain levies, the higher cost for transportation because it was their own duty to send the forced levies to the signed locations. In some families, all family members—as old as a sixty-year-old man and as young as a twelve-year-old daughter—participated in the transportation. The situation for those who did not have grain to submit was even worse. Grain levy collectors stayed at these houses until grain levies were turned in. Some people were sent to the government to be "temporarily detained" or even "tortured." Grain levy collections became "violent" and the landlords and rich peasants suffered "attacks" both economically and physically. When the government could not collect enough grain levies from landlords and rich peasants, it started to target at ordinary peasants.[14] The stories of Jiangjin reflect the general situation in Sichuan. When the peasants could not survive and therefore had nothing to lose, they risked participating in insurrections (Figure 10.2).

FIGURE 10.2 Peasants sell their produce at a rural market in Sichuan. *Source*: Photograph by Sidney D. Gamble, ca. 1917–1919. Reproduced courtesy of Sidney D. Gamble Photographs, David M. Rubenstein Rare Book & Manuscript Library, Duke University.

Chongyiqiao, the real name of Shen Baoyuan's fictive Hope Township, might have been the birthplace of the anti-tax disturbance. In January 1950, as discussed, cadres had come into Xinfan County for the purpose of raising grain for PLA troops. On January 28 they went to Chongyiqiao. It was late, so the team decided to camp. That night, "bandits robbed the locale," and the team threatened the bandits and scared them off with loud shouts and gunshot. At dawn, they continued to march, arriving in Xinfan County that evening. Personnel of the military, the police, the Paoge, and bandits themselves, headed by He Zaizhi, launched an insurrection in February.[15] Thirty of the grain-levy team were killed. "Rumors" began to spread, and a childlike rhyming ditty rose through the county:

Empty, empty, empty,
All Sichuan grain to be centralized.
The poor folk to be starved to death,
The rich old coots will die of anger.[16]

Clearly, the "bandit insurrections" reflected growers' resistance to grain collection; it was not a case of what the government called "trying to destroy the people's new administration." Under the PLA's suppression, the riots disappeared quickly.[17] During the process, more than six hundred people were publicly executed in Xinfan County. The largest public execution took place on a single day: nine townships held public trials, and over a hundred "band chiefs" and "bullies" were sentenced to death and executed on site. He Zaizhi turned himself in to the Bureau of Public Security and was arrested. He later died in jail.[18]

★   ★   ★

When the Paoge's interests were threatened by the CCP, they used violence to resist, just as they had done during the Qing and GMD periods in Nationalist causes. But the CCP's power was different: it was buoyed and strengthened by a wave of support all over China in thousands of local, rural places. It increased that power through brute force used against not only opposition combatants but also those with the wrong political alignment in their past. When the Paoge chose to fight this harsh, new government, their day as local leaders all across Sichuan and other provinces ended. Chongyiqiao and Xinfan County were near each other, and therefore historical material regarding Xinfan can be collated with the inferences regarding the Paoge's final days in Chongyiqiao—or should we say "Hope Township"? Undoubtedly, the cadres of the new government also took grain from the small-holders of Chongyiqiao.

Was the fall of the Paoge also the final fall of the already stumbling Lei Mingyuan? How did he respond to the new government's orders? He might have joined the organized resistance in its confronting the Communist regime; or he might have become a nobody to survive a bit longer, making sure not to get involved in any open activity. Why should he have, since he had no property of his own to protect? By this time, the opium might have already completed its devastation of Lei's body. Probably, when the CCP came, his grave had already been covered by grass. We cannot know for sure, or where and how he died, but Lei's fate and trajectory were so well established that our mind's eye can easily picture it.

CHAPTER 11

Looking for the Storyteller

THIS BOOK HAS MAINLY BEEN CONCERNED with two people: Paoge leader Lei Mingyuan (and his family) and Shen Baoyuan, the storyteller of Lei's life and family. They lived in two completely different worlds and had wildly different geographical, educational, social, and economic backgrounds, but they intersected in the summer of 1945. One was investigated and described, while the other was the investigator and narrator. Both played a role in retelling a moving piece of human history. However, we can also regard this book as a three-way narrative: in addition to Lei and Shen, I am engaging in dialogue with them. I have tried to understand Lei Mingyuan from Shen Baoyuan's account.

This book observes and tells its history in three layers: the first is the protagonist Lei Mingyuan and his family; the second is Shen, who recorded their stories and observable patterns, observing Paoge activities and Paoge families from a Western-trained sociological student's perspective; and the third layer is that of a modern-day researcher who uses today's views to explore the nature of Sichuan's secret society in a historical context. The first two layers are tightly entwined: the report that functioned as Shen's thesis requirement was completed in April 1946, and the discussions about and stories concerning Lei Mingyuan and his family ended chronologically around February of the same year. From her writing, we see that she established an unusually close relationship with the Lei family. Shen stayed in touch with Woman Lei and her daughter, Shuying, between August 1945 and February 1946—and perhaps for a short time after that.

This chapter takes up some of the work of the third layer, in which I step in more blatantly with the goal of sorting out aspects of Shen Baoyuan's life and her narratives about the Paoge. By questioning the known facts, I seek to understand how it was that Shen got to be the type of person who thought and acted as she did. To do that, even to elicit a few more items or any small pearl of insight, we need to frame a backdrop of influences, as human influences are very much a bloodline of the shape of all intellectual and cultural growth. During Shen's adolescent and college years, she likely would have been influenced by the three aspects: (1) her family's tradition of intellectual pursuit, in which her father, once a student in America, encouraged his daughter toward a certain Western style of open-mindedness in her thinking and assumptions; (2) left-wing and Communist influence; and (3) the academic and theoretical processes and activities typical at Yenching University and its Department of Sociology at the time.

★   ★   ★

As research for this book evolved, I realized that further information about the young academic sociologist sent to Hope Township might reveal at least one or two new bits of information. To find Shen Baoyuan in person, though, seemed likely to be difficult, since almost seventy years had elapsed: from the standard searches, I could not easily tell if she were even still alive. After some sleuthing in media reports, I found out that Shen Baoyuan and her relatives had set up a scholarship at Sun Yat-sen University in 2005. Through a friend at the university, I was able to gain Shen's phone number. I reached her by phone in the summer of 2014, but unfortunately she has lost most of her memory due to Alzheimer's disease. I learned some basics from her daughter, however. Below, we'll explore some of that family history, but for now let's start with Shen's birth year: 1924. When she traveled to Hope Township in the summer of 1945 for her sociological investigation, Shen was twenty-one and a junior in Yenching University's Department of Sociology.

   Although Shen could not sit down with me and establish revised narratives, or check the those I have deduced concerning Hope Township in the 1940s, my deductions are no less valuable. Her 1946 report was, after all, a contemporaneous record of her original investigation. Moreover, given the nature of Alzheimer's, whatever she could have told me about events that occurred in the 1940s might be skewed current memory producing an unreliable "new and revised" report. To make matters more complex, after 1946 and the completion of Shen's report, Chinese Communist Party politics began to interfere with and change narratives of known events, complex social realities, and even individual and national memory. For decades, people's minds underwent subtle changes as the CCP, with unparalleled vigor, undertook a massive campaign of historical revisionism. Therefore, rather than working to understand Shen's current, possibly problematic memories, let's dig deeper into the three primary influences: her family, her ideological orientation, and the shape of her knowledge and studies.

I discovered that Shen came from a prestigious family. Her father, Shen Zurong (Samuel T. Y. Seng, 1883–1977), founder of the academic field of library science in China, started life in a poor family. His grandfather was a tracker on the Yangtze River and later his father opened a small restaurant on the waterfront, where he worked for many years. At fifteen, Shen Zurong worked for the Protestant Episcopal Church in Yichang, Hubei, and then studied at Boone University, a missionary school in Wuhan. After graduation, Shen Zurong was employed by the Boone Library (Wenhua gongshulin), which had been founded by American professional librarian Mary Elizabeth Wood (1861–1931). In 1914, he was funded by Wood to study library science in the United States, where he earned his bachelor's degree from Columbia University in 1916. He was the first person from China awarded a degree in library science from that university. After returning to China, Shen Zurong continued to work for the Boone Library. In 1920, Wood collaborated with Boone University to create a library major, and both Shen Zurong and Wood taught courses in that program. In the 1920s, he initiated the Chinese Library Association and participated in the first general assembly of the International Federation of Library Associations as the sole representative of China. Later he served as president of the Boone Library School. During the 1930s and 1940s, Shen Zurong trained many library professionals. In 1952 his position, along with the Boone Library School, was merged into Wuhan University. He died in 1977.[1]

In 2005, Shen Baoyuan and her relatives set up the Shen Zurong and Shen Baohuan Memorial Scholarship at Sun Yat-sen University. Shen Zurong's eldest son, Shen Baohuan went to the United States in 1946 and after the Communist Revolution toppled China in 1949, father and son were permanently separated. For the rest of his life, Shen Zurong could not get any news about or from his son, and thus he did not know that Shen Baohuan had later on moved from the United States to Taiwan and continued his father's mission of library development. Shen Baohuan was in the United States when he died in 2004.[2] Although Baohuan's sister, Shen Baoyuan, had also been provided by the family with the best education and a foundation to become an open-minded and new-style young woman, she nonetheless did not become known in her field or in the wider world, as had her famous father. This lack of a high profile does not impede our ability to characterize her intellectual habits and contours as having come under the influence of the academics in her own family. As professionals, they had taken up so-called modern methods of scientific bibliography and cataloging as practiced in the Western world, with all the earmarks of inclusiveness and rational inquiry that generally came along with these methods. Based on Shen's questioning and her reactions documented in her 1946 report, she seems to have been quite comfortable as an intrepid detective and interrogator, despite her youthful emotions about the disturbing events that were uncovered in Hope Township.

★   ★   ★

Next, what about any leftism, even indirect or subtle inclinations toward the Communist cadres and their ideologies that may have affected Shen Baoyuan's thinking? Her investigation could not be entirely separated from politics and ideologies. At this time, students in Yenching University went to rural areas having been influenced not only by sociology and anthropology professors but also because they responded to a more energetic and widespread call by the Communist Party to China's youth to "go to the countryside." On October 15, 1944, left-wing activists at Chengdu universities held an assembly and set up a Chengdu Democratic Youth Association (Chengdu minzhu qingnian xiehui), which included Communists at Yenching University. In the spring of 1945, to motivate college students in large numbers to get to the countryside and begin empathizing and working with peasants and rural affairs, the association organized students into "rural work teams" that would operate near Chengdu during university summer break. The cadres, using funds from numerous sources, sent doctors and medicines, set up evening schools, propagandized for support of the War of Resistance against the Japanese, conducted surveys, and so on. These activities were meant to "make students understand the importance for intellectuals to enter the world of workers and peasants." One student said: "The rural life for a month has decided my future life. I have learned a lot from the reality of the countryside, so I have decided to join the revolution."[3] Although I did not find a direct clue that Shen's fieldwork was organized by the CCP, it seems to me that a close connection existed.

Although lacking direct evidence of a connection with the CCP, Shen clearly was a left-wing student, specifically an active member of the university's Sea Swallows Troupe (Haiyan jutuan), founded in the fall of 1942 and named after the famous poem "Sea Swallows" by Maxim Gorky— the Russian writer who was famously devoted to international Communist revolution and to the Soviet Union. In the Chinese New Year period of 1943 the troupe performed its first drama, *Wind and Clouds Beyond the Great Wall* (Saishang fengyun) by Yang Hansheng, a story about the Han people and the Mongols uniting to fight the Japanese. Later, the troupe performed *Fragrant Grass at the Edges of the Sky* (Fangcao tianya) by Xia Yan, a drama of modern intellectuals' lives and loves.[4] Furthermore, Shen's name appeared on an item titled "An Appeal from Chengdu's Cultural Circle about the Current Political Situation" (Chengdu wenhua jie dui shiju de huyu), signed by 248 people on September 29, 1945, including celebrities in the world of Chinese literature and the arts. They demanded that the Guomindang government "immediately end the one-party dictatorship" and "unconditionally protect basic human rights, including freedom of speech, press, assembly, association, and religions."[5] At this moment in time, Mao Zedong had arrived in Chongqing, in eastern Sichuan, for a U.S.-sponsored negotiation session (held from August 29 through October 10, 1945) with Chiang Kai-shek concerning the ongoing civil war. These intellectuals' "appeal" seems to have been coordinated with the CCP propaganda being directed at what is known as the Chongqing Negotiation.

Later, Shen went to Hong Kong and became a secretary in the Office of Women Workers of the YWCA. In early 1950 five Hong Kong evening schools for women were closed, affecting more than a thousand women workers; Shen and thirty-three teachers and staff issued "A Letter of Public Appeal," calling for "Christians, co-workers, and all people who enthusiastically support the YMCA" to work together "to save the schools."[6] Her name disappeared from media reports after that. She had apparently decided not to continue in academia after 1950.

★ ★ ★

We turn now to the training Shen Baoyuan received at Yenching University—another important influence. In the preface of her thesis, she thanked her teacher, Lin Yaohua, for teaching her the "operational method (*jisuan fangfa*) and functionalism" (this refers to early sociology's theory of "structural functionalism," discussed in the Introduction and in some detail in Chapter 7). Shen said that she used the "operational method" to "measure interactions among people." She explained that the operational method was a new approach, coming after critical theory and functionalism in American social anthropology; it resulted from synthesizing both approaches. The new method could be applied using mathematical methods, such as statistics, for studying human phenomena and could "predict the occurrence of future events." She tried to use her thesis to make an "experiment" in this new research method.[7] Shen believed that the "narrative of relations" (*guanxi xushu*) was important, being "an essential element in the operational method."

In reading her thesis, however, I did not find any actual application of such methods. The operational method is generally a macro perspective, using statistical theories and mathematical methods to calculate formulas related to quantifiable and changing conditions in people's lives.[8] Shen might have planned to use the method more explicitly for a next step in her study, but once she completed the thesis, she did not have a chance to go back to the project. Today, it is not critical to try to reconstruct Shen's understanding and even implicit use of methods and theories. It would give us very little and would be utterly speculative. What is more commanding are the stories that she recounted about Lei and his family. Although she often made comments that reflected her Westernized, educated-elite point of view, Shen was still trying to understand Lei and his family's lives and their inner world and to make objective observations. In my opinion, she actually combined certain microscopic methods together with her individual visits and observations about the visits—all of which were approaches being used in field investigations generally.

Shen Baoyuan's thesis remarked that Professor Lin Yaohua had taught her mathematical methods, but about this method even Lin himself did not say much in his book *Teaching Notes on Social Anthropology*, a comprehensive summary of his own lifetime of teaching and research. When he commented on the contemporary school of critical theory (*piping pai*) in anthropology, he wrote: "As for methodologies of study, applying statistics to analyze culture is not beneficial; using it to recover ethnic cultural history is too mechanical."[9] It seems Lin did not give much credit to this methodology. However, the theses written by Lin Yaohua's students repeatedly referred to the use of the theory under Professor Lin's supervision. For instance, in his thesis "A Rural Handicraft Family: A Report on the Du Family in Shiyangchang," Yang Shuyin said that in a class on "social systems" during 1942 and 1943, Professor Lin "introduced this perspective to students," stressing use of the comparative mathematical method to "examine the interaction between people using standardized units and predictions of the future."[10]

To understand to what extent Lin Yaohua influenced his students methodologically requires more study. However, it is clear that Lin encouraged them to go to rural areas so that they might better understand peasant lives. Shen Baoyuan was one of these students, and the result for posterity was her valuable records from field investigations. Because her investigations were directly part of a rising trend since the 1920s in sociology and anthropology that emphasized rural issues, this dictated her modus operandi—rural lifestyles in the context of local control, education, health, justice, women's statuses, and so forth. Thus Shen also made it clear that the purpose of her thesis was to "study a secret society, and the family profile of one of its leaders." Her motivation was "purely academic exploration and personal interest" rather than to "explore secrets of members, families, or organizations."[11]

Shen may have felt secure and convinced in her academic purposes, but the Paoge members, she noted, were "very cautious about leaking secrets of the organization." Therefore, after Shen became familiar with Lei and his wife, she "was still afraid of telling them she was making an investigation, so as to avoid their suspicion." With the relationships getting closer, she started to ask more questions. We see evidence in her report, however, that she was quite dissatisfied with the progress—for example, she "often could not achieve the desired requirements." Sometimes she took a lot of time to "circle round" with them but "failed to get the slightest material" or often "tried very hard just to get a little sporadic information."[12] It is possible to deduce if Shen was attempting to see if a case about the Leis and the Paoge could contain data that she could work up (their motives, their thoughts, their actions) and then those could be collected and subjected to analysis according to the operational method and structural functionalism. Whether that was her intention, it is obvious that it was difficult for Shen to get inside this family and the worlds of the Paoge.

At the time, the usual sort of sociological and anthropological investigations being conducted by those academic departments in China concerned industry, economy, social organizations, lifestyles, and local customs; they did not typically try to capture sensitive information on specific social groups, much less specific families or local secret society bands. Although the secret society was semipublic, it was explicitly banned. Furthermore, groups like the Paoge maintained stringent rules to protect themselves and punish violators. Shen's study was potentially dangerous. Of course, her going ahead and deciding in favor of making the investigation was propelled to some extent by specific logistical advantages. The site was close to Chengdu, where her school had been relocated from Beijing. Moreover, she would be relatively safe, unlike the conditions that beset her teacher Lin Yaohua, who had made long, difficult journeys three times to Xiaoliangshan and Xikang during 1943 and 1945, experiencing various hardships and life-threatening circumstances (see Map 1).[13]

The tragic story of another scholar, Fei Xiaotong, and his new bride, Wang Tonghui was likely well-known to Shen. They had gone to Yao Mountain (Dayaoshan), Guangxi Province, for fieldwork in 1935, where Wang disappeared forever.[14] Shen likely also realized that being such a short distance to Chengdu, she could keep in frequent contact with the Lei family even after the summer fieldwork. Without this ability to continue her exchanges with the Leis, it would not have been up to the quality of investigations among her peers. In hindsight, any decision about post-fieldwork energies spent on the project turned out to be useful, given the events the Leis experienced after the summer of 1945 (discussed in Chapters 8 and 9, with additional details below).

★ ★ ★

Shen acknowledged in the preface of her report that she did not have a clear idea what she would study before she arrived in Hope Township. Subsequently, however, she recognized the Paoge everywhere and found that they

occupied the center of local energies and forces. This observed phenomenon caused her to gain an "interest in the study of such an organization,"
and her willingness "to take this opportunity to gather information about
them" eventually became the "real motivation for this thesis."[15] Apparently,
to understand 1940s rural society in the Chengdu Plain, one simply had to
examine the Paoge.

When Shen Baoyuan and her classmates arrived in Hope Township, they
sought to establish a good foundation based on "friendly exchanges" with
villagers. According to her report, Shen tried to understand "the conditions
of rural life, the situation of farm families, and structure of local forces."
She knew that to really understand "local forces," she had to start from the
top for the access to "local relationships." As suggested by villagers, she first
visited the head of the township, the security chief, and heads of the *baojia*,
who "mostly were members of the Society."[16] Here, "the Society" meant
the secret society, the Paoge (see Chapter 2 for a discussion of the way Shen
used variations on the word *shehui* in her report to refer in some cases to a
society generally and in others to the band of local populists and their so-
called secret organization).

Shen got to know Lei Mingyuan mostly through his wife, Woman Lei.
Lei's youngest daughter, Shuying, and son, Julong, enrolled in the summer
school that was set up by Yenching professors and students. Accordingly,
Shen had more opportunities to become close to the family, and she began
to treat them "as the beginning of a study of the Paoge secret society." At
that time, although peasants' children had opportunities to go to a rural
school, they also carried a heavy work burden, usually helping in the fields
after school; they did not get tutored after school, and many had difficulties in learning. When the Yenching college students provided the summer
school, it was a boon for peasant families. Lei and his wife enthusiastically supported it and helped set up equipment. They also became "voluntary propagandists for the school," and when the school needed it, the Leis
helped keep students in order. Shen felt that their methods in doing so were
"not very appropriate," but they certainly provided much-needed support.[17]

The Lei couple played a "decisive role" in Shen's investigation. As an
illiterate man, Lei Mingyuan "respected" educated people and probably because of this showed "extreme friendliness" to Shen and her classmates. He
liked to talk to these young people about guns and military knowledge. He
often carried and displayed his Browning pistol, carefully wiping it daily
with a piece of cloth. He was known to possess excellent marksmanship and
taught shooting to whichever students wanted to learn. He had owned this
pistol for nearly twenty years and claimed that he had used it to "kill countless lives."[18] Here, through Shen's portrayal, we see the complexity of Lei's
character—a man who killed his daughter and his rivals in cold blood, who

could also be very friendly toward the young students around him at another time in his life. Every afternoon Shen investigated by visiting all kinds of people, and in the evening she wrote in her working diary. She gradually discovered that the scope of the investigation should be limited to the Lei family, which thus helped her to keep the focus on the Paoge. She began to collect and sort her materials in this manner.[19]

But Shen experienced difficulties because of the secretiveness. Her inquiries faced "either support or obstruction by local forces," thus she made an effort to gather all kinds of information through daily chats, "intentionally or unintentionally asking questions," thereby gaining "totally honest answers" through her approach and the spontaneous reactions she elicited.[20] For example, she sometimes deliberately asked Woman Lei about traditional medicines or recipes while in the kitchen; these were opportunities to know about the family's life and "the inside stories of the Paoge society."[21] She did not explain to the Leis that she was collecting information for her thesis, only that she acted from "curiosity."[22] Shen often visited their house; her report states: "In many a long evening, when the sunshine made the rice fields a golden color, I sat in their living room as a guest." When Lei's daughter Shuying asked Shen to be her English tutor, Shen deepened the relationship and "established a friendship."[23] Shen was idealistically inspired by the world of rural people, which makes it easy to suppose that she believed her friendship with Woman Lei and Shuying was genuine.

Shen stayed in Hope for only a month and ten days, unlike many anthropologists who lived in a village for a long period. However, because it was not a long distance between Hope Township and Chengdu, she kept in close touch after the end of her fieldwork; some of the stories in her report actually happened after leaving Hope. Shen went back several times in August and September of 1945 as well as in January 1946. In the fall and winter of 1945, Woman Lei and Shuying visited the Chengdu campus of Yenching a few times, and Shuying even once watched the student performance of *Fragrant Grass at the Edges of the Sky* and stayed overnight at the school, returning home the next day.[24] After Shuying started her middle school, located on the same street as Yenching, Shen and the girl could meet each other almost every day.[25] This ongoing friendship helped Shen complete her materials. Many stories in her report, especially the Lei family struggles explored in Chapters 8 and 9, were going on while Shen was writing her thesis, told to her by Woman Lei and Shuying. On January 19, 1946, Shen brought a British woman and her classmate named Jinjuan (Bai Jinjuan as mentioned in Chapter 1) to Hope Township; they were treated with "warm hospitality" by "country friends."[26] When Shen returned to school, she brought Shuying with her, who Shuying stayed at school overnight and returned home the next afternoon. On January 26, Shuying again came

FIGURE 11.1 Farmers entering Chengdu from the North Gate. *Source*: Photograph by Sidney D. Gamble, ca. 1917–1919. Reproduced courtesy of Sidney D. Gamble Photographs, David M. Rubenstein Rare Book & Manuscript Library, Duke University.

to Chengdu to visit Shen and told her "many fresh materials." After that, almost every Sunday, Shuying would come to school, sometimes with her mother. After her middle school started up, Shuying moved into its buildings on Shaanxi Street, so Shen and Shuying could see each other every day, which made it even more convenient for Shen to collect information and complete her thesis (Figure 11.1).[27]

Although Shen did not disclose the name of Shuying's middle school, it would have been Huamei Girls' Middle School (Huamei nüzhong), a missionary school on Shaanxi Street. Years before, because of air raids, the school and a primary school next door were closed; students were evacuated to the countryside in 1939. The Chengdu campus of Yenching University then took the space of these two sites, and thus the physical campuses of Yenching and Huamei Girls' were conjoined. Despite no indication of the place Huamei evacuated to, based on other accounts it probably was Hope Township. With this in mind, we can logically deduce that Shuying attended Huamei.[28] After the war, the middle school moved back to Chengdu, so in 1946 Shen and Shuying lived for a time almost in the same place. In early summer of 1946, after her graduation, Shen (as well as Yenching University) left Chengdu to return to Beijing.[29]

★   ★   ★

Thinking about the work Shen performed, and all the legwork it entailed, as well as the odd places her work took her and her conscience, we might be a bit surprised (or not) that the report overall was somewhat superficial. There was little in-depth analysis using data-oriented social science methods or analytic templates, and there was little extensive discussion. After all, the investigation was done by an undergraduate student whose ideas about those theories and methods were still relatively immature. However, its merits are the data concerning everyday lives. To some extent, my aim has been to continue Shen's task concerning the Paoge. Although it has been many years since her work was completed, I am surprised to find that today our understanding of the Paoge still is slight. Although historical accounts provide a great deal of cases of Paoge activity and presence, no other source brings us so close to them and their organization—to their culture and their real, complicated motives and actions.[30] Shen Baoyuan's thesis perhaps was not as solid as a mature academic research would likely be, especially in China of a more modern bent, but this was because her lack of the ability to process the information, which in turn makes her more trustworthy.

CHAPTER 12

Untangling Paoge Myth

IN HIS BOOK *Primitive Rebels*, British historian E. J. Hobsbawm found that a certain type of person he called the "social bandit" emerged from rural areas rather than cities, and that locals usually did not help the authorities in their pursuit of these culprits but instead protected them. Only bandits who harassed peasants were usually sold out by local people.[1] In another work, *Bandits*, Hobsbawm states: "First, the noble robber begins his career of outlawry not by crime, but as the victim of injustice, or through being persecuted by the authorities for some act which they, but not the custom of his people, consider as criminal." These saints from the lower depths often righted wrongs and took "from the rich to give to the poor." They never killed "but in self-defence or just revenge." If they survived, he wrote, they returned to their people as "honourable citizen[s] and member[s] of the community."[2] Although Hobsbawm might have idealized "social bandits," he reminds us that in some sense the "bandits" then were different from today's criminals because some of the mythical greats among them longed for the establishment of a just world. He pointed out that social bandits were peasants, making the case for the need to understand peasant cultures.

Hobsbawm thought that noble bandits had a "programme." Such robbers wanted to defend or to restore "the traditional order of things" as "it should be." They wanted to "right wrongs" and to "correct and avenge cases of injustice." Therefore, these characters applied "a more general criterion of just and fair relations between men in general, and especially between the rich and the poor, the strong and the weak." They were not radical; they even allowed "the rich to exploit the poor" but "no more than is traditionally accepted as 'fair.'" These bandits could admit that "the strong oppress the weak" but "within the limits of what is equitable, and mindful of their social and moral duties." As a result, in this sense "social bandits are reformers, not revolutionaries."[3] To Hobsbawm, "reformist or revolutionary, banditry itself does not constitute a social movement," but they might "be a surrogate for it"; to him they might emerge in suppressed economies and areas of stagnancy and unemployment—that is, places with surplus laborers. He noticed that surplus labor often existed in nomadic economies and in mountainous and barren areas. People who were "not integrated into rural society" were "forced into marginality of outlawry."[4]

★   ★   ★

This book looks closely at the Paoge, and I have noticed similarities and differences in relation to Hobsbawm's ideas about social bandits. Comparing the Paoge in the Qing era with Hobsbawm's bandits, we see similarities: both are antiestablishment groups and warriors fighting the state machine. Whereas Hobsbawm's social bandits mostly came from rural areas, the Paoge in China were widely distributed throughout both urban and rural areas. There was even a clearer distinction between the two worlds of bandits: in the 1940s, China's rural Paoge made a significant mark by becoming part of local civil authorities. On the one hand, they were not legally recognized by the top-down government, but on the other hand, they played an important role in local administrations, especially in rural and market townships.

We are certainly dealing with bandits and with a secret society. Yet the Paoge were not necessarily Hobsbawmian, so what were they? Were the Paoge in the Chengdu Plain in the 1930s and 1940s laudable social bandits? Were they unreformed protorevolutionaries? And if so, as protor-evolutionaries where did they fit on the pro–Chinese Communist Party/pro–Guomindang spectrum? Or were they ad hoc political trouble makers in dozens of little towns? Later on, did they get their own Hobsbawm—that is, someone who could raise a flag of legitimacy for them? Could that person have been our Shen Baoyuan? Before 1949, essays and reports on the Paoge in local newspapers were relatively positive. However, the Paoge was crushed after 1949 (described in Chapter 10). The existing sources are so manipulated by more than three hundred years of image-shaping on the part of government officials and local elites—from the early Qing period through today—that it is hard to tell who supported the Paoge in principle, or who might have contributed to a legitimizing myth about them. Was 1949 the critical moment in China when noble robbers, like Zhuangzi's Robber Zhi, or *The Water Margin*'s Song Jiang (a bandit who hankered after justice) became, instead, subhuman enemies of the "people"? This chapter touches on these themes.

Despite a highly manipulated image of the Paoge, which turned sharply negative in 1949, we have a way to look through it all. The fall of the Paoge was definitely a result of attacks by the CCP state machinery; in a sense, it was the inevitable fate of an organization that up until 1949 was continually challenging power structures, while increasingly becoming the power structure itself at lower levels of local society. The Paoge tried to cooperate with the CCP, but the CCP never could allow into their tent such an organization, with the potential force to mount a challenge. The secret society was destroyed, leaving huge questions to be answered. We have our youthful, even if on occasion inconsistent, attempt by Shen Baoyuan to judge and perhaps scold the Paoge in the Chengdu Plain just before 1949. Through her we possess a true image of Paoge leader Lei Mingyuan, "true" in a special and mediated way but at least not a caricature. Shen's report has become an indispensable part of historical memory.

Shen's investigation tells us that before the arrival of the CCP, Lei had gone into his own personal decline, not only an economic and political decline but a physical one as well. She considered Lei's fading as the result of a "metabolic force" (*xinchen daixie liliang*) within the Paoge organization.[5] Although she did not give a specific description how this "metabolism" happened, a leader of the Paoge would rely on morality (loyalty), power (violence), and finance (earnings and spending) to support his leadership. All three of these aspects were complementary and each linked with another and could not be interrupted. When Lei's finances went wrong, someone inside the Paoge took this as a pending opportunity to make a mark for himself. When Lei canceled the traditional banquet during the Chinese New Year, for example, someone else in the Paoge took over the event. The lower-level Paoge brothers also noticed such changes. If they received better treatment regarding meals and money, their loyalty naturally would transfer elsewhere. As Shen predicted, "Probably in one or two years, Master Lei might disappear in this new environment. Lei's future will undoubtedly be pitiful."[6]

Of course, the Paoge's decline was a problem not only for Lei Mingyuan but also for the entire organization. Shen Baoyuan thought that the fundamental reason for it was that the Paoge abandoned its "task of anti-Qing and anti-corruption" and forgot its own "historical significance and value." This organization "grew from people"—that is, an organization with "reformist" and "revolutionary" characteristics; but they ultimately "betrayed the people's interests" and were in cahoots with the "corrupt bureaucracy." If such "corruption and deterioration" of the Paoge continued and the Paoge did not actively transform themselves, they "would not have a future." Shen continues by saying that the Paoge "do not have a positive goal and do not produce, but came together as a gang of vagrants, thieves, and robbers, who carry guns, smuggle opium, host gambling, and suppress people."

Especially, "heads of townships who hold two identities as Paoge leaders and as local officials can squeeze money out of people and lay unreasonable taxes on them." They also "bully and oppress women" and "make shameless deals." Such acts "will make the Paoge's lot in Hope Township encounter a severe blow," as they also contributed to the decline of the Paoge leaders' reputations.

Shen believed that her investigation revealed "the pitiful internal factors that caused the Paoge's decline." She predicted that "this decadent organization in the rural area will be drowned in the wave of a new era."[7] Obviously, she basically held a negative attitude toward the actions and values of Hope Township Paoge, as she witnessed them, but she favored an ideal sort of Paoge that could become fighters for revolutionary "progress." Shen's judgment on the Paoge was actually close to the CCP's characterization of them after 1949. At the time of Shen's writing, CCP cadres had made inroads in a number of local places in south, west, and northwest China, and CCP propaganda and agendas had had successes among faculty and students in the major universities. There had even been some successes in limited armed skirmishes with GMD forces. Despite all that, an inexperienced Beijing college youth could not have sensed that there would soon be an enormous regime change in store for the Chengdu Plain.

As a college student of sociology, and an academic, Shen seems to have wavered: going from apolitical records of her subjects' actions and motives to reactive judgments on the moral failure of her subjects—a fairly clear political judgment that aligned with the leftist approach at the time. She thought that the Paoge could still have a future if it undertook serious reforms, because she found that there existed some "enterprising and revolutionary Paoge organizations." She also thought that those were the "enlightened and progressive Paoge" (*kaiming jinbu Paoge*), who were "heading toward a bright future." She gave an example of an opinion from a journal called *Righteousness Weekly* (Dayi zhoukan) published in Chengdu. This periodical claimed to represent the "correct political views" (*yanlun zhengque*) of the Paoge. Through a series of political mechanisms it was not simply a naïve booster club for the Paoge but essentially a tool of the Communist Party. Its articles tried to "bring forward the Paoge's inherent virtues and spirit" and elaborated ideas concerning the "theoretical basis of the association." Shen appreciated the magazine, finding that it made "appeals for peace and democracy" and had "numerous incisive and unique points that were worth being set to practice by the general public." For Shen Baoyuan, these reformist Paoge were "commendable" because they were "not out of touch with the Chinese people."[8] In other words, Shen thought the direction of the Paoge, as framed by *Righteousness Weekly*, represented the future of the secret society. She saw only the surface and was unaware (as were others) of the secret agendas in the background. In short, it was a tool of the CCP to use the Paoge for their revolutionary ideology and activities.

★   ★   ★

Righteousness Weekly was founded by the China Democratic League (Zhong-guo minzhu tongmeng) chaired by Zhang Lan, but the CCP was behind the scenes.[9] Only many years later would these details be disclosed. In September 1944 the original Democracy Political League (Minzhu zhengtuan tongmeng) was reorganized into the China Democratic League. At that time, the CCP believed that any GMD-CCP cooperation was over but also that the CCP members in the league "should absolutely not be exposed." To facilitate "democratic activity" and the "United Front" in the eyes of intellectuals, the CCP needed "democrats" (*minzhu renshi*) to aid in propaganda work, especially to be involved in publications. Therefore, Du Chongshi, a CCP member with a Paoge identity, joined the league and began to prepare the publication.

Du met with Zhang Lan and shared the details of his mission: to organize the Paoge branch named Sichuan Moral Society (Shude she) to do "united front work" in the military and government in Sichuan and Xikang Provinces (the latter being established in 1939 by the GMD but dispensed with in 1950, as soon as the CCP took power; see Map 1). At this point the slogan "GMD-CCP cooperation to solve the national crisis" was "no longer applicable," so the new goals were "anti–civil war, demanding peace, anti-authoritarian, and struggling for democracy." The CCP intended to ask the Paoge to publish *Righteousness Weekly*, and Du hoped Zhang Lan would be a sponsor; all the other sponsors were Paoge masters who were military generals in Sichuan and Xikang. To get approval for this from the Nationalist government, they claimed that the aim of the journal was "to promote the Paoge's national consciousness and patriotism, and to inspire the Paoge to join the War of Resistance against the Japanese."[10]

Yet the magazine's founder ultimately played a role in the CCP's agenda, by supporting the so-called struggle for democracy. In July 1946 two prominent leaders of the China Democratic League, Li Gongpu and Wen Yiduo, were assassinated in Kunming.[11] In the memorial service held in Chengdu, Du wrote an elegiac couplet and condemned the Nationalist government, deduced by most people to be the agent of the killings: "To achieve the Three People's Principles, they were murdered; but we still pledge our life to struggle for democracy. Someone set up a conspiracy in order to further their Fascist regime, but we are determined to get rid of dictatorships." The military police immediately took away the couplet and then shut down Du's *Righteousness Weekly*. They arrested Du Chongshi under the accusation of his "being a hooligan Paoge and involved in opium and gambling." In winter of the same year, Du was released from prison.[12]

But there was more to it. According to an article in *The Joyful Grove* (Kuaihuo lin), a supplement of the *Daily News* (Xinwenbao, a GMD-controlled and Shanghai-based newspaper), Zhang Lan had also attended the memorial service. Zhang had studied in Japan and then served as governor of Sichuan, as president of Chengdu University, and as a member of the National Council (Guomin canyiyuan). Interestingly, he was also a "big brother" in the Paoge. Because of his seniority and leadership in the Paoge, Zhang became president of the China Democratic League. According to the article, there is this curious fact: "Unexpectedly, a famous Paoge big brother was beaten up at the recent memorial service for Wen Yiduo and Li Gongpu. How does that not destroy the Paoge's stance?"[13]

The writer seems to have disapproved of Zhang's participation in pro-CCP politics. He continues: "The Paoge has a very restrictive organization and they avoid engaging in politics but focus on society. However, this big brother, with a status of Paoge leader, has attempted to enter political circles. He has quit social undertakings and wants to play a role in the political arena. To serve national salvation, he should be doing grassroots work, so now having been beaten up: doesn't that let down the Paoge?"[14] Based on another account, during the memorial service, when Zhang Lan, representing the China Democratic League, conveyed condolences to the families of Li Gongpu and Wen Yiduo, secret GMD agents in the audience whistled and shouted, "Down with the CCP's running dog Democratic League!" as they beat on the tables and chairs, making such a large noise that the place erupted into chaos. Someone threw rubbish at Zhang. Du Chongshi's writing was subsequently removed by those same agents.[15]

Although the descriptions of the event vary, there is no doubt that Zhang Lan participated in the memorial service and that a conflict and a breakdown of order took place. Zhang's previous reputation as an activist in the Communist Party's "democratic movement," which targeted the GMD (calling it a one-party dictatorship), naturally brought him a wide appeal. But the partisan politics produced criticisms too. The essay in *The Joyful Grove* criticized Zhang's recent involvement in politics, yet Paoge involvement in politics was nothing new. What the article resented specifically was that unlike most other Paoge members, Zhang did not stand with the GMD Nationalist government; rather, he had turned into a leftist. After the CCP took power, Zhang Lan's contributions to the CCP were fully recognized. He served the new regime as vice chairman of the Central People's government. In the ceremony that established the takeover of the People's Republic of China, carried out in Tiananmen Square on October 1, 1949, the man with a long beard, standing by Mao Zedong, was Zhang Lan.

Du Chongshi was not as lucky as Zhang. He devoted his life to the Communist Revolution, but his experience after the CCP's victory became merely another of many tragedies. Du was a consultant, he ranked as a major general, and he was also a Paoge master. He supported the Red Army, participated in the Battle of Shanghai during the War of Resistance, went to Yan'an (the wartime headquarters of CCP), and studied at the Chinese People's Anti-Japanese Military and Political College (Kangda). He met Mao Zedong twice and was a "special member" of the CCP. In 1948 he joined the Revolutionary Committee of the Chinese Guomindang in Hong Kong and then he was elected as a member of the Central Executive Committee of the party. In December 1949 he arrived in Chengdu with the First Field Army under PLA leader He Long.[16] Du served as He's political representative and made contributions to the "liberation of the Southwest" by using his social relations in Sichuan and Xikang.

Because of Du's Paoge identity, however, he ultimately could not gain the trust of the CCP. Thus, in 1950 he was demoted from being a member of the Central Executive Committee to being just a regular member of the Party. Subsequently, Du decided to go outside of the inner political circle and to open a lumber business with friends in Shanghai. In 1956, during the socialist transformation, he was relocated to a state-run timber company, with a monthly salary of only 43 yuan, a difficult sum for supporting his family of six, so he became a public-school Chinese teacher. In 1957 he was categorized as a rightist and sent to labor camps because of his being judged a "historical counterrevolutionary." Du returned to Shanghai in 1976, and in 1980 his name was finally cleared.[17] History is baffling. As a leader of the Paoge, he used his associations to help in the establishment of the regime that ultimately turned around and entirely destroyed the Paoge. He had to pay the price of thirty horrible years because of his Paoge identity.

★　★　★

The point of the twisting background into the publication that interested Shen Baoyuan during the 1945–46 period (we know that she read *Righteousness Weekly*) is that what stood for boosterism was frequently manipulated editorials; what stood for news was frequently an assault on an activist for his or her politics. Such puzzles help us to understand some of the possible inputs into Shen's thinking about Lei Mingyuan and the Paoge in Hope Township—namely, her idea that the Paoge were not going in the reformist, "progressive," direction that *Righteousness Weekly* apparently favored. She most likely did not realize that the periodical was secretly led by a pro-Communist Paoge member. At the end of her report, Shen summarized Lei's life, and she regarded her investigation as "his brief biographical history, about his rise and fall"—one that was "closely linked with the Paoge's growth and decline." Lei was an important figure indeed: it was his brothers who "lifted him onto the stage of the Paoge." However, when he did not have money to splurge, no power to display, no capability to demonstrate, and no confidants to aid him, he was "abandoned to public contempt."[18] One might say that Shen was more emotionally reactive than politically astute.

We do not know Lei Mingyuan's fate under the new regime, nor if he lived until 1949, when the CCP arrived and took over Sichuan and the Chengdu Plain. Given that he had become devastated by opium, we might imagine that he did not live a long life. Shen's investigation did not touch on Lei's life and actions after February 1946, but as Chapter 8 demonstrated, his position as a deputy helmsman had for some time been difficult to maintain. The fact that he was growing weak may have been a blessing, because if he lived under the radar after 1949, his diminished status could have saved him from the mass persecutions of Paoge undertaken by the new socialist regime. Having been a deputy helmsman, and having killed a few people, would have made Lei a target of Communist attack. If we he had lived through 1950, his life might have had one of several possible endings: (1) as a Paoge leader, he might have been executed; (2) if he were punished but not executed, he might have suffered in the CCP's ground-shaking and sometimes violent political campaigns; or (3) because he had been broken and frustrated, the CCP might have merely considered him a poor peasant—that is, a member of a "class" with many advantages. As a tenant without land, Lei might even have been given a piece of land during the Land Revolution.

Shen's depiction of Lei Mingyuan's was not quite the portrait of evil that characterized the life of He Song of Jintang as described by local historians (explored in Chapters 2 and 6). Lei was a complex person: he fought bandits for the aim of preserving local security; for a long time he enjoyed prestige and respect as a Paoge leader, but he killed his daughter and was regarded as a cold-blooded and cruel father; he helped the students from Yenching University, just like an ordinary peasant would have done. Stubborn and conservative, Lei did not hesitate to threaten a relative who he felt had violated his version of a code of a woman's virtues. Once a heroic figure, he was an opium user morphing into a weak man; he was an uncompromising character, but he often made concessions when he faced his sometimes domineering wife. Lei was a tenant and increasingly became poor, yet he had two wives and even intended to get a third; he treated visitors generously, but sometimes his wife did not have any money to buy food. The point is to emphasize how difficult it is to determine, using a binary of good/bad, such a complex life.

★ ★ ★

Those who understand how local culture has always worked in China may not have realized that the Paoge as an organization, even after the post-1949 purges, was actually completely destroyed. In fact, we can see the organization's stubborn undergrowth in many places and in many ways. Their argot has survived in daily life, becoming a part of local popular culture in today's Sichuan. Many of these words have entered the everyday spoken language. For example, "fell from a horse" (*luoma*) once meant that a Paoge brother died; today, it refers to a government official dismissed as a result of corruption or other reasons. "Having a diarrhea attack" (*laxi*) meant that someone could not take responsibility; today, it points to a coward facing a confrontation. "Taking firewood off the stove" (*choudihuo*) meant revealing secrets; today, it means to undermine someone's interest. "Knowing the lesson" (*luojiao*) meant doing things by following rules; today, it means keeping promises to friends.

Some argot expressions are used today without any extension of the original meaning, such as "becoming a rolling dragon" (*dagunlong*), which is to lead a miserable life; "standing behind" (*zhaqi*), giving support in a conflict; "laying a soft egg" (*xiapadan*), being threatened upon facing a confrontation; "a stove keeper" (*guanhuo*), one who makes decisions; and "carrying the burden of fire" (*shenghuo*), to take responsibility. This phenomenon is not unique to China. Writing about the United States and Canada, linguist David Maurer has noted that "today many of the [argot] terms... are familiar in the dominant culture. This is due to the gradual diffusion of the criminal subcultures and their exploitation in fiction and motion pictures, which, incidentally, were very slow to use authentic language."[19]

In the post-Mao and Reform eras, once the government relaxed social control, secret societies and underground societies, sometimes called the "black society" (*heishehui*) by the authorities, revived throughout China. Of course, most organizations reemerged with a different look. In some places "black societies" have affected local economy and politics.[20] In 2007 the political star Bo Xilai, a member of the Politburo, was placed in charge of Chongqing, a mega city that had been separated from Sichuan Province in 1997 because of the construction of the Three Gorges Dam and put directly under the central government. In an effort to accumulate political capital, he launched a movement called "Singing Red Songs and Crushing Underworld (literally "Black") Forces" (*changhong dahei*). After Bo's fall in 2012, we learned that he had used the "crushing underworld forces" movement to strip wealth from the owners of large, private enterprises and solidify his own power base.[21] However, in Chongqing there were underworld forces that one had to navigate especially to compete for privileges and contracts.

Some private companies could use the power of this underworld, and if necessary, be helped by intimidation and violence. Some local governments have preserved the age-old political tradition of developing tangled relationships with these underground societies.

Bizarre stories have circulated: When a certain city's development project could not reach an agreement about compensation for condemned residences, for example, people's houses were destroyed at night by "unidentified" people. But this local government "also could not find who did it." There is an implication that underworld activities continue to have deep roots within local governments. It has been no secret that local governments have recently colluded with the underworld to punish certain "disobedient" people. Du Daozheng, director of the *Yanhuang Annals* (Yanhuang chunqiu)—China's only surviving liberal journal (forced to shut down in the summer of 2016)—wrote an article titled "Fundamental Revelation from the Zhou Yongkang Case" (Zhou was a former member of the highest-level Politburo Standing Committee). Du wrote: "The matter of Zhou Yongkang is not isolated; many people—a few dozen and even over a hundred—are linked together and have become a group. Now seven to eight of his people who were at the provincial and ministry level have been dismissed. The power of officialdom has joined together with the armed police, and in some places they have joined up with the underworld. The power that they have in their hands also joins with that of monopolistic groups. It is a huge interest group that cannot be disposed of."[22]

A good example is that of Liu Han, former board chairman of the Sichuan Hanlong Group (Hanlong jituan), the largest private enterprise in the entire province. The media hailed Liu as a hero after the great Wenchuan earthquake of 2008, when the school buildings that his company built and donated were the only such buildings that did not collapse. Ironically, Liu was accused later of conducting "Paoge-style" underworld activities, including murder, and was sentenced to death. The media called the entrepreneur and philanthropist a "true representative of the Paoge." It was noted that in the background of Liu Han's world were certain principles of the Paoge organization. Journalists implied that Liu's companies operated with such gangster notions as "mutual aid for the insider group but destruction to outsiders." They claimed that there were "striking similarities" with the Paoge and to expand his power, Liu Han had killed, wounded, detained, and committed other crimes, yielding a victims list of eight killed and many wounded. As a "big brother," Liu demanded total loyalty, and the company promoted violence in its interests by purchasing firearms, ammunition, and vehicles; it provided funds for the insiders to help them elude authorities, to repay loans and gambling debts, and to buy housing. He is said to have established a "responsible and thoughtful patriarchal image" for his own people.[23] This was a volatile combination of philanthropy, secret society culture, and political power. More important, it is a realistic depiction of the complex background of many Chinese businessmen and a true reflection of an underworld that has existed since the Qing dynasty.

In CCP officialdom, local headmen are secretly called "elder brother" (*laoda*), as senior brothers in secret societies were called in the past. Such a moniker is used sometimes in a humorous way, but it hints at internal networks inside the Party's operations and management, underscoring at least indirectly certain similarities, or even direct ties, with underworld organizations. Moreover, scholars have pointed out the close relationship between the Communist Revolution and secret societies. The CCP recognized the tradition of the organization in its enduring operations, which usually worked against older, established systems; the Party has understood that it can use this tradition for its own agendas. However, after the Communist regime was established, it was this very antiestablishment tendency that led to the destruction of the Paoge organization.[24]

★ ★ ★

In the view of Marxist historian E. J. Hobsbawm, "social bandits" and robbers were antigovernment forces looking for justice in an unjust society. He pointed out that they were "peasant outlaws," regarded by the lords and state as criminals but "considered by their people as heroes, as champions, avengers, fighters for justice, perhaps even leaders of liberation, and in any case as men to be admired, helped and supported." Therefore, such a "relation between the ordinary peasant and the rebel, outlaw and robber is what makes social banditry interesting and significant." Hobsbawm believed that when traditional "peasant society" no longer existed, "social bandits" also disappeared. For example, Europe used to be a Robin Hood's world, but such bandits were not seen after the seventeenth century.[25]

Recent scholars' investigations and oral histories in Sichuan, to a certain extent, show images similar to those Hobsbawm described. For instance, when people in Yuantong Township, Chongzhou, talked about the famous Paoge Huang brothers, they praised them as "good people." Every Chinese New Year "they [the Huang brothers] conducted charitable activities, such as giving away rice to the poor. They did not bully common people, although their followers sometimes took advantage of their power to suppress local folks." The Huang brothers ran a medicine shop and provided free medicine to the poor. Before the New Year they sometimes "exempted poor people's debts for medicines. They called on heads of *baojia* and asked them to donate rice for the poor.[26] A considerable number of Paoge members were more like the Liangshan heroes in the Chinese classic novel *Water*

Margin. Hobsbawm regarded bandits, mafia, mobs, and so on as "primitive rebels" who violently resisted the state. If Hobsbawm had studied the Paoge, almost certainly he would have placed them in this category, a sharp contrast to modern Chinese Marxist historiography, in which the Paoge were seen as the complete antithesis: simply as oppressors.

The ingrained myths about the Paoge started out with easily transformable, shifting stories about the honorable fighters against the Manchu Qing—rather in the vein of Hobsbawm's noble bandits. These secret societies of old seemingly possessed a sense of justice for the small Han folk of the villages against the non-Han empire, and they also possessed a "programme" for doing so. But unlike the mythic, noble cause of the marginalized, as imagined by Hobsbawm, the Sichuan secret societies turned into mundane local powerbrokers after the fall of the Qing. Thus we have a kind of a myth and myth-making (the Qing authorities treated and persecuted these marginals as insurgents, which converts easily to "noble"), but that would transform into a myth of mundane powerbrokering, which one might argue is not material for a myth: there's no punch there. Has China pushed forward anyone to herald and judge any part of that transformative and evolving Paoge myth, in whatever form it took? Was there ever a legitimizer of the Paoge men and their stories? We saw a bit of this in scenes from fiction. But also, the role of Shen Baoyuan must be pondered, even though her report and insights had no impact on other scholars or on society in general.

Shen was a young academic and a naïve analyst of the nuts-and-bolts, crude life in the villages. She wavered between theory and her own pro-leftist opinions, some of which were moralizing and reactionary in their own way. Whatever intellectual constructions and theories were created by her teachers, they were not as important as the sociologists and anthropologists' promotion of their social agenda (bringing "progress" to the "people" and distributing benefits to them). This required sending students into the field. Once the fieldwork began, there was no way an inexperienced student of sociology could easily square abstract theories (such as structural functionalism) with what went on in real, everyday rural Sichuan. Shen was confronted with "face" and ritual, male hierarchical bonding, criminal societies, and misogynist violence. These realities could not be treated as merely the results of poverty and civil wars, and they were not easily fixed with social programs, professional empathy, and monetary and direct aid. Shen, having been influenced by both leftist and Communists at her school, ironically ended up proposing an ideal agenda that she heard about that called for a new, progressivist Paoge. At the same time, she offered no particularly decisive judgment about Lei Mingyuan as a violent, misogynist killer. In the end, academic quasi-theory and leftist ideals trumped common everyday criminal justice and common sense.

Shen cannot be considered a legitimizer of this massive Sichuan secret society of drug smugglers and drug users, murderers, and manipulators of local governments and national parties. But in her own tender and sometimes complicated way, she navigated political currents (probably unconsciously) and came up with a partly academic and partly emotional legitimation of the Paoge as innately containing an ideal of real progressive, pro-commoner motives, but on the verge of losing that ideal. It was a muted legitimization, which fed into a post-1949 tragedy for the brothers.

As to the survival of Paoge culture, one might say that things have come out a bit better than Hobsbawm's social bandits. The Paoge had no clear-cut Hobsbawmian myth of the noble bandit, but they did not necessarily lose out over time, nor even for that reason. It may be that the Hobsbawmian myth—which holds that noble bandits no longer remained noble in modern times—translates differently when we revert to the China case. That is, the turning point in Paoge history was their gaining control of local administrations. It helped their culture (their argot, their insider-gangster model, an so on) to survive. The Hobsbawmian bandit vanished, but the Chinese Paoge, having set down roots in local control (and then roots in corporate culture), may turn out to last much longer.

Appendix 1:
Paoge Ranks

Brothers (ge)	Masters (ye)	Rows (pai)	Other Names
First Brother (*dage*)	First Master (*daye*)	First Row (*yipai*)	Helmsman (*duobazi*) Dragon Head (*longtou daye*) Head of Society (*shezhang*)
Second Brother (*erge*)	Second Master (*erye*)	Second Row (*erpai*)	Vice Helmsman (*fu duobazi*) Sage Second Master (*shengxian erye*)
Third Brother (*sange*)	Third Master (*sanye*)	Third Row (*sanpai*)	Powerful Third Master (*dangjia sanye*)
Fifth Brother (*wuge*)	Fifth Master (*wuye*)	Fifth Row (*wupai*)	Manager Fifth Master (*guanshi wuye*). Two positions: Manager Internal Affairs (*nei guanshi*) or Black Flag Manager (*heiqi guanshi*); Manager External Affairs (*wai guanshi*) or Red Flag Manager (*hongqi guanshi*)
Sixth Brother (*liuge*)	Sixth Master (*liuye*)	Sixth Row (*liupai*)	Old Six (*laoliu*)
Eighth Brother (*bage*)	Eighth Master (*baye*)	Eighth Row (*bapai*)	Old Eight (*laoba*)
Ninth Brother (*jiuge*)	Ninth Master (*jiuye*)	Ninth Row (*jiupai*)	Old Nine (*laojiu*)
Tenth Brother (*shige*)	Tenth Master (*shiye*)	Tenth Row (*shipai*)	Youngest (*laoyao*)

Appendix 2:
Lei Family Tree (1945)

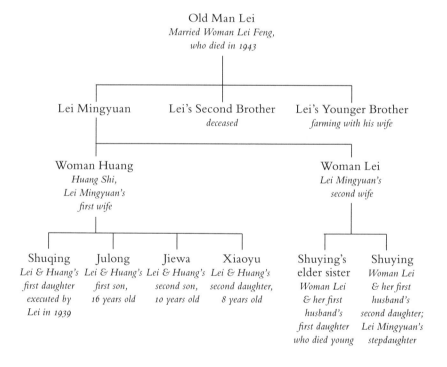

Old Man Lei
Married Woman Lei Feng,
who died in 1943

Lei Mingyuan

Lei's Second Brother
deceased

Lei's Younger Brother
farming with his wife

Woman Huang
Huang Shi,
Lei Mingyuan's
first wife

Woman Lei
Lei Mingyuan's
second wife

Shuqing
Lei & Huang's
first daughter
executed by
Lei in 1939

Julong
Lei & Huang's
first son,
16 years old

Jiewa
Lei & Huang's
second son,
10 years old

Xiaoyu
Lei & Huang's
second daughter,
8 years old

Shuying's
elder sister
Woman Lei
& her first
husband's
first daughter
who died young

Shuying
Woman Lei
& her first
husband's
second daughter;
Lei Mingyuan's
stepdaughter

Appendix 3:
Selected Ritual/Festival Events

Lunar Month/Day	Name of Festival Events	Activities
I/1	New Year ceremonies	Rites to gods, ancestors; verbal good-luck greetings
I/9	Guanyin Festival (Guanyin hui)	Celebration; attendance at Guanyin Temple for worship
I/9–16	Lantern Festival (Shangyuan hui)	Various operas performed on streets; lanterns hung; lion and dragon dance performances
II/3	Festival of God of Literature (Wenchang hui)	Literati banquets and gatherings; essay and poetry writing
III/(date is changeable)	Pure Brightness Day (Qingming hui)	Visits to graveyards for sweeping and rites to ancestors
IV/8	Washing Buddhas (Yufo hui)	Release of fish, turtles, and birds
V/5	Dragon Boat Race Festival (Duanwu jie)	Making of rice balls, placing herbs on doorways, and drinking realgar wine (*xionghuang jiu*); also, dragon-boat races
V/13	Guandi Festival (Guandi hui)	Local operas performed
V/28	City God Festival (Chenghuang chujia)	Statue of City God paraded on street; local operas performed
VI/6	Drying Cloth Festival (Shaiyi hui)	Clothes and books put out under sunshine to prevent spoilage

Lunar Month/Day	*Name of Festival Events*	*Activities*
VII/7	Patron Deity Festival (Tudi hui) Double-seven Day (Qiqiao jie or Qixi jie)	Ceremony for the god; also people offered wine and fruit to the astral goddess Weaving Maid (Zhinü)
VII/15	Ghost Festival (Zhongyuan jie)	Celebration of ancestors
VIII/15	Moon Festival (Zhongqiu jie)	Family reunions; observing full moon
IX/9	Double-Nine Festival (Chongyang jie) Ascending Heights Festival (Denggao hui)	Drinking of Double-Nine Festival wine (*Chongyang jiu*), climbing high places
X/1	Ox King Festival (Niuwang hui)	Cooking of rice balls; tying them on horns of ox to celebrate the animal's work
XII/8	Rice Porridge Festival (Laba jie)	Eating of rice porridge
XII/23–31	Nian Festival (Nian jie)	Cleaning one's house, renew peach-wood charms against evil (*yitaofu*), and stay awake to "keep" New Year's eve (*shousui*)

Appendix 4:
Chinese Texts of Sayings and Poems

The first number indicates the chapter and the second number, the footnote where the English translations appear. For example, if the numbers are 3-8, they mean that English translation is on Note 8 in Chapter 3.

3-8:
聖賢聖賢
結義桃園
忠肝義膽
萬古流傳
聖賢聖賢
荊州保全
徐州失散
古城團圓

3-11:
金木水火土五行
法力如來五行真
位台能知天文事
可算湖海一高明

4-11:
三仙原來明望家
英雄到處好逍遙
昔日桃園三結義
烏牛白馬祭天地

4-18:
天開黃道日
龍門大吉昌

英雄齊聚會
稟開忠義堂

4-19:
黃道大開大吉昌
英雄齊集忠義堂
自古當仁原不讓
各歸方位序排行

4-20:
天下袍哥本一家
漢留意義總堪夸
結義異姓同胞日
儼以春風棠棣花

4-21:
忠義堂前喜洋洋
福新大爺擺鳳凰
擺鳳凰來擺鳳凰
要效桃園劉關張
咱們弟兄來結拜
擺龍擺鳳降吉祥
忠義堂，喜洋洋
我弟上前擺鳳凰
一張桌子四角方
我將鳳凰擺中央

4-26:
兄弟來的魯莽
望哥哥高抬一膀
久聞哥哥有仁有義
有志有仁
在此招旗掛帥
著集天下英雄
栽下桃李樹
結下萬年紅
將來與你哥隨班護駕
初在貴地寶碼頭
理當先用草字單片
到你哥龍虎寶帳請安

不知哥哥到此來
未曾收拾早安排
未早接駕休見怪
哥哥仁義賽桃園

4-27:
不知你哥哥水路來，旱路來
兄弟水路也來，旱路也來
旱路有多少山，水路有多少灘
霧氣騰騰不見山，大水茫茫不見灘
有何為証
有憑為証

5-6:
此雞生來賽鳳凰
生穿五色錦衣裳
文官聽得金雞叫
手指朝笏入朝堂
武將聽得金雞叫
整頓人馬到校場
我們聽得金雞叫
整頓衣冠到香堂

雞呀雞
非是我今來殺你，
弟兄們借你賀財喜
喜喜你
賀喜你
脫了衣裳穿布衣

5-10:
木楊城裡是乾坤
結義全憑一點洪
今日義兄來考問
莫把洪英當外人

5-11:
雙龍戲水喜洋洋
好比韓信訪張良
今日兄弟來相會
暫把此茶作商量

5-12:
單刀獨馬走天涯
受盡塵埃到此來
變化金龍逢太吉
保主登基坐禪台

5-17:
七星寶劍擺當中
鐵面無情逞英雄
傳斬英雄千千萬
不妨洪家半毫分

5-18:
我亦不就干
我亦不就滿
我本心中漢
持起飲杯盞

5-19:
反鬥窮原蓋舊時
清人強佔我京畿
複回天下尊師順
明月中興起義人

5-20:
江山開基本是洪
五湖四海共一宗
殺絕滿洲西韃子
洪家兄弟保真龍

5-21:
一朵蓮花在盆中
端記蓮花洗牙唇
一口吞下大清國
吐出青煙萬丈虹

5-22:
單手使金槍
手執是雙銅
打破你城池
救出我真主

5-23:
四方疆土盡歸明
惟有中央未滅清
未必忠良分疆土
兄弟齊心盡反清

10-15:
空空空
四川糧食要集中
餓死貧窮漢
氣死富人翁

Appendix 5:
Brief Comments on Texts, Myth, and History

In the past, when scholars studied secret societies, we had only a few types of source material—archives, personal memories, local history writing, newspapers, and social surveys. With the recent trends to broaden our fields of study, tapping into the methods of what is called the new cultural history, for example, literature too becomes integrated with other sources. Files from the many newly tapped archives provide a basic form of information, regarded as reliable to historical research. However, historians increasingly recognize the limitations of archives because of the inherent distortions in them, as discussed by Natalie Zemon Davis in her famous book *Fiction in the Archives: Pardon Tales and Their Tellers in Sixteenth-century France*. Moreover, in *Soulstealers: The Chinese Sorcery Scare of 1768*, Philip Kuhn has pointed out that many of the confessions found in China's state archives were the result of torture, so these must be considered unreliable.[1] Therefore, when we use archival materials, we treat them as both veritable records and records requiring interpretation. We must understand the background history of the historical accounts; we must ask how an archive was made and preserved. And when we use it for its texts of events, people, and policy outcomes, we ought to discern hidden meanings and indications that lead elsewhere.

Archival materials on the Paoge are quite limited (such archives, for example, the case of Huang Chunian of Weiyuan County, are discussed in Chapter 3). Most extant files were collected by local officials at all levels and the data provided by informants who identified themselves, sometimes several persons using an anonymizing cover, as "gentry and people" (*shenmin*), and they usually were brief—without much detail. Because of the need for covering up and anonymity, the information collected might be thought of as unreliable, even though it was placed in archives. As discussed previously, from the Qing dynasty to the Republic, governments had always been hostile toward secret societies, and they gathered their intelligence for the purpose of control. Secret reports from these local "gentry and people" had several motivations: First, according to government decree, locals had to report what they knew, otherwise they would be punished. Second, they might have been experiencing harassment by the Paoge and wanted protection from the authorities. Third, such persons might have been contenders for local power and were using government to gain an advantage over their competition. However, from these archival records, we know how and what information the government held about the Paoge.

With these flags in place concerning archival reports, let us touch briefly on how research on the Paoge can broaden. Throughout the book we encountered various kinds of narratives written about the Paoge in the form of journalism, academic projects, or as part of local historiography. Naturally, these forms of prose were made at different times, for different purposes, and from different political backgrounds. Some were done by contemporaries of writers (for example, newspaper accounts in the 1940s). Some were produced by officials, and others by intellectuals, including academic sociologists. Many of these accounts were written after 1949, thus having a bit of distance from the time period in which the accounts themselves were set. We also encountered writing that reflected an official point of view. Although government did take some measures to limit Paoge activities, it had little success. Before the Communists took over Sichuan in late 1949, local governments had failed to stop the expansion of the Paoge and their avenues of control. Although governments in Republican times issued many bans on the Paoge, we cannot find any real or effective movement against them. Overall, I need to emphasize that such accounts, as used in this book, cannot be seen simply as true history; they are merely different perspectives for us to gather up and to use for focusing on the Paoge in a new way.

On occasion, the Paoge were enemies of bandits and played an active role in local security. But in the official records, from the Qing to the Republic to the Chinese Communist Party, the Paoge were often connected with bandits. Especially in the Qing period, Paoge branches, often referred to as the Gelaohui, were considered to be "bandit gangs" (*huifei*), and Chinese Marxist historiography basically inherited this manner of characterization, partly for the reason that some brothers did have connections with unaffiliated bandits, but the overall negative image was also based on official discourse—the party line.[2]

The CCP government remade the Paoge's image after 1949, and in their official, didactic discourse that laid out a political world of enemies, loyalists, and temporarily useful friends, the Paoge were pegged as evil villains. Yet, just before 1949, Shen Baoyuan established separate friendships within the Lei family, and she also wrote descriptions of members of a Paoge family that were unguarded and politically naïve: they showed the family going through stressful and unfortunate times. Even the Paoge master himself appears without any charisma, power, or hierarchical hold on anyone. The implication is that only a couple of years before the Communists succeeded in claiming power and reshaping political life, there was plenty of room in the minds of academics, and probably in the minds of local Sichuanese as well, to view the Paoge as merely common, everyday people, or as social bosses who did good things. The bottom line is that there is room to doubt how solid of a grip the early socialist political discourse and propaganda had on people—and room to doubt the veracity of archival material and local historiography, which were to a certain extent created to nourish that very discourse.

Moreover, we have literary works, mostly novels, that before roughly 1970 were hardly used by historical researchers on China in addressing their subjects or developing a view of society. But now literature is being meaningfully interpreted for these purposes. As French philosopher and historian Michel de Certeau once pointed out: "And whereas historiography recounts in the past tense the strategies of instituted powers, these 'fabulous' stories offer their audience a repertory of tactics for future use."[3] Li Jieren wrote historical novels, including *Citizens' Self-Protection* (Shimin de ziwei), *Ripples in Stagnant Water* (Sishui weilan), *Before the Storm* (Baofengyu qian), and *Great Waves* (Dabo) (Chapter 7 looked at Li's setting of a love relationship that involved a Paoge leader). His novels were criticized for being more like "records of chronological events."[4] Their settings were the townships and market towns around Chengdu, which had almost the same natural and social conditions as Chongyiqiao (Shen's "Hope Township").

Turning to the novelist Sha Ting, his stories too often came from real life in rural Sichuan (as explored in Chapter 5); they seem like documentary reports based on his observations and experiences in rural Sichuan. For example, *In Fragrant Chamber Teahouse* describes teahouse-goers, teahouse talk and culture, and social practices that were based on real historical contexts. He mentions a director of joint security, conscripted soldiers (*zhuangding*), the county draft office, drinking negotiation tea, calling for tea money, heads of local militia, the Paoge, and so on. When Sha Ting later recalled the process of writing the novel, he described it as basically drawn from actual events. "The fictional description is only minor," he said, "and placed at the end of the novel for bringing out the theme." The scene of drinking negotiation tea was one that was "often found in teahouses in rural market towns." The teahouse in the story "synthesized various situations of such teahouses.... As long as I closed my eyes, the atmosphere would appear in my mind."[5] That means that the characters and scenes Sha Ting described were as real as any report in an archive; they offer us scenes of action, confrontation, reaction, and even inner conflicts and values, like a background scene of everyday life and people that we ponder in Early Master paintings.

People's personal experiences make up precious material in the form of oral and memoirist history. The Paoge master Cai Xinghua's memoir had considerable information, but we must be aware of the problems. First, a former Paoge member might not be willing to tell all; thus what we know about him might not be complete, but only what he wanted people to know. In addition, since the CCP took power, the state and its master myth of revolution have been strikingly dominant. When the elderly recall history, they inevitably fall into political line, and consequently class and ideological struggles, the state and the self pitted against various enemies, and revolution versus counterrevolution often take over a person's conception of events. We cannot rely unquestioningly on such memories when constructing our histories; we need other materials and other evidence to construct what we sense as the veritable event.

We should be especially careful when using certain kinds of official history and locally sponsored or encouraged historiography. Although often filled with detail and vivid emotion, the real value of the material may be bent out of shape because of the political orientation. Consider the narrative about He Song discussed in Chapters 2 and 6. It employed emotional adjectives and phrases such as "arbitrary dictator," "cruel and cunning," "harming the revolution," "monstrous crimes," "too numerous evil-doings to be listed," and so on—a typical lexicon of local history writing after 1949, representing the official evaluation of persons who were deemed "negative" influences on socialist history. Such local historians found it difficult to avoid politics, and other factors—the local government, history, culture, and habits—also affected their projects. Furthermore, the format and style expected of local history gave authors only limited space. In the end, however, the long-term efforts of these history sleuths and political admonishers in fact rescued many forgotten figures and events that would surely have otherwise disappeared from memory. The story of the grain-levy team (see Chapter 10) is an example of gaining rare details about local people's confrontation with taxation policy and the causes of violent resistance.

★   ★   ★

This book is a study devoted to the lower classes and to marginalized people. In that regard, we have to find where their voices are heard, hardly apparent in much of the historical material, and whatever information is lodged in people's remembrance, the accounts themselves were often shaped by elites, who were framing the historiography or gathering the information for policy purposes. Above, I touched on the manipulated nature of facts, accounts, and data gathered by officials and testimonies taken from people held by officials. Italian historian Carlo Ginzburg has noted that "the thoughts, the beliefs, and the aspirations of the peasants and artisans of the past reach us (if and when they do) almost always through distorting viewpoints and intermediaries." This has led some historians to raise the question, "Can the subaltern speak?"[6] In the 1950s, British Marxist E. J. Hobsbawm studied "primitive rebels" (touched on in Chapter 12), and in doing so regarded their letters, conversations, oaths, and so on as their own voices, and there one could reconstruct marginalized people's history by using their own language."[7] For that matter, Shen Baoyuan's investigation was also an effort to find the voices of a specific social group. From the Lei family's affairs and goings-on, she described not just events but also people's pleasures, angers, and sorrows.

This book used the voice of secret society members, especially the Paoge foundational text, *The Bottom of the Ocean* (Haidi); it was the canon of the Gowned Brothers, employing a somewhat closed language (argot and signs). *The Bottom of the Ocean* acted as a history of the Gowned Brothers and a true expression of their own voices, thus, to a certain extent understandable as a "hidden transcript"—a term used by anthropologist James Scott to refer to a text showing a kind of "subordinate group politics," or in historian Ranajit Guha's terms, "the small voice of history." Taking the model of the history of the subaltern and by interpreting a "hidden transcript" and the "small voice," we get to "the public discourse of subordinate groups."[8] The secret language and the canon of the Paoge, which reflected the wider politics and society, resulted from a subculture that dates back to the Qing dynasty.[9] We saw in Chapters 4 and 5 how a special canon and special language can directly reflect the members' activities and helps us understand their thought, behavior, organization, regulations, membership, internal and external relationships, and subculture.

The Bottom of the Ocean contains sources of fact and myth about the Paoge's early history: it was an organization that participated in the anti-Manchu movement. Through the compilation of their canon, the Paoge could highlight their real or imagined roots in a lineage of anti-Manchu movements and identify themselves as proud members of an insurgency. From local officials and description of official documents in the Qing, we can see that the Paoge had a completely different view of the origins of their history. We should recognize that the different versions held different purposes. The officials defined the Paoge as riffraff and robbers because of their prejudice as well as their political purpose—attacking the organization. But the Paoge's own description of their history was a part of their image-building as well as the recognition of an identity. This identity was an important foundation for the expansion of their organization and cohesion. We are unable to confirm the credibility of descriptions by the government and by the Paoge, but there is no doubt that both had some historical basis, although both had artificially constructed the Paoge's history.

The Bottom of the Ocean provides not just a skeletal history of the Paoge, and the way hand gestures and teacup formations could signal anti-Manchu sentiment in an earlier time, but also how the organization interrelated with local Sichuan culture and social networks. The argot gave expression to an emergent antigovernment counterculture in these locales, which influenced, and was influenced by, popular sentiment and legends. Using the text and its encoded gestures, strangers from outside a Paoge lodge's locale could perform their connection, as it were, to the larger community of brothers. Moreover, by moving teacups, reciting poems, and participating in call-and-response dialogues, members from all walks of life could engage in political and in-group ritual activities and legitimize illegal actions. In their own language, the Paoge became righteous warriors who were trying to overthrow Manchu rule. In the government's words, they were a criminal gang of rebels and ruffians—an organization to be marginalized and suppressed or exterminated. The general populace, however, had more complex feelings about the Paoge, depending on the individual experiences, and the words of ordinary outsiders reflect these mixed sentiments.

Character List

anweiling 安位令
bage 八哥
bai chawan zhen 擺茶碗陣
Bai Jinjuan 白錦娟
bai matou 拜碼頭
bai matou shu 拜碼頭書
baidiba 擺地壩
bangke 棒客
bao 保
Baofengyu qian 暴風雨前
baojian zhen 寶劍陣
baoju 保舉
baotongzi 抱童子
baozheng 保正
bapai 八排
bata maole 把他毛了
Baxian tuanshou paituan tiaoli 巴縣團首牌團條例
baye 八爺
Beibei 北碚
Beiping shehui diaochasuo 北平社會調查所
Biancha baojia tiaogui 編查保甲條規
Bo Xilai 薄熙來
Cai Xinghua 蔡興華
caile 裁了
caisheng 裁牲
caozi danpian 草字單片
chaguan jiangli 茶館講理
chahu shi 茶壺式
changhong dahei 唱紅打黑
changyue 場約

Chaozhou 潮州
chayang jiu 插秧酒
Chen Hansheng 陳翰笙
Chen Jinnan 陳近南
Chengdu jianghu haidi 成都江湖海底
Chengdu jianghu haidi quanji 成都江湖海底全集
Chengdu jiexiang zhi 成都街巷志
Chengdu minzhu qingnian xiehui 成都民主青年協會
Chengdu tonglan 成都通覽
Chengdu wenhua jie dui shiju de huyu 成都文化界對時局的呼吁
Chengdu wenming shuju 成都文明書局
Chengdu zhi jianghu yanci 成都之江湖言詞
Chengdu zhi Paoge hua 成都之袍哥話
Chenggu suanmingfa 稱骨算命法
chenghuang 城隍
chenghuang chujia 城隍出駕
chijiangcha 吃講茶
chong 崇
Chongqing 重慶
Chongyang jie 重陽節
Chongyang jiu 重陽酒
Chongyi dadui 崇義大隊
Chongyi xiang renmin gongshe 崇義鄉人民公社
Chongyiqiao 崇義橋
Chongyiqiao pu 崇義橋鋪
Chongzhou 崇州

choudihuo 抽底火

chuan da che ri 川大車日

Chuanjun 川軍

chuanliao 傳了

chuantie 传帖

chundian 春點

Chunmei 春梅

cunzhi 村治

Cunzhi yanjiu yuan 村治研究院

da dianhu 大佃戶

da qingjiao 打清醮

Dabo 大波

dachuantang 大傳堂

Dafeng xiang renmin gongshe 大豐鄉人民公社

dage 大哥

dagunlong 打滾龍

Dahoufang 大後方

daizhao 待詔

dajie maxiang 打街罵巷

dan 担

dan 石

danbian zhen 單鞭陣

dandao hui 單刀會

dangjia sanye 當家三爺

daoke 刀客

Daxia daxue 大夏大學

Dayaoshan 大瑤山

daye 大爺

Dayi zhoukan 大義周刊

Dazu 大足

Deng Xihou 鄧錫候

Denggao hui 登高會

deye xiangquan 德業相勸

Dianshang 店上

difang wenshi ziliao 地方文史資料

Dingxian shehui gaikuang diaocha 定縣社會概況調查

Dingzhou 定州

dingzi Paoge 腚子袍哥

Dongsansheng zhi yimin yu fanzui 東三省之移民與犯罪

Du Chongshi 杜重石

Du Daozheng 杜導正

Duanwu jie 端午節

Dujun 督軍

duobazi 舵把子

enxiong 恩兄

erge 二哥

erpai 二排

erye 二爺

fan Qing fu Ming 反清复明

Fangcao tianya 芳草天涯

fangqu shiqi 防區時期

fangqu zhi 防區制

Fei Xiaotong 費孝通

feimuji 肥母雞

feishou 匪首

fencheng zhi 分成制

Fenghuangcun 鳳凰村

fengjian fandong shili 封建反動勢力

fengjian huimen 封建會門

fengjian naojin 封建腦筋

Fengyi gongshe 鳳儀公社

fu duobazi 副舵把子

fude buxiu 婦德不修

Gantian dongdi Dou E yuan 感天動地竇娥冤

Gao quan Chuan minzhong shu 告全川民眾書

Gaojiaxiang cun 高家巷村

ge 哥

Gelaohui 哥老會

gongkou 公口

gongneng 功能

gongneng fangfa 功能方法

Gu Jiegang 顧頡剛

guaheipai 掛黑牌

Guan Hanqing 關漢卿

Guan Yu 關羽

guanchang Paoge 官場袍哥

Guandi 關帝

Guandi hui 關帝會

guanggun 光棍

Guanghan xian 广汉县

guanhuo 關火

guanshi wuye 管事五爺

guanshi 管事

guanxi xushu 關係敘述

Guanxian 灌縣

Guanyin 觀音

Guanyin hui 觀音會

guanzhengmen 官政門

guixian 規限

gun dingban 滾釘板

Guo Yongtai 郭永泰

guofei 咽匪

Guolu 咽嚕

Guomin canyiyuan 國民參議員

guoshi xianggui 過失相規

Haidi 海底

hailiao 海了

Haiyan jutuan 海燕劇團

han chaqian 喊茶錢

hangjia tai sanfen, kongzi ya sanfen 行家抬三分, 空子壓三分

hanliu 漢留

Hanliu ling 漢留令

Hanliu quanshi 漢留全史

Hanlong jituan 漢龍集團

hanshu guanxi 函數關係

He Long 賀龍

He Song 賀松

He Zaizhi 何載之

Hedeng chang 禾登場

heihua 黑話

heiqi wuye 黑旗五爺

heishehui 黑社會

heping jiefang 和平解放

heping qiyi 和平起義

heiqi guanshi 黑旗管事

hongbang 紅幫

hongfei heipian 紅飛黑片

Hongmen 洪門

hongqi daguansu, 紅旗大管束

hongqi guanshi 紅旗管事

hongqi wuye 紅旗五爺

Hu Zongnan 胡宗南

Huamei nüzhong 華美女中

Huang Shi 黃氏

huanguo 換过

huannan xiangxu 患難相恤

Huaxi daxue 華西大學

Huayang yizhen jiuzai zonghui 華洋義賑會救災總會

Huguang tian Sichuan 湖廣填四川

huidang 會黨

huifei 會匪

Huixian 輝縣

huiyide 會意的

Hujiang daxue 滬江大學

Hunan fangshou pian 湖南防守篇

hunshui 渾水

hunshui paoge 渾水袍哥

jia 甲

jianghu 江湖

Jianghu qieyao 江湖切要

Jianghuhui 江湖會

Jiangjin 江津

jianye 贱业

jiaofei 剿匪

jie 截

jie 節

jie gaizi 揭盖子

jie Guanyin 接觀音

jie lingguan 接靈官

jiegou gongneng 結構功能

jieke 接客

Jiewa 潔娃

jigongche 雞公車

jinbu renshi 進步人士

jinbu xuesheng 進步學生

Jingzhongshan 精忠山

Jinling daxue 金陵大學

Jinling nüzi daxue 金陵女子大學

Jintaishan 金台山

Jintaishan shilu 金台山實錄

Jintang 金堂

Jintang xian qingnian dang 金堂縣青年黨

jisuan fangfa 計算方法

jiuge 九哥

Jiuhe gongshe 九合公社

Jiuliqiao 九里橋

jiupai 九排

jiuye 九爺

Julong 具龍

junheng zhuangtai 均衡狀態

kai longmen 開龍門

kaiguang 開光

kaiming jinbu Paoge 開明進步袍哥

kaishan 開山

kaitang 開堂

Kaixian 開縣

Kaixiangong cun 開弦弓村
kancaixi 看財喜
Kangda 抗大
kongzi 空子
kuagan rou 垮杆肉
Kuaihuo lin 快活林
Kunlun 昆仑
Laba jie 臘八節
lafeizhu 拉肥豬
Laijiayuan 賴家院
laoba 老八
laoda 老大
laojiu 老九
laoliu 老六
laoyao 老么
laxi 拉稀
Lei Daniang 雷大娘
Lei Daye 雷大爷
Lei Mingyuan 雷明遠
Leshan 乐山
Li 禮
Li Anzhai 李安宅
Li Gongpu 李公朴
Li Jinghan 李景漢
Lianbao banshichu 聯保辦事處
lianbao zhuren 聯保主任
Liang Shuming 梁漱溟
liangdi 亮底
liangfu 粮賦
Liangshan 涼山
Liao Taichu 廖泰初
lie 烈
lienü 烈女
Lin Yaohua 林耀華
Linjiangsi 臨江寺
linli xiangdang 鄰里鄉黨
lisu xiangjiao 禮俗相交
liu 劉
liu 流
liu 留
Liu Bei 刘备
Liu Han 劉漢
Liu Shiliang 劉師亮
Liu Wenhui 劉文輝
Liu Xiang 劉湘
liuge 六哥
liupai 六排

liuye 六爺
Longqiao 龍橋
Longquanyi 龍泉驛
longtou 龍頭
longtou daye 龍頭大爺
Lu Yongji 陸永箕
Lu Zuofu 盧作孚
luojiao 落教
luoma 落馬
man 滿
Maoding 帽頂
matou 碼頭
Mianzhu xian 綿竹縣
Mile 彌勒
mimi huishe 秘密會社
Mingyuan tang 明遠堂
minzhengzhi 民政志
minzhi 民職
minzhu renshi 民主人士
Minzhu zhengtuan tongmeng 民主政
    團同盟
mixin 迷信
mozhuang 摸莊
Muyang cheng 木楊城
muyang zhen 木楊陣
Nanhua gong 南華宮
Nanji gongshe 南集公社
nei guanshi 內管事
Neijiang 內江
neipanhua 內盤話
Nian jie 年節
Niuwang hui 牛王會
nongcun buxi xuexiao 農村補習學校
nongcun gongzuo dui 農村工作隊
nongcun gongzuo zhe 農村工作者
Nongcun shehui xue 農村社會學
Nongcun yanjiu fuwu zhan 農村研究
    服務站
Nongmin xiaoxi yuekan 農民消息月刊
nongmin xuexiao 農民學校
Nüzi baolu tongzhi xiehui 女子保路
    同志協會
pai 排
pai 牌
pan Haidi 盤海底
Pan Wenhua 潘文華
pao jianghu 跑江湖

Paoge 袍哥
Paoge lingji juli 袍哥令集舉例
paopinao 袍皮鬧
paotan 跑灘
paotanzhe 跑灘者
pi 皮
pidu 批牘
piguanjie 皮管街
pingheng 平衡
Pingxiang 平鄉
pinjia efu 貧家惡婦
piping pai 批評派
Pixian 郫縣
puqiandao 撲前刀
qie 竊
qiekou 切口
Qin Mu 秦牧
Qinghe 清河
Qingjiao hui 清醮會
Qinglongchang 青龍場
Qingming hui 清明會
qingshui 清水
Qiqiao jie 乞巧節
Qixi jie 七夕節
Quandian 全店
quanzi 圈子
Ren 仁
renshi 人市
Renshou 仁壽
Renshugong 仁恕公
Renzi qi 仁字旗
Rongxian 榮縣
Saishang fengyun 塞上風雲
sandao liugeyan, ziji zhao diandian 三
    刀六個眼，自己找點點
Sandianhui 三點會
sange 三哥
sanhu zhuyi 三壺主義
sanpai 三排
sanye 三爺
Sha Ting 沙汀
Shaiyi hui 晒衣會
Shanghai shijie shuju 上海世界書局
shangsipai 上四牌
Shangyuan hui 上元會
shantang 山堂
shecang 社倉

shegong 社公
Shehui diaocha bu 社會調查部
Shehui kexue yanjiu suo 社會科學研
    究所
shehui tuanti 社會團體
Shehui yuezhi 社會約製
shehui zhicai 社會製裁
shehui zhiyue 社會製約
Shen Baohuan 沈寶環
Shen Baoyuan 沈寶媛
Shen Zurong 沈祖榮
shenghuo 乘火
shengxian erye 聖賢二爺
shenmin 紳民
shenzai caoying xinzai han 身在曹營
    心在漢
sheshen 社神
shetuan 社團
shexue 社學
shezhang 社長
shi (or dan) 石
shi paifang 石牌坊
Shibantan 石板灘
Shigandang 石敢當
shige 十哥
Shimin de ziwei 市民的自衛
shipai 十排
shiwu dizu 實物地租
shiye 十爺
shou Paoge 瘦袍哥
shougui 收鬼
shousui 守歲
Shu 蜀
shuanglong zhen 雙龍陣
Shude she 蜀德社
Shuihu 水滸
shuijindehen 水緊得很
shuizhangle 水漲了
Shun tian zhuan ming 順天轉明
Shuqing 淑清
Shuying 淑英
Sichuan Jialingjiang Sanxia de
    xiangcun jianshe yundong 四川嘉陵
    江三峽的鄉村建設運動
Sichuan tongzhi 四川通志
Sihexing she 四和興社
Sishui weilan 死水微瀾

Sixing, renshi, xue de shangwan 私
   刑, 人市, 血的賞玩
Su Yu 蘇予
Suiyuan chashe 随园茶社
Sun Benwen 孫本文
Tadashi Negishi 根岸佶
Taiping xiang 太平鄉
Taishan Shigandang 泰山石敢當
Tao Menghe 陶孟和
Taoyuan sanjieyi 桃園三結義
ti honglong 提烘籠
tian di jun qin shi 天地君親師
Tian Jiaying 田家英
Tiandihui 天地會
Tianhuizhen 天回鎮
Tianyi gongshe 天一公社
Tong Niansheng 佟念生
Tongle she 同樂社
Tongrengong 同仁公
tongshuxing 同属性
tongyangxi 童養媳
toupian 投片
tuan tiaozi 團條子
tuanfang 團防
tuanlian 團練
tudi 土地
Tudi hui 土地會
tufei baoluan 土匪暴亂
tufei touzi 土匪頭子
Tuqiaochang 土橋場
tusu 土俗
wai guanshi 外管事
wan Paoge 玩袍哥
Wang 望
Wang Chuanshan 王船山
Wang Erge 王二哥
Wang Kaiyun 王闿運
Wang Lingji 王陵基
Wang Shiliang 王世良
Wang Tonghui 王同惠
wangwu chifan 望屋吃飯
Wangzhen 望鎮
Wen Yiduo 聞一多
Wenchang hui 文昌會
Wenchuan 汶川
Wenhua gongshulin 文華公書林

wenshi ziliao 文史資料
Wenwu miao 文武廟
Wu Wenzao 吳文藻
Wu Zelin 吳澤霖
wuge 五哥
wuke naihe 無可奈何
wukui cha 五魁茶
wulide 武力的
wupai 五排
wuye 五爺
Xia Yan 夏衍
Xiajiasi 夏家寺
Xialian 夏蓮
xian canyihui 縣參議會
xian daye 閑大爺
Xian geji zuzhi gangyao 縣各級組織
   綱要
xiangcun gongzuo fuwutuan 鄉村工
   作服務團
xiangcun jianshe 鄉村建設
Xiangcun jianshe yanjiuyuan 鄉村建
   設研究院
xianggongsuo 鄉公所
Xiangjun zhi 湘軍志
xiangyue 乡约
xiangyue zhidu 鄉約製度
xiangzhang 鄉長
xiangzhen 鄉鎮
xiao 孝
Xiaoliangshan 小涼山
Xiaoyihui 孝義會
Xiaoyu 小玉
xiapadan 下火巴蛋
xiasipai 下四牌
Xiehe gongshe 協和公社
xietaikou 寫台口
Xikang 西康
Ximen beixiangzi 西門北巷子
Xin zhexue shehuixue jieshi cidian 新
   哲學社會學解釋辭典
Xinchang 新場
xinchen daixie liliang 新陳代謝力量
Xindu 新都
Xinfan 新繁
Xinfan renmin gongshe 新繁人民公社
Xinke jianghu qieyao 新刻江湖切要

Xinwenbao 新聞報
Xiong Kewu 熊克武
xionghuang jiu 雄黃酒
Xipuchang 犀埔場
xishen 喜神
Xi Liang 錫良
Xu Yongshun 徐雍舜
Xuesheng jiuji hui 學生救濟會
Yamamoto Shin 山本真
Yan Yangchu 晏陽初
Yang Hansheng 陽翰笙
Yang Kaidao 楊開道
Yang Shuyin 楊樹因
Yanhuang chunqiu 炎黃春秋
Yanjing daxue biye lunwen 燕京大學
　　畢業論文
Yanjing daxue shigao 燕京大學史稿
yanlun zhengque 言論正確
yanna feitu 嚴拿匪徒
yaodian 腰店
Yaodianzi 幺店子
Yaojiadu 姚家渡
yasui qian 壓歲錢
yazu 押租
ye 爺
Ye Shengtao 葉聖陶
yi 義
Yichang 宜昌
yige guanggun, shijia bangmang 一個
　　光棍，十家幫忙
Yige nongcun shetuan jiating 一個農
　　村社團家庭
yilong zhen 一龍陣
yingsheng 迎聖
yinjin 引進
yinyu 隱語
yinzi 隱字
yipai 一排
yitaofu 易桃符
yu tian tongxing 與天同姓
yuan 園
Yuan Tiangang 袁天罡
Yuantong 元通
Yufo hui 浴佛會

yuzu 預租
zan xiangzhu 贊香燭
zaoshen 灶神
zhaqi 扎起
Zhang Fei 張飛
Zhang Henshui 張恨水
Zhang Lan 張瀾
Zhang Xianzhong 張獻忠
Zhang Xun 張洵
zhen 貞
Zheng Chenggong 鄭成功
Zheng Keshuang 鄭克塽
Zheng Linzhuang 鄭林莊
zhengliang 征糧
zhi 智
Zhinü 織女
Zhongguo minzhu tongmeng 中國民
　　主同盟
Zhongguo minzhu zhengtuan
　　tongmeng 中國民主政團同盟
Zhonghua jiaoyu wenhua jijin
　　dongshihui 中華教育文化基金董事會
Zhonghua pingmin jiaoyu cujinhui 中
　　華平民教育促進會
Zhongqiu jie 中秋節
zhongxin yiqi cha 忠心義氣茶
Zhongyang daxue 中央大學
Zhongyihao 忠義號
Zhongyuan jie 中元節
Zhou Xun 周詢
Zhou Yongkang 周永康
zhuan Qing Ming cha 轉清明茶
zhuangding 狀丁
Zhugao 竹篙
Zhugao diqu Paoge jiushan lianhe
　　zongshe 竹篙地區袍哥九山聯合總社
zhuo hanlin 捉寒林
Zigong 自貢
ziyou jiehun ge 自由結婚歌
zou hongdan 走紅單
Zouping 鄒平
zoushuile 走水了
zuole 做了

Introduction

1. Throughout the book, except in a few circumstances, I use "the Paoge" as a plural term. The secret society had many branches but no unified headquarters. "The Paoge" could mean both the organizations and their members. For the latter, I sometimes use "the Paoge brothers" and "the Gowned Brothers."

2. Wang 1993, 2003, 2008a, 2008b, and 2010.

3. Regarding microhistories, see Ladurie 1978; Ginzburg 1982; Darnton 1985; and Davis 1984. Microhistory is almost absent in the writings of Chinese history, however, although a few books might be exceptions. William T. Rowe's *Crimson Rain: Seven Centuries of Violence in a Chinese County* (2007) reveals a seven-hundred-year history of violence in Macheng county, Hubei province. Henrietta Harrison's *The Man Awakened from Dreams* (2005) uses local elite Liu Dapeng's diary to describe his life as a literati, dutiful son, merchant, and farmer. Jonathan Spence's *Death of Woman Wang* (1978) also has a perspective of microhistory. Done in the 1970s, before the rise of microhistory in the West, there had been some relevant works in Italy and France, but they had not been translated into English. Spence's methodology is very close to those used by microhistorians. The book began with an earthquake, allowing us to see how natural disasters influenced people's lives and changed the ecosystem, how women lived, how a widow survived, how children were educated, and what family violence looked like. Although the title is about Woman Wang, only the last chapter is about her. All other chapters talk about something else. From a strict definition it might not be a real microhistory.

4. Chesneaux 1971 and 1972; Davis 1977; Cai Shaoqing 1987 and 1990; Dai Xuanzhi 1990; Zhou Yumin and Shao Yong 1993; Yu Songqing 1994; Li Fuhua and Feng Zuozhe 1994; Zhuang Jifa 1994; Wang Jianchuan and Jiang Zhushan 1996; Sakai Tadao 1992; Ownby and Heidhues 1993; Ownby 1996; Ter Haar 1998; and Booth 1999. Studies of the Paoge in China mainly are general history and informative, although there have been a few articles published in English. There is no in-depth research tome on the Paoge, however. Regarding studies of the Paoge, see Hu Hansheng 1988; Wang Chunwu 1993; Qin Heping 2001a; Stapleton 1996; McIsaac 2000; and Wang 2008b and 2010. Japanese anthropologist Yamamoto Shin (2010) has also studied the Paoge of the 1940s.

5. Liu Shiliang 1939 [1975]; Shi De 1946; Wu Cang 1946; Xiao Tiezhui 1946; Zhang San 1946; Li Mufeng 1947; Guan Qun 1948; and Ling Guangfu 1949.

6. In this book I use such materials as Wang Yunzi 1981; Fan Shaozeng 1982; Chen Maozhao 1983; Deng Xihou 1986; Wang Shiliang and Diao Chunjin 1990; Wang Dayu 1993; Cao Yunsheng 1999; and Liang Xisheng et al. 1999.

7. Ownby 2001.

8. Shen Baoyuan 1946: 1.

9. Dittmer 1918; Gamble and Burgess 1921; Kulp 1925; and Han Mingmo 1997.

10. Malone and Tagler 1924.

11. Buck 1930 and 1937. The former was translated into Chinese by Zhang Lüluan and published in 1936.

12. Educated in the United States and Europe, Chen Hancheng (1897–2004), also known as Chen Han-seng and Geoffrey Chen, is considered a pioneer of modern Chinese social science.

13. Regarding the Movement of Rural Construction, see Zheng Dahua 2000; Li Weizhong 2009; Liu Chonglai 2006; Lu Zhenxiang 1987; Zhao Xudong 2008b; He Jianhua 2008; Hayford 1990; and Keehn 1993.

14. *Dingxian shehui gaikuang diaocha* (Investigation of the social conditions in Ding County) has seventeen chapters, including geography, history, county government and other local organizations, population, education, health, and so forth (Li Jinghan 1933). Also see Han Mingmo 1997.

15. Yang Kaidao (1899–1981) studied at Iowa State College and Michigan Agricultural College (now Michigan State University), where he earned a doctorate in sociology. After his return to China, he taught rural sociology at both Shanghai and Fudan Universities, and in 1928 he taught at the Department of Sociology at Yenching University. Yang Kaidao was in charge of an experimental district in Qinghe township, a suburb of Beijing, to investigate local history, environment, economy, population, families, hygiene, education, and so on. The investigation resulted in *Ching Ho: A Sociological Analysis: The Report of a Preliminary Survey of the Town of Ching Ho, Hopei, North China 1930* (Yen-ching ta hsüeh, Shê hui hsüeh hsi 1930). Li Jinghan (1895–1986) studied in the United States in his early years and then taught in the Department of Sociology at Yenching University. In the mid-1920s he guided students conducting surveys of population, families, family income, and family lives in four villages in the Beijing suburbs. He later published *A Survey of Rural Families Past Beiping's Suburbs* (Li Jinghan 1929). From 1924 to 1931, Li Jinghan was in charge of the famous survey of Dingxian, Hebei, and wrote *Investigation of the Social Conditions in Ding County* (see Li Jinghan 1933). Wu Wenzao (1901–1985) earned his doctoral degree from Columbia University in 1929, after which he returned to China and became a professor in Yenching University. By applying methodologies of community studies and field investigation of British functionalism of cultural anthropology, he promoted studies of rural community (Wu Wenzao 1934, 1935, 1936).

16. Similar books include those by Gu Fu 1924; Yang Kaidao 1929; Feng Hefa 1932; and Yan Xinzhe 1934.

17. Lei Jieqiong and Shui Shizheng 1989.

18. Park's works include *Introduction to the Science of Sociology* (with Ernest Bur-

gess, 1921) and *The City: Suggestions for the Study of Human Nature in the Urban Environment* (with R. D. McKenzie & Ernest Burgess, 1925).

19. Radcliffe-Brown's works include *Social Organization of Australian Tribes* (1931) and *The Andaman Islanders* (1933).

20. Fei Xiaotong's works include *Social Organization of Hualanyao* (Fei Hsiao-tung [Fei Xiaotong] and Wang Tonghui 1988), *Three Villages in Yunnan* (1990), "Fifty Years Investigation in the Yao Mountains" (1991), and *From the Soil: The Foundations of Chinese Society* (1992). There are many studies of Fei's scholarship, such as Zhao Xudong 2008a; Wang Jianmin 2010; Arkush 1981; Fong 1997; and Pan 1992.

21. It was written in English (Fei Hsiao-tung [Fei Xiaotong] 1939). Also see Han Mingmo 1997.

22. Xu Yongshun 1931.

23. Liang Shuming (1893–1988) taught at Peking University from 1917 through 1924. Regarding studies of Liang Shuming and rural construction, see Lu 2010; Thøgersen 2009; and Wu and Tong 2009.

24. Lu Zuofu (1893–1952) was an entrepreneur, educator, social activist, and founder of the Minsheng Shipping Company. For studies of his ideas on rural construction, see Liu Chonglai 2007.

25. Li Zaiquan 2006: 132–36.

26. Liu Chonglai 2006 and Cheng Bicheng 2014.

27. Zhou Yong 2006: 373–74; Yanjing daxue Chengdu xiaoyou hui 2007: 344; and Zhang Weiying, Wang Baiqiang et al. 1999: 1314.

28. Yanjing daxue Chengdu xiaoyou hui 2007: 344; and Zhang Weiying, Wang Baiqiang et al. 1999: 1314.

29. Li Anzhai 1934, 1935, and 1945.

30. Lin Yaohua 1935a, 1935b, (Yao-hua Lin) 1947a (original in English; for two Chinese translations, see Lin Yaohua 1977 and 1989), 1947b, 1985, 1990, 1997, 2003a, and 2003b. For a study about Lin Yaohua, see Zhang Haiyang 2001.

31. Wang Xiaoting and Huang Wenyi 1993: 100–101. Regarding Yenching University, see Stuart 1946; Edwards 1959; and West 1976. Regarding the university's student movement, see Perry 2013.

32. Here, Shen used English.

33. Shen Baoyuan 1946: 1.

34. Zhang Weiying, Wang Baiqiang et al. 1999: 1320; and Lin Yaohua 2003a: 457–60 and 2003b.

35. During the Chengdu period (1942–1945) of Yenching University, he visited the Yi people's area in Liangshan three times. See Lin Yaohua 2003a: 456–60 and 2003b.

36. The Department of Sociology was under Yenching University's School of Law.

37. Li Wenhai edited a large source collection of social investigators in the Republican period. Among it, volumes of "Marriage and Family" (Li Wenhai 2005a), "Social Organizations" (Li Wenhai 2005b), and "Rural Society" (Li Wenhai 2009) do not include Shen's thesis.

Chapter 1. A Public Execution

1. Shen Baoyuan 1946: 23.

2. Skinner 1964–65.

3. Wang 1993. Before the outbreak of World War II, the population of Chengdu was about half a million, due mainly to even newer immigrants—namely, the refugees steadily resituated away from the major eastern and northeastern cities after the Japanese invasion. By 1945, Chengdu's population had risen to more than seven hundred thousand.

4. He Yimin 2002: 583.

5. Zhang Xianzhong (1606–1647), a leader of the peasant uprising in the late Ming, established the Daxi regime. Battles and bloodshed would return later, in the first part of the twentieth century.

6. Lü Zuoxie 1982; Wang 1993; Wang Dongjie 2008; Liu Zhenggang 1991; Lan Yong 1996; Golas 1977; Rowe 1984: chapters 8 and 9; and Ho Ping-ti 1966.

7. Huang 1985: chapter 3.

8. Lu Yongji as quoted in Fang Zhirong and Zhou Jianhua 2011: 84.

9. Bai Jinjuan 1946: 19.

10. Bai Jinjuan 1946: 22.

11. Wang 1993: chapter 4.

12. "Baxian Bamiao chang changshi guizhang"; and Skinner 1964–65.

13. Zhang Fengzhu n.d.: vol. 4, "tusu."

14. Wang Qingyuan 1944: 32.

15. Zhang Weiying, Wang Baiqiang et al. 1999: 1331.

16. Shen Baoyuan 1946: 3.

17. Shen Baoyuan 1946: 2.

18. Su Yu 1993: 205. Su Yu (b. 1926) graduated from the Department of Journalism of Yenching University and became an editor for several newspapers and journals.

19. Lei Jieqiong and Shui Shizheng 1989.

20. Zhang Weiying, Wang Baiqiang et al. 1999: 1320–21.

21. Beijing shi shehui kexue yanjiusuo shehuixue yanjiushi 1984: 276.

22. See "Thirty Years of the Department of Sociology of Yenching University," in Yanda wenshi ziliao bianweihui 1989: 55.

23. Zhang Dezeng 1992: 263–70 (the work is about Liao). There were several tasks: provide law students summer practical activities; facilitate a school for dropout rural students; help with local illiteracy; develop manufacturing; promote new agricultural knowledge; and provide public health education as well as simple medical services.

24. Liao T'ai-ch'u 1947: 161–73.

25. Shen Baoyuan 1946: 23.

26. Yuan Tingdong 2010: 275 (Yuan is the author of the gazetteer).

27. Shen Baoyuan 1946: 8.

28. Huang Tinggui et al. 1733: 3830.

29. Ye Shengtao 2004: 305–6.

30. Chengdu shi difangzhi bianzhuan weiyuanhui 2009: 425; and Jinniuqu difangzhi bianzhuan weiyuanhui 1996: 51. In January 1950, when the People's Lib-

eration Army took over Chengdu County, Chongyiqiao was changed to Chongyi Township, as one of four townships in the Second District of Chengdu County. In 1952, Chengdu County was restructured, then Chongyi Township was put under the jurisdiction of Xinfan County (Xinfan xian). During the Commune Movement in 1958, it became Chongyi Production Brigade (Chongyi dadui) of Xinfan Commune (Xinfan renmin gongshe). In 1959 the Chongyi Township Commune (Chongyi xiang renmin gongshe) was established and soon Chongyi Township was changed to Dafeng Township Commune (Dafeng xiang renmin gongshe). In 1965, when Xinfan County was annexed by Xindu County (Xindu xian), Dafeng Township was also incorporated into Xindu County (see Map 2). In 1982, with the abandon of communes, Dafeng Township administration was established, which had thirteen villages (Sichuan sheng Xindu xiangzhi bianzhuan weiyuanhui 1994: 84–85; and Jinniuqu difangzhi bianzhuan weiyuanhui 1996: 51). This book covers the period when Chongyiqiao was still a part of Chengdu County.

31. Li Yonghui 2009: 17–19; and Peng Yaxin 1988: 166–87.

32. These included the Culture and Militance Temple (Wenwu miao, 1770) put up by the Hubei and Hunan Native Place Association, the South China Temple (Nanhua gong, 1782) by the Native Place Association for Guangdong People, and others of this type (Zhengxie Chengdu shi Xindu qu wenshi ziliao bianji weiyuanhui 2006: 18–19).

33. Wang Qingyuan 1944: 34.

34. As of this writing, Tie Liu is eighty-six years old and a dissident writer. In 1957 he was categorized as a "rightist" and sent to labor camp for twenty-three years. On September 14, 2014, eight days after I read this memoir, he was arrested for criticizing China's political situation; see www.voachinese.com/content/chinese-writer-20140915/2449892.html, September 15, 2014; accessed on October 1, 2014.

35. Shen Baoyuan 1946: 23.

36. Shen Baoyuan 1946: 23.

37. Shen Baoyuan 1946: 24.

38. In *Soulstealers*, Philip Kuhn discusses the separation of soul and body (Kuhn 1990: chapter 5). However, here I discuss the opposite of Kuhn's example. The activity of calling the soul was to call the soul back to the body and to let the deceased come back to life. Lei Mingyuan did not want his daughter's soul coming back home.

39. Shen Baoyuan 1946: 24.

40. Shen Baoyuan 1946: 25.

41. Shen Baoyuan 1946: 26.

42. Shen Baoyuan 1946: 25.

43. Shen Baoyuan 1946: 26.

44. Fawu bianji xiaozu 2001: 57. The "Criminal Laws of Republican China" in 1928 had similar punishments. In Item 282 of Chart 21, "Homicide," the murderer could be sentenced to death, life imprisonment, or ten or more years of imprisonment. In Item 283 the one who killed a member of the immediate family would be sentenced to death or life imprisonment (Wang Chonghui 2006: 74–75). Regarding studies of criminal laws during the Republican period, see Guo Jian et al. 1998; Liu,

Zhang, and Messner 2001; Mühlhahn 2007; Neighbors 2009; and Luo Xunan 2012. Regarding the laws and punishment of adultery in the Qing period, see Sommer 2000. For a comparison of laws and their practices in the Qing and the Republican period, see Huang 2001 (Huang's book focuses on civil not criminal laws, however).

45. Regarding the New Cultural Movement, see Wu Qiyuan 1934; Goldman 1977; Chen Shaoting 1979; Geng Yunzhi and Chen Yuwu 2009; and Fung 2010. Regarding the New Life Movement, see Xin shenghuo yundong cujin zonghui n.d.; Eastman 1986; Zuo Yuhe 1990; Guan Zhigang 1992; Oldstone-Moore 2000; Qiao Zhaohong 2005; Zhou Lei 2009; and Liu Wennan 2013.

46. Qin Mu 1983 [1943]: 359–65.

47. Lü Simian 2011: 16; and Zeng Xianyi 2011.

48. Hu Guotai 1993: 267–311.

49. Shen Baoyuan 1946: 26.

Chapter 2. A Local Band of the Gowned Brothers

1. See my discussion of the historical field concerning secret societies in the Introduction (and the citations there).

2. Shi De 1946: 10.

3. Li Mufeng 1947; Guan Qun 1948: 14; Fan Shaozeng 1982: 236; and Liao T'ai-ch'u 1947: 162. Liao's investigation estimated that more than 70 percent of male adults in Sichuan were members.

4. *Chengdu shi wenhua ju dang'an* 124-2-133. Based on "A Survey of Gangsters in Sichuan" in 1949 and "A Survey of Gangsters in Chongqing" in 1950, the Paoge in Chongqing had "over five hundred branches" and the Paoge members counted for "70–80 percent of the total population of the city." One estimate said that the Paoge have near one hundred thousand in the professions: the distributions were 90 percent of heads of *baojia* (local security system), 70 percent of guild members, 80 percent of professional associations, 50 percent of policemen, 90 percent of secret agents, 20 percent of apprentices and shop workers, and 100 percent of bandits, petty thieves, hooligans, and owners of brothels, lodges, teahouses, and public bathhouses. According to a government estimate in 1949, "over 70 percent of Sichuan population have the Paoge membership," and the number of professional and semiprofessional the Paoge had approached seventeen million (Zhao Qin 1990: 220, 224). Based on an investigation done by a Japanese anthropologist in 2008, the Paoge had great power in Yuantong town, Chongzhou, and they mainly conducted their activities in teahouses. "About 60 percent of local people joined the Paoge"; for commoners, "joining the Paoge was to secure personal security and to avoid being forced into military" (Yamamoto Shin 2008).

5. Zhang San 1946: 3.

6. Guan Qun 1948: 14.

7. Zhang San 1946: 3.

8. Li Mufeng 1947.

9. Shen Baoyuan 1946: 1, 6.

10. Liao T'ai-ch'u 1947: 161.

11. Sha Tiefan 1936: 51.

12. For example, Sichuan difang shiji wenti yanjiuhui 1940; and Wu Cang 1946.

13. Zuo Zongtang 2009: vol. 31; Li Rong 1922: "pidu," vol. 1; and Fu Chongju 1987 [1909–10]: vol. 2, 48. Some studies claimed that the Paoge were the Red Gang (*hongbang*) but others that they were one of three secret societies, along with the Green Gang and Red Gang (Li Mufeng 1947: 81; and Shi De 1946: 10–11).

14. Fu Chongju 1987 [1909–10]: vol. 2, 47–50.

15. Shen Baoyuan 1946: 17.

16. Liu Shiliang 1975 [1939]. One explanation for the phrase "bottom of the ocean" is that the book "is spacious and huge and can contain everything" (Li Zifeng 1940: 1).

17. Shen Baoyuan 1946: 44.

18. Liu Shiliang 1975 [1939]: 4. The origin of the Sworn Brotherhood Society is debatable. This book does not attempt to discuss this issue but rather uses the origin stories to explore the cultural phenomena. Regarding the debate, see Cai Shaoqing 1987: 210–16; and Qin Baoqi and Meng Chao 2000.

19. Hobsbawm 1983: 1.

20. *The Bottom of the Ocean* is among the several titles listed in Shen Baoyuan's appendixes (1946: 46). We know that there were many versions. I have collected three editions (none matches the editions in Shen's appendix). They are (1) *A Complete Collection for the Bottom of Ocean of Chengdu River and Lake Runners* (Chengdu jianghu haidi quanji 1932); (2) *The Bottom of the Ocean of Chengdu River and Lake Runners* (Chengdu jianghu haidi 1934); and (3) *The Bottom of the Ocean* (Li Zifeng 1940). The first two editions were woodblock-printed in Chengdu (the two woodcut-printed versions were provided by Cynthia Brokaw); the third was done with moveable type, at 334 pages, the most complete and widely distributed.

21. Schoppa 1973.

22. In the *baojia* system ten households was a *jia* and ten *jia* was a *bao*. Each *jia* and *bao* had a head.

23. Zhang Ji et al. n.d.: vol. 3, "minzhengzhi."

24. "Baxian tuanshou paituan tiaoli" 1813; and "Biancha baojia tiaogui" 1850.

25. Lan Bingkui et al. n.d.: vol. 7, "guanzhengmen, minzhi."

26. Ran Jinhui and Li Huiyu 2005: 147.

27. Zhongguo diyi lishi dang'an guan and Beijing shifan daxue lishi xi 1986: 746.

28. Wei Yingtao and Zhao Qing 1981: vol. 1, 35.

29. Zhongguo diyi lishi dang'an guan and Beijing shifan daxue lishi xi 1986: 792.

30. Wang Kaiyun 2007: "Hunan fangshou pian," 25; Zuo Zongtang n.d.: vol. 25; and Chen Xulu, Gu Tinglong, and Wang Xi 1979: 161.

31. *Sichuan guanbao*, no. 9, 1911.

32. Liu Shiliang 1975 [1939]: 12.

33. "Sichuan tongsheng jingcha zhangcheng" 1903.

34. Wu Jinhang 1981; Wang Yunzi 1981; and Wei Yingtao and He Yimin 1983.

35. Qin Heping 2000: 94–95.

36. Wang Shiliang and Diao Chunjin 1990.

37. Wang Shiliang and Diao Chunjin 1990.

38. Liu Shiliang 1975 [1939]: 12.

39. Wei Yingtao and Zhao Qing 1981: vol. 1, 134.

40. *Sichuan guanbao*, no. 9, 1911.

41. Wu Jinhang 1981; Chen Shunong 1981; and Wang Yunzi 1981.

42. Wei Yingtao and Zhao Qing 1981: vol. 1, 134.

43. *Sichuan guanbao*, no. 9, 1911.

44. Shen Baoyuan 1946: 3.

45. Shen Baoyuan 1946: 22; Li Rong 1922: "pidu," vol. 1; *Sichuan guanbao* no. 9, 1911; and Fu Chongju 1987 [1909–10]: vol. 2, 47–48.

46. Guomindang shengzhiwei 1942: 158–60.

47. Regarding the role of the patron deity associations, see Wang 2003: chapter 2.

48. In 1916, Yuan Shikai's forces and various Sichuan (and neighboring) armies fought for power in Sichuan; in 1917 street battles took place in Chengdu, with great losses. To avoid warlord miseries, Xiong Kewu, the military governor (*dujun*) of Sichuan Province, set up "designated defense zones" (*fangqu zhi*) in 1918 so that power was distributed. In 1927 the Nationalist government nominally unified the nation, but Sichuan stayed relatively independent until 1935. On Sichuan warlords, see Kuang Shanji and Yang Guangyan 1991; Tu Minggao 1980; Fu Zengyang 1989; Tang Xuefeng 1990; Zhang Jianji 2003; Liu Zhengmei 1997; Huang Tianhua 2008; Wang Youping 1999; and Kapp 1973.

49. Xiao Tiezhui 1946.

50. Ling Guangfu 1949: chapter 3.

51. Wang Shiliang and Diao Chunjin 1990.

52. Wang Dayu 1993: 159–60.

53. Li Mufeng 1947: 82.

54. Wenjiang xianzhi bianzhuan weiyuanhui 1990: 840.

55. Shen Baoyuan 1946: 7.

Chapter 3. Spirituality and Customs

1. Shen Baoyuan 1946: 23.

2. Regarding to the worship of the patron deity, see Wang Yongqian 1994.

3. During the time, 1,100 yuan could buy ten pound rice (see note 45 of Chapter 9)..

4. Fu Chongju 1987 [1909–10]: vol. 1, 546–61.

5. Fu Chongju 1987 [1909–10]: vol. 1, 546–61.

6. Liu Yuan 1986 [ca. 1790]: 126–27; *West China Missionary News*, no. 3, 1905: 57; Vale, no. 10, 1906: 237–38, no. 11, 1906: 262; and Grainger 1917: 8.

7. Guan Hanqing 1958a. Regarding Guandi worship and the historical figure of Guan Yu, see Duara 1988b. Discussion of Guandi worship is taken up further in this chapter.

8. Shen Baoyuan 1946: 18–19.

9. Shen Baoyuan 1946: 18–19.

10. Xiang Qifen 2003: 65–69.

11. Hirayama Shu 1911: 64–65; and Li Zifeng 1940: 220, 227.

12. Liu Shiliang 1975 [1939]: 36.

13. Wang Dayu 1993.

14. Duara 1988a and 1988b.

Chapter 4. Secret Codes and Language

1. Hobsbawm 1981: 38.

2. Shen Baoyuan 1946: 44. *Paopinao*: the Paoge called themselves *pi* (leather), which implies *ge* (revolution), "to reform and to change corrupted politics, social customs, education, and ideologies." Here, *nao* means "action" to create an ideal world. In "Appendix V: Examples of the Paoge Argots" of her report, Shen included twenty-two words the locals used for the Paoge. They can be generalized into categories of daily life, things, activities, and people (Shen Baoyuan 1946: 46).

3. David Maurer (1981: 1) was a pioneer in studying the language of the underworld; he believes that "a subculture is a group of individuals—such as social, occupational, ethnic, or racial groups—who share certain common attitudes, associations, behavior patterns, and speech patterns."

4. Leslau 1964: 7; and Kaplan, Kämpe, and Farfán 1990: 143–44, 146. Here I do not attempt to discuss "professional languages" (jargons) used by various occupations; instead, I focus on the languages used by secret societies. Generally speaking, the professional languages were merely conveniences for work; unlike argots, they were not secret. But argots had connections with jargons.

5. Kaplan, Kämpe, and Farfán 1990: 144–45. Almost all studies of argots in the West and in China have been by linguists, who claim that they are unique when compared to standard languages. See Maurer 1981; Kaplan, Kämpe, and Farfán 1990; Davie 1997; Leng Xueren 1991; and Wang Hui 2003. Some historians, however, have noticed the importance of argots and secret signs used by Chinese secret societies, regarding them as a propaganda tool rather than a means of communication; see, for example, Boris Novikov's systematic analysis of political meanings in the poems of the Triad Society (Novikov 1972).

6. One explanation for the title *The Bottom of the Ocean* is that the book "is spacious and huge and can contain everything" (like the ocean). An early account explores the name from the organization's history (Li Zifeng 1940: 1).

7. Wang Chunwu 1993: 61. A *diao* (a string) of money was one thousand coins in copper yuan.

8. *Zhongguo shehui kexueyuan yuyan yanjiusuo* 1997: 515; Zhuo Tingzi 1991: 243–74; and Leng Xueren 1991: 7–24. In the Republican period more books were printed, such as the *Jargons of All Professions in China* (Quanguo gejie qiekou dacidian) (Wu Hanchi 1924).

9. Fu Chongju listed 126 words used by the Gowned Brotherhood, which could be divided into six categories: membership (14 words), criminal activities (30), situations (12), behaviors (36), and objects (34) (Fu Chongju 1987 [1909–10]: vol. 2, 48–50). Because of the nature of their activities, in fact, they had many language taboos to avoid bad luck. But Fu Chongju also provided an entry for "Argots of River and Lake Runners in Chengdu" (*Chengdu zhi jianghu yanci*), which had 22 categories, including astronomy, geography, seasons, people, shops, artisans, professions, medicines, fortune-telling, prostitutes and actors, beggars, robbers and thieves, Buddhist

monks and Daoist priests, the human body, daily items, boats, clothing, drinks and foods, numbers, illnesses, life and death, and things (Fu Chongju 1987 [1909–10]: vol. 2, 47, 50–66).

10. Kaplan, Kämpe, and Farfán 1990: 142–43.

11. Hirayama Shu 1911: 64–65; and Liu Shiliang 1975 [1939]: 2.

12. Liu Shiliang 1975 [1939]: 3.

13. Liu Shiliang 1975 [1939]: 38. Wang Fuzhi (Chuanshan, 1619–1692) was a writer and philosopher who professed a strong anti-Manchu ideology. Zheng Chenggong (1624–1662), known as Koxinga, organized resistance against the Manchu troops; he campaigned in the south and took Taiwan from the Dutch in 1661. See further discussion of Zheng later in this chapter.

14. Stanton 1900: 97–98.

15. Liao T'ai-ch'u 1947: 164.

16. Wang Dayu 1993: 148.

17. Schlegel 1974 [1866]: 193; Stanton 1900: 96–98; Davis 1977: 129–30; Booth 1999: 122–28; and Liu Shiliang 1975 [1939]: 38.

18. Shen Baoyuan 1946: 45.

19. Shen Baoyuan 1946: 45.

20. Shen Baoyuan 1946: 45.

21. *Chengdu jianghu haidi* 1934. Thanks to Cynthia Brokaw for providing this material.

22. Shen Baoyuan 1946: 20.

23. Headquarters of the Paoge were commonly called "harbors" (*matou*); the term "public gates" (*gongkou*) was also widely used, where *gong* means "unanimous agreement" and *kou*, a place of entrance and exit. *The Bottom of the Ocean* explained that the *gongkou* was a "place of entrance and exit for all members" (Liu Shiliang 1975 [1939]: 3–4; and Wang Shunwu 1993: 62).

24. Zhongguo diyi lishi dang'an guan and Beijing shifan daxue lishi xi 1986: vol. 2, 792.

25. Chen Shunong 1981: 176.

26. Shen Baoyuan 1946: 20–21.

27. Shen Baoyuan 1946: 20–21.

28. Liu Shiliang 1975 [1939]: 5, 36; Zhongguo shehui kexueyuan 1996: 469; and Fu Chongju 1987 [1909–10]: vol. 2, 48.

29. Li Zifeng 1940: 269.

30. Yun Tao 1933: 16; Fu Chongju 1987 [1909–10]: vol. 2, 48–50; Qin Heping 2001a; and Zhou Xun 1987 [1936]: 17–18.

31. Leslau 1964: 7.

32. Li Zifeng 1940: 266–67. In addition to the argot, when a member went to an area controlled by a different lodge and wanted to contact local fellows, he had to show his "red and black board" (*hongfei heipian*), which functioned as an ID card or a certificate. An urgent and important letter would have a hole in it with a piece of feather attached. The invented characters could often be seen on such documents.

33. Fu Chongju 1987 [1909–10]: vol. 2, 48–50.

34. Fu Chongju 1987 [1909–10]: vol. 2, 48–50; and Zhang Guanghai and Liang Hongou 1987: 111.

Chapter 5. Disciplines and Dominance

1. Chen Shunong 1981: 176.

2. Brace 1936: 178.

3. Shen Baoyuan 1946: 45.

4. Shen Baoyuan 1946: 20.

5. Author interview with Zhou Shaojie, seventy-five years old, Joy Teahouse, June 22, 1997; and Li Jieren 1980 [1936a]: 339.

6. Shen Baoyuan 1946: 18.

7. For this, see Stanton 1900 and Li Zifeng 1940.

8. These formations were recorded in the *The Bottom of the Ocean* (Li Zifeng 1940: 210–36). When William Stanton studied Chinese secret societies in the late nineteenth century, he wrote in detail about this practice (Stanton 1900).

9. The "Regulations for the Inspection of Gambling, Thieves' Dens, the Elder Brothers Society, and Heterodox Sects," enacted in the late Qing, stated that police should stop and question men in groups of three to five, wearing strange clothing, and behaving with excited or violent gestures ("Sichuan tongsheng jingcha zhangcheng" 1903; and Cui Xianchang 1982: 96).

10. Stanton 1900: 99; and Li Zifeng 1940: 210. Here, *hong* is a reference to a related secret society, in some sense a name that was synonymous with Gelaohui and indirectly with the Paoge, who shared some aspect of their origins with the Hongmen ("Hong" may refer to the Ming-dynasty's Hongwu emperor). For details, see Qin Baoqi and Meng Chao 2000.

11. Stanton 1900: 100; and Li Zifeng 1940: 210.

12. Stanton 1900: 99; and Li Zifeng 1940: 210.

13. It was said that Han Xin, who came from a poor family and served as a low-ranking official in Liu's army, ran away from Liu's camp because of his disappointment at the treatment he received. Zhang Liang, a major adviser to Liu, heard Han was a talented man and chased him back and persuaded Han to serve Liu.

14. Regarding the culture of the dragon, see Pang Jin 1993.

15. The next position down from "dragon head" was the "chief of incense sticks" (*xiangzhang*), who managed the routine affairs of the lodge (Liu Shiliang 1975 [1939]: 31–32).

16. Regarding the violent factors in Chinese culture, refer to William Rowe's book *Crimson Rain* (Rowe 2007).

17. Li Zifeng 1940: 227.

18. Li Zifeng 1940: 213.

19. Li Zifeng 1940: 218.

20. Li Zifeng 1940: 230.

21. Li Zifeng 1940: 210.

22. Li Zifeng 1940: 275.

23. Li Zifeng 1940: 276.

24. Shen Baoyuan 1946: 22.

25. Shen Baoyuan 1946: 22.

26. Shen Baoyuan 1946: 7.

27. Shen Baoyuan 1946: 10.

28. In 1930, Wu published *Social Control* (Shehui yuezhi), one in a series of

sociology studies edited by Sun Benwen, a PhD from New York University and chair of the Department of Sociology of National Central University (Zhongyang daxue); it was published by Shanghai World Books (Shanghai shijie shuju).

29. Wu Zelin 1930: 8.

30. Wu Zelin 1930.

31. *The New Dictionary of Philosophy and Sociology* (Xin zhexue shehuixue jieshi cidian) published in 1947 did not include the term *social control* but only *social norm*, which was defined as the following: "Sociology generally calls the various forced forms of 'regulations and restrictions' (*guixian*) in social life as moral norms, and is divided into moral norm, order norms, and legal norm" (Cishu bianyishe 1947: 288).

32. Liang Shuming 2011: 172–74, 180–81.

33. Shen Baoyuan 1946: 10.

34. Wang Shiliang and Diao Chunjin 1990: 451–52.

35. Shen Baoyuan 1946: 14, 29.

36. Except an article by me (see Wang 2010).

37. Sha Ting 1982 [1940]: 140–56.

38. "Director of mutual security" was equivalent to "head of township" (*xiangzhang*) later. In 1939 the Nationalist government abandoned offices of the mutual security agency (*lianbao banshichu*) and established the public office of township (*xianggongsuo*) and the former director of mutual security (*lianbao zhuren*) was renamed "head of township."

39. Sha Ting 1982 [1940]: 140–56.

40. Sha Ting 1982 [1940]: 140–56.

41. Chen Maozhao 1983: 181–82. Also, Fu Chongju's investigation of social customs collected many Paoge words (Fu Chongju 1987 [1909–10]: vol. 2, 43).

42. Li Jieren, for example, described a scene of "calling for tea money." After paying for his own tea, a man saw two acquaintances coming in and immediately looked away. He later pretended that he just then saw them and said with a smile: "Just arrived? Your tea is on me!" He waved bills at the waiter. But the two acquaintances called the waiter over and said, "Take our money to pay for the tea at that table [pointing to the first man]." The waiter, who knew that both gestures were only symbolic, announced, "Both sides thank each other." He did not bother to take money from the first one, which is precisely what was expected. See Li Jieren 1980 [1937]: 602; Chen Shisong 1999: 205–6; and Wang 2003: chapter 4.

43. The celebration of the Pure Brightness Day all over China was also a strong indication of community solidarity. Anthropologists have studied the significance of the Pure Brightness Day Festival; according to Myron Cohen's study of North China, participation in it emphasized kinship associations. Rituals were performed in a communal setting, with each local lineage arranged as "Qingming associations" (*Qingming hui*), which combined each individual lineage into a collective. In Chengdu the Patron Deity Association (Qingjiao hui, or Tudi hui) had a similar function—to organize the ceremony for worship of neighborhood patron deities. Leaders were selected from among local residents. These associations were mostly Daoist and were called "thanksgiving societies" by Western missionaries, because they referred to neighborhood peace. The celebration organized by patron deity as-

sociations, as C. K. Yang wrote, provided "a collective symbol" for local community (Cohen 1990: 509–34; Grainger 1918: 5; and Yang 1961: 81).

44. Ci Jun 1942.

45. Rankin 1986, 1990; and Rowe 1989, 1990. Regarding conflicts and resolutions in rural communities, also see Huang 1996.

Chapter 6. A Tenant Farmer and Paoge Master

1. Wu Cang 1946: 9.

2. Guomindang shengzhiwei 1942.

3. Bai Jinjuan 1946: 12–13.

4. Guan Qun 1948: 14.

5. Guan Qun 1948: 14.

6. Shen Baoyuan 1946: 4.

7. Shen Baoyuan 1946: 17.

8. Shen Baoyuan 1946: 7.

9. Cai Xinghua 2008 (the memoir was originally written in 1987).

10. Kapp 1973.

11. Cai Xinghua 2008.

12. All of the narratives about He Song, unless stated otherwise, are taken from Wang Shiliang and Diao Chunjin 1990.

13. Examples of this local, politicized historiography are Cai Xinghua 2008; Cao Yunsheng 1999; and Chen Maozhao 1983.

14. Wu Yu 1984: 10.

15. Shen Baoyuan 1946: 15.

16. Shen Baoyuan 1946: 18.

17. But with rapid inflation after the war, the price soared to 44,100 yuan in April 1946—the year Shen completed her report (Li Zhuxi, Zeng Dejiu, and Huang Weihu 1987: 370–71).

18. Fu Chongju 1987: vol. 1, 103; and Li Zhuxi, Zeng Dejiu, and Huang Weihu 1987: 377. In the early Qing period, 1 *mu* produced roughly 118 *jin* of grain, and therefore a five-person family could live by working 31 *mu*. If half the harvest went to rent, a tenant needed to lease at least 60 *mu*, depending on the level of productivity. In the mid-Qing period the yield went up to 151 *jin* (correlating to a 48-*mu* requirement), and in the late Qing the per-*mu* yield rose to 215 *jin* (correlating to a minimum of 34 *mu*, with the usual contingencies of soil, weather, management, and so on).

19. In July 1945, based on 18,633 yuan per *dan,* 20,000 yuan could buy about 300 *jin* rice. Therefore, (280 x 2) + 300 = 860 *jin*. The 20,000 yuan of purchase power has been added to the 860 *jin* of rice.

20. Wang 1993: 132.

21. Guo Hanming and Meng Guangyu 1944: 15–19.

22. Shen Baoyuan 1946: 15.

23. Li Deying 2006: 152; and Lü Pingdeng 1936: 185.

24. Wang 2008b: 265.

25. Shen Baoyuan 1946: 15.

26. Wang 1993: 124.

27. Li Yingfa 1985. These data are from analyses of the Baxian Archives; the other Chongqing ratios were less, almost all being 6:4, in which the landlord held six-tenths and the tenant four-tenths.

28. Wang 1993: 124–30. For discussion on rent rate in different parts of China, see Gao Wangling 2005.

29. Li Deying 2006: 137–47.

30. Shen Baoyuan 1946: 15–16.

31. See Wang 1993: 132–33.

Chapter 7. Entering the Paoge

1. Shen Baoyuan 1946: 8.

2. Shen Baoyuan 1946: 8.

3. Wei Yingtao and Zhao Qing 1981: vol. 1, 516–17, 551.

4. Shen Baoyuan 1946: 8.

5. Shen Baoyuan 1946: 9.

6. Shen Baoyuan 1946: 9–10.

7. Shen Baoyuan 1946: 9–10.

8. Shen Baoyuan 1946: 11.

9. Shen Baoyuan 1946: 11.

10. Shen Baoyuan 1946: 11.

11. Shen Baoyuan 1946: 3–4, 12.

12. Zhang Henshui (1897–1967) was a representative of the Mandarin Ducks and Butterflies School in the 1920s and 1930s. There are many studies of him and his novels. See Wei Shouzhong 1989; Zheng Ling 2000; and Chen Jing 2001. For the study of the Mandarin Ducks and Butterflies School, see Link 1981.

13. Shen Baoyuan 1946: 12. The meaning is unclear from the source but probably can be regarded as bad luck signs.

14. Wen Shu, Wu Jianzhou, and Cui Xianchang 1984.

15. Shen Baoyuan 1946: 12.

16. Shen Baoyuan 1946: 13.

17. Shen Baoyuan 1946: 12.

18. Shen Baoyuan 1946: 14.

19. Shen Baoyuan 1946: 13.

20. Fu Chongju 1987 [1909-10]: vol. 1, 112–13. *Guomin gongbao*, August 2, 1914; October 15 and December 9, 1927. *Tongsu ribao*, October 27 and December 10, 1909.

21. Both Dorothy Ko (1994) and Susan Mann (1997) have pointed out that in traditional Chinese society, women in certain areas or of certain classes could live lives that were unusual compared that of other women; both authors basically study elite women in the Jiangnan region.

22. Shen Baoyuan 1946: 14.

23. Li Jieren 1980 [1936b].

Chapter 8. The Decline of Power

  1. Shen Baoyuan 1946: 16.

  2. Wang Shiliang and Diao Chunjin 1990: 441–55.

  3. Shen Baoyuan 1946: 33.

  4. Shen Baoyuan 1946: 32.

  5. Shen Baoyuan 1946: 33.

  6. Shen Baoyuan 1946: 32. In Shen's report this is the only time she used the character *dan* 担 (a unit of weight), but when she mentioned this rice elsewhere, she used the character *dan* 石 (a unit of volume; also pronounced *shi* in early Chinese sources); 50 *dan* of rice was not a small number. By using the correlation of 100 *jin* to 1 *dan*, the total was 5,000 *jin*. However, by using the correlation of 220 *jin* to 1 *dan* (or *shi*), the total indicated a larger amount/weight (11,000 *jin*; for a more detailed discussion of *dan* [or *shi*], see Chapter 6, note 19).

  7. Shen Baoyuan 1946: 33.

  8. Shen Baoyuan 1946: 33.

  9. Liao Taichu and Yang Shusheng 1941.

  10. Liao Taichu and Yang Shusheng 1941.

  11. Shen Baoyuan 1946: 34.

  12. Shen Baoyuan 1946: 34. Weaving was a common handicraft among farmers in the Chengdu Plain, an important supplement to their income. In the 1940s, Yang Shuyin investigated a farming family nearby Chengdu (Yang Shuyin 1944).

  13. Shen Baoyuan 1946: 35. Yunxiang Yan has studied the functions of gift giving, one of the most important tools of establishing social networks and social relations (Yan 1996).

  14. Cai Xinghua 2008: 240.

  15. Cai Xinghua 2008: 240.

  16. Shen Baoyuan 1946: 34.

Chapter 9. A Family Crisis and a Rural Woman's Fate

  1. Shen Baoyuan 1946: 33.

  2. Shen Baoyuan 1946: 34.

  3. Shen Baoyuan 1946: 36.

  4. Shen Baoyuan 1946: 36.

  5. Shen Baoyuan 1946: 36.

  6. Shen Baoyuan 1946: 37.

  7. Shen Baoyuan 1946: 35.

  8. The report appears in *Decennial Reports on the Trade* 1891.

  9. Tadashi Negishi 1906: 148–52; and Wang 1993: 153–55.

  10. Wang 1993: 643.

  11. Based on the official budget of the Sichuan government in 1937, of 86.3 million yuan of total income, taxes were 60 million yuan, including 24 million yuan in opium tax. In 1938 annual production of opium in Sichuan was 1.2 million to 1.4 million *dan*, 70 percent of which were exported outside the province; see Lin Shourong and Long Dai 1984.

  12. Qin Heping 2000.

13. Xie Zaosheng 2002. Another account estimated that in 1932, among the total seventy million people, four million used opium (Wang Jinxiang 2005: 176). Based on another observation by a foreigner, "there are countless people using opium in Sichuan." He said that during the time people often believed half of Sichuan's population used opium, and he claimed a German told him that 90 percent of adults in Chongqing used opium. See *Sichuan yuebao* 3, no. 5 (1930): 15. Such a statement might be exaggerated, but it shows how serious opium use had become.

14. Xie Zaosheng 1996: 492.

15. Qin Heping 2001b: 191.

16. Xie Zaosheng 2002: 585–96.

17. Qin Heping 2001b: 71, 328–29; Wenjiang xianzhi bianzhuan weiyuanhui 1990: 839; and Fan Shaozeng 1982: 236.

18. Shen Baoyuan 1946: 37.

19. Shen Baoyuan 1946: 37.

20. Shen Baoyuan 1946: 38.

21. Shen Baoyuan 1946: 37.

22. The Tang work is quoted in Jiang Bo 2010 and Yuan Tiangang n.d.

23. Woman Lei, or perhaps Shen's reporting or transcribing, may have erred by claiming "1.2." In Yuan's text "2.1 taels" is the lowest bone number.

24. For the commentary in Yuan's work quoted here, see Jiang Bo 2010: 75.

25. As in Jiang Bo 2010: 71.

26. Shen Baoyuan 1946: 38.

27. Shen Baoyuan 1946: 37.

28. Wang 2003: chapter 6.

29. Shen Baoyuan 1946: 26. Regarding social positions and situations of Chinese women in traditional society, see Jaschok and Miers 1994; and Bernhardt 1999. Regarding the modern transformation of Chinese women, see Gilmartin et al. 1994; Bossen 2002; and Diamant 2000.

30. Wang 1993: 626.

31. *Sichuan xuebao*, no. 5, 1907; and Wang 1993: 631.

32. "Newsletter of the Association for Sichuan Railroad Protection," no. 24 in Wei Yingtao and Zhao Qing 1981: vol. 1, 240; and Wang 1993: 632.

33. Shen Baoyuan 1946: 27.

34. Shen Baoyuan 1946: 27.

35. Jonathan Spence's *Death of Woman Wang* described the tragic story of a woman who tried to run away from her husband (Spence 1978). In Lu Xun's writing, Xianglin's wife had a similar fate (Lu Xun 1981).

36. A neighbor owed widowed Woman Cai money, so the neighbor offered his seven-year-old daughter for Cai's eight-year-old son; see Guan Hanqing 1958b.

37. Scott 1985.

38. Qin Mu 1983: 359–65.

39. Ba Jin 1985 [1932]: 230, 240. Kristen Stapleton has fully discussed this character in her new book, *Fact in Fiction: 1920s China and Ba Jin's Family* (Stapleton 2016: chapter 1).

40. Shen Baoyuan 1946: 28.

41. Shen Baoyuan 1946: 29.

42. *Fengjian* (a modern locution) has been used by elites and by Marxist histori-ography since the early twentieth century to criticize popular religions, which are often signaled as *mixin* (superstition).

43. Shen Baoyuan 1946: 30–31. Lu Xun's short story *Xianglin's Wife* is a good example of "old moral and ethic code" killing people (Lu Xun 1981).

44. Shen Baoyuan 1946: 30–31.

45. In July 1945 rice price was 18,600 yuan per *dan*. After the war prices soared. In February 1946 the price reached 36,000 yuan per *dan* (Li Zhuxi, Zeng Dejiu, and Huang Weihu 1987: 371). Therefore, by selling 2 *dan* of rice, Lei might receive more than 70,000 yuan.

46. Shen Baoyuan 1946: 39.

47. Shen Baoyuan 1946: 39. Regarding studies of concubines, see Cheng Yu 2005.

48. Shen Baoyuan 1946: 40–41.

49. Shen Baoyuan 1946: 40.

50. Shen Baoyuan 1946: 40–41.

Chapter 10. Fall of the Paoge

1. Sun Jiang has published extensive studies on the relationship between the GMD and the Communist revolution and secret societies; see Sun Jiang 2000, 2001, 2007, 2012a, and 2012b.

2. Cai Xinghua 2008: 240.

3. The narrative is cited in Wang Shiliang and Diao Chunjin 1990.

4. Four of the five branches had existed from the Qing dynasty Guangxu period (1875–1908): the Harmony and Peace Public Society (Xiehe gongshe), in the area of the West and East City Gates; the South Market Public Society (Nanji gongshe), in the area of the South and North City Gates; the Heaven Unity Public Society (Tianyi gongshe), downtown; and the Phoenix Protocol Public Society (Fengyi gongshe), around the Rice Market (Hedeng chang). The fifth branch was estab-lished in the late Qing by the county clerks, called the Joined Nines Public Society (Jiuhe gongshe), with the mission to help common people in lawsuits. See Xinfanx-ian gonganju 1950. I am indebted to Zhao Qing, who shared this document with me over twenty years ago. The original is held by the Bureau of Public Security in Sichuan and bears no file number or page numbers. All quotations in this chapter about the Paoge in Xinfan are derived from this work.

5. Xinfanxian gonganju 1950.

6. During the warlord period in Sichuan (namely, 1916–35), the organized army there under the local generals was called the Sichuan Army (Chuanjun), and even after Chiang controlled Sichuan in 1935 the force was organized under the Nation-alists but people still called it the Sichuan Army. Deng was general of the Sichuan Army from the 1920s through the 1940s. In 1937 he had led his army out of Sichuan to fight the Japanese. After 1949 he held the position as vice governor of Sichuan under the Communist government. Liu Wenhui was at the same time a general in the Sichuan Army; formerly he was governor of Sichuan and Xikang Provinces. After 1949 he served as minister of agriculture in the Communist government. Pan

Wenhua was a general in the Sichuan Army as well, but he died of illness right after the Communist takeover.

7. Deng Xihou 1986. Hu Zongnan (1896–1962) advised the president on military strategy after the retreat of the Nationalists to Taiwan in 1949.

8. Sichuanese landlords and better-off peasants had already paid the land tax (*liangfu*) in the fall of 1949 to the GMD government; now the Communist government was going after them as well. The land tax often meant, or included, the grain levy and could even be called *zhengliang*.

9. Cao Yunsheng 1999: 1–2.

10. Liang Xisheng et al. 1999: 7–8.

11. See the relationship of land tax to grain levy earlier in the chapter.

12. Liang Xisheng et al. 1999: 7–8.

13. Liang Xisheng et al. 1999: 7–8.

14. Cao Shuji and Liu Shigu 2015: 185–94.

15. Liang Xisheng et al. 1999.

16. Cao Yunsheng 1999: 1–2.

17. Cao Yunsheng 1999: 1–2.

18. Liang Xisheng et al. 1999. According to anthropologist Yamamoto Shin's investigation of Yuantong Township, Chongzhou, after 1949 the Paoge was categorized as a "feudal secret society" (*fengjian huimen*), and the result of only three trials was that ninety "rich and powerful Paoge leaders were executed" (Yamamoto Shin 2008).

Chapter 11. Looking for the Storyteller

1. Regarding Shen Zurong's contributions to library science in China, see Boettcher 1989.

2. Cheng Huanwen 2007; and Chen Weizun 2010.

3. Wang Xiaoting and Huang Wenyi 1993: 100–101.

4. Zhang Weiying, Wang Baiqiang et al. 1999: 558. The story in *Fragrant Grass at the Edges of the Sky* by Xia Yan concerns a group of intellectuals' experiences during the war, their love lives, struggles for survival, and participation in the War of Resistance (Xia Yan 1949).

5. *Xinhua ribao*, September 29, 1945.

6. *Xingdao ribao*, January 30, 1950.

7. In his late years, Lin Yaohua (2003a: 22–24) wrote *Teaching Notes on Social Anthropology* in which he reviewed the schools of critical theory and functionalism. Regarding studies of them in China, see Qiao Jian 1996 and Wang Mingming 1996. Regarding the historical school and Franz Boas's representative works, see Boas 1929 as well as Boas and Stocking 1974. For major works of functionalism, see Malinowski 1926; Radcliffe-Brown 1933; Firth 1957; and Kuper 2004.

8. Cai Jiaqi 1987: 25–52.

9. Lin Yaohua 2003a: 25.

10. Yang Shuyin 1944. Other theses written by Lin Yaohua's students who used this method include "A Study of Factory Workers: A Printing Factory in Chengdu" and "The Lama Temple in Zagunao" (Zhao Li and Zhu Hu 2007: 95–96).

11. Shen Baoyuan 1946: 6.

12. Shen Baoyuan 1946: 6.

13. Lin Yaohua 2003a: 457–60.

14. Fei got caught in a tiger trap, and Wang presumably died while traveling to get help for him (Fei Hsiao-tung [Fei Xiaotong] 2006: 268–71; and Arkush 1981: 66–67).

15. Shen Baoyuan 1946: 2.

16. Shen Baoyuan 1946: 2.

17. Shen Baoyuan 1946: 2.

18. Shen Baoyuan 1946: 17.

19. Shen Baoyuan 1946: 2.

20. Shen Baoyuan 1946: 3.

21. Shen Baoyuan 1946: 3–4.

22. Shen Baoyuan 1946: 5.

23. Shen Baoyuan 1946: 4.

24. Shen Baoyuan 1946: 4.

25. Shen Baoyuan 1946: 5.

26. Bai Jinjuan wrote "Peasant Education in Jiuliqiao" (Bai Jinjuan 1946); she was advised by Liao Taichu and graduated from Yenchjing University in the same year as Shen Baoyuan.

27. Shen Baoyuan 1946: 5.

28. According to his diary entry on November 18, 1940, Ye Shengtao (1894–1988) traveled with Gu Jiegang to Chongyiqiao (i.e., Hope Township) to visit Huamei Middle School and was treated to a meal by its president (Ye Shengtao 2004: 311). Ye was a famous educator; Gu Jiegang (1893–1980), a very famous historian. Under the jurisdiction of Hope Township, there were thirteen villages, one of which was called Huamei—likely getting the name from the time when Huamei Female Middle School relocated there (Chengdu shi difangzhi bianzuan weiyuanhui 2009: 425).

29. On August 15, 1945, the Japanese surrendered. The Chengdu campus of Yenching University returned to Beijing in the summer of 1946 (Yanjing daxue Chengdu xiaoyou hui 2007: 353).

30. Shen Baoyuan 1946: 10.

Chapter 12. Untangling Paoge Myth

1. Hobsbawm 1959: chapter 2.

2. Hobsbawm 1981: 42–43.

3. Hobsbawm 1981: 26.

4. Hobsbawm 1981: 26, 33.

5. Shen Baoyuan 1946: 42.

6. Shen Baoyuan 1946: 42.

7. Shen Baoyuan 1946: 43.

8. Shen Baoyuan 1946: 42–43.

9. Zhang Lan (1872–1955) was a Sichuan native and governor of the province in the early Republic. In 1941 he organized the Chinese League of Democratic

Organizations (Zhongguo minzhu zhengtuan tongmeng), which was renamed the China Democratic League in 1944 and Zhang was named president. He held several important positions in the early Communist government, including vice president of the Central People's Government, vice president of the People's Congress, and vice president of the Chinese People's Political Consultative Conference.

10. Wu Yue 2010: 150–55.

11. Li Gongpu (1900–1946) was an early leader of the China Democratic League and an educator. Wen Yiduo (1899–1946), another early leader of the league, was a well-known writer; his assassination occurred only a few days after Li's. Both actions were carried out by local military authorities in Yunnan Province.

12. Ran Chongquan n.d.

13. There are several biographies of Zhang Lan; see Feng Weigang 1991; An Ran 2005; and Xie Zengshou 2011.

14. Ou Shi 1946: 2.

15. Wu Yue 2010: 311.

16. One of ten marshals, He Long (1896–1969) was purged during the Cultural Revolution.

17. Wu Yue 2010.

18. Shen Baoyuan 1946: 41.

19. Fu Chongju 1987 [1909–10]: vol. 2, 48–50; Hirayama Shu 1911: 63; Wang Shunwu 1993: 61–65; and Maurer 1981: 37.

20. Regarding studies of underworlds in contemporary China, see Zhang Renshan 2001; Wang Dazhong 2002; Fan Hongfei 2003; Kang Shuhua 2004; Zhang Guoqi 2004; Dai Meiping 2005; and Zhao Ying 2011.

21. Li Zhuang 2012.

22. Tu Daozheng 2014. Zhou Yongkang (b. 1942) was a member of the Politburo Standing Committee, China's highest decision-making body, and the secretary of the Central Political and Legal Affairs Commission between 2007 and 2012. In that position he oversaw China's security apparatus and law enforcement agencies. Zhou became the first Standing Committee member to be tried. In June 2015 he was convicted of bribery, abuse of power, and the intentional disclosure of state secrets by the Court. Zhou was sentenced to life in prison.

23. "Liu Han, Liu Wei yishen beipanchu sixing" 2014; Areddy 2013; and Zhang Jing, Gui Tao, and Yu Li 2014.

24. Sun Jiang 2007.

25. Hobsbawm 1981: 17–19.

26. Yamamoto Shin 2008.

Appendix 5. Brief Comments on Texts, Myth, and History

1. Davis 1990; Kuhn 1990.

2. As a result, some studies, such as *Gowned Brothers and Bandits* (Paoge yu tufei), put the two together (Zhao Qing 1990).

3. de Certeau 1984: 23.

4. Li Jieren 1947 [1926]: 124–35; and Li Jieren 1980a [1936], 1980b [1936], and 1980 [1937]. For studies of Li Jieren's novels, see Wu Jialun and Wang Jinhou 1981;

Qin Gong 2002; Lei Bing 2005; Ding Fan and Li Xingyang 2007; Ng 2009; Yang Daixin 2011; and Yang Haitao 2012.

5. Wu Fuhui 1990: 264. Regarding the realist aspect of Sha Ting's novels, see Huang Manjun 1980, 1981, 1993; Sun Weike and Ji Wenjun 2012; and Ma Xueyong 2013.

6. Ginzburg 1982: xv; Spivak 1988; and Hershatter 1993: 117–18. Based on her study of widows in India, Gayatri Chakravorty Spivak (1988) believes that we cannot find their voice.

7. Hobsbawm 1959: 175.

8. Scott 1990: 18–19; and Guha 1996: 12. James Scott uses the term "hidden transcript" to characterize "discourse that takes place 'offstage,' beyond direct observation by powerholders." Therefore, the hidden transcript is derivative "in the sense that it consists of those offstage speeches, gestures, and practices that confirm, contradict, or inflect what appears in the public transcript" (Scott 1990: 4–5).

9. David W. Maurer (1981: 1) was a pioneer in studying the language of the underworld; he believes that "a subculture is a group of individuals—such as social, occupational, ethnic, or racial groups—who share certain common attitudes, associations, behavior patterns, and speech patterns."

Works Cited

An Ran. 2005. *Zhang Lan* [Zhang Lan]. Beijing: Taihai chubanshe.

Areddy, James T. 2013. "Amid Probe, Chinese Moguls Vanish: Prominent Executives Are Being Detained, Associates Say, in Sign of New Round of Political Infighting." *Wall Street Journal*, September 26.

Arkush, R. David. 1981. *Fei Xiaotong and Sociology in Revolutionary China*. Cambridge, Mass.: Council on East Asian Studies.

Ba Jin. 1985 [1932]. *Jia* [Family]. Beijing: Renmin wenxue chubanshe.

Bai Jinjuan. 1946. "Jiuliqiao de nongjia jiaoyu" [Peasant education in Jiuliqiao]. Thesis, Department of Sociology, Yenching University. Peking University Library.

"Baxian bamiao chang changshi guizhang" [Regulations of Bamiao market, Baxian]. N.d. Handwritten copy of Baxian Archives. Department of History, Sichuan University.

"Baxian tuanshou paituan tiaoli" [Regulations of local Baxian militia]. 1813. Handwritten copy of Baxian Archives. Department of History, Sichuan University.

Beijing shi shehui kexue yanjiusuo shehuixue yanjiushi, ed. 1984. *Shehuixue yanjiu yu yingyong* [Sociology research and applications]. Beijing: Beijing shi shehui kexue yanjiusuo shehuixue yanjiushi.

Bernhardt, Kathryn. 1999. *Women and Property in China, 960–1949*. Stanford: Stanford University Press.

"Biancha baojia tiaogui" [Compiling baojia regulations]. 1850. Handwritten copy of Baxian Archives. Department of History, Sichuan University.

Boas, Franz. 1929. *Anthropology and Modern Life*. Crows Nest, New South Wales, Australia: George Allen & Unwin Ltd.

Boas, Franz, and George W. Stocking Jr. 1974. *A Franz Boas Reader: The Shaping of American Anthropology, 1883–1911*. Chicago: University of Chicago Press.

Boettcher, Cheryl. 1989. "Samuel T. Y. Seng and the Boone Library School." *Libraries and Culture* 24, no. 3 (Summer): 269–94.

Booth, Martin. 1999. *The Dragon Syndicates: The Global Phenomenon of the Triads*. New York: Carroll & Graf Publishers, Inc.

Bossen, Laurel. 2002. *Chinese Women and Rural Development: Sixty Years of Change in Lu Village, Yunnan*. Lanham, Md.: Rowman & Littlefield Publishers.

Brace, A. J. 1936. "Some Secret Societies in Szechwan." *Journal of the West China Border Research Society* 8 (1936): 178.

Buck, John Lossing. 1930. *Chinese Farm Economy.* Chicago: University of Chicago Press. Chinese translation by Zhang Lüluan, *Zhongguo nongjia jingji.* Shanghai: Shangwu yinshuguan, 1936.

———. 1937. *Land Utilization in China.* Shanghai: University of Nanking.

Cai Jiaqi. 1987. "Shilun minzuxue tianye diaocha de lilun yu fangfa" [Theories and methodologies in ethnological fieldwork], in Yunnansheng minzu yanjiusuo, ed., *Minzu yanjiu wenji: Yunnansheng minzu yanjiusuo jiansuo sanshi zhounian jinian* [An essay collection: The thirtieth anniversary of the establishment of the Institute of Minority Studies in Yunnan], 22–52. Kunming: Yunnan minzu chubanshe.

Cai Shaoqing. 1987. *Zhongguo jindai huidang shi yanjiu* [A study of Chinese secret societies]. Beijing: Zhonghua shuju.

———. 1990. *Zhongguo mimi shehui* [Chinese secret societies]. Hangzhou: Zhejiang renmin chubanshe.

Cai Xinghua. 2008. "Wode paoge jingli" [My experiences in the Gowned Brothers], in Zhengxie Kaixian weiyuanhui, ed., *Kaixian wenshi ziliao* [Kaixian literary and historical materials], no. 4, 234–40. Shenyang: Liaoning jiaoyu chubanshe.

Cao Shuji. 2001. *Zhongguo renkou shi* [History of Chinese population], vol. 5, *The Qing.* Shanghai: Fudan daxue chubanshe.

Cao Shuji and Liu Shigu. 2015. *Chuantong Zhongguo diquan jiegou jiqi yanbian* [The structure and transformation of landownership in traditional China]. Shanghai: Shanghai jiaotong daxue chubanshe.

Cao Yunsheng. 1999. "Jiefang chuqi wojun jieguan Xinfanxian de gaikuang" [The general situation of the PLA's early stage of takeover in Xinfan county], in Zhengxie Sichuan sheng Xindu xian weiyuanhui wenshi ziliao weiyuanhui, ed., *Xindu wenshi* [Historical materials of Xindu county], vol. 15, 1–2. Xindu.

Chen Jing. 2001. "Zhang Henshui yanjiu shuping" [A review of studies of Zhang Henshui studies]. *Nanjing shifan daxue wenxueyuan xuebao* [Journal of the college of liberal arts of Nanjing Normal University], no. 3: 48–53.

Chen Maozhao. 1983. "Chengdu de chaguan" [Chengdu Teahouses]. *Chengdu wenshi ziliao xuanji* [Selection of Chengdu literary and historical materials] 4: 178–93.

Chen Shaoting. 1979. *Wusi xin wenhua yundong de yiyi* [Significance of the May Fourth New Culture Movement]. Taipei: Baijie chubanshe.

Chen Shisong. 2005. *Daqianxi: "Huguang tian Sichuan" lishi jiedu* [Great migration: Historical materials on flood of Hubei and Hunan migrants into Sichuan]. Chengdu: Sichuan renmin chubanshe.

Chen Shunong. 1981. "Sichuan paoge yu Xinhai geming" [Gowned Brothers in Sichuan and the 1911 Revolution], in *Xinhai geming huiyi lu* [A collection of memories of the 1911 Revolution], vol. 3, 174–76. Beijing: Wenshi ziliao chubanshe.

Chen Weizun. 2010. "Wujinde aisi shenshende huainian: Huiyi waizufu Shen Zurong xiansheng" [Endless sadness and deep remembrances: Memories of my grandfather Shen Zurong]. September 12, 2010. http://zwf251.blog.sohu.com/. Accessed July 2, 2014.

Chen Xulu, Gu Tinglong, and Wang Xi, eds. 1979. *Xinhai geming qianhou: Sheng*

Xuanhuai dang'an ziliao xuanji zhiyi [Before and after the 1911 Revolution: Collection of Sheng Xuanhuai's archives, part I]. Shanghai: Shanghai renmin chubanshe.

Cheng Bicheng. 2014. "Minguo xiangcun jiaoyu yundong jiqi dui nongcun jiaoyu gaige de qishi" [The rural education movement in Republican China and its inspiration for rural educational reforms]. *Jiaoxue yu guanli* [Teaching and administration]. February 22.

Cheng Huanwen. 2007. "Shen Zurong guju xunli" [A note about visiting Shen Zurong's former residence]. *Tushu qingbao zhishi* [Knowledge about library information], no. 6: 104–107.

Cheng Yu. 2005. "Qing zhi Minguo de xuqie xisu yu shehui bianqian" [Practice of concubinage and the social transformation from Qing to Republican China]. PhD dissertation, Fudan University.

Chengdu jianghu haidi [The Bottom of the Ocean of Chengdu River and Lake Runners]. 1934. Chengdu: Liushuang heke ban.

Chengdu jianghu haidi quanji [A complete collection for the Bottom of the Ocean of Chengdu River and Lake Runners]. 1922. Chengdu: Zhonghuan xinjuan.

Chengdu shi difangzhi bianzuan weiyuanhui, ed. 2009. *Chengdu shizhi, zongzhi* [Gazetteer of Chengdu, general annual]. Chengdu: Chengdu shidai chubanshe.

Chesneaux, Jean. 1971. *Secret Societies in the Nineteenth and Twentieth Centuries.* Ann Arbor: University of Michigan Press.

———, ed. 1972. *Popular Movements and Secret Societies in China 1840–1950.* Stanford: Stanford University Press.

"Chongqing banghui diaocha" [Survey of gangsters in Chongqing]. 1950. Manuscript copy (no archival category number). Bureau of Sichuan Provincial Public Security.

Ci Jun. 1942. "Chengdu de chaguan" [Teahouses in Chengdu]. Parts 1–2, *Huaxi wanbao* [Huaxi evening news], January 28–29.

Cishu bianyishe. 1947. *Xin zhexue shehuixue jieshi cidian* [New analytic dictionary of philosophy and sociology]. Shanghai: Guanghua chubanshe.

Cohen, Myron L. 1990. "Lineage Organization in North China." *Journal of Asian Studies* 49, no. 3: 509–34.

Cui Xianchang. 1982. "Jiu Chengdu chaguan sumiao" [A literary sketch of Chengdu teahouses]. *Longmenzhen* [Folk tales] no. 12: 92–102.

Dai Meiping. 2005. "Shilun dangdai Zhongguo de heishehui xingzhi zuzhi fanzui" [On the organized crimes of contemparary China underworlds]. PhD dissertation, East China Political Science and Law College.

Dai Xuanzhi. 1990. *Zhongguo mimi zongjiao yu mimi huishe* [Chinese secret religions and secret societies]. Taipei: Shangwu yinshu guan.

Darnton, Robert. 1985. *The Great Cat Massacre and Other Episodes in French Cultural History.* New York: Vintage Books.

Davie, James D. 1997. "Missing Presumed Dead? The Baikovyi Iazyk of the St. Petersburg Mazuriki and Other Pre-Soviet Argots." *Slavonica* 4, no. 1: 28–45.

Davis, Fei-Ling. 1977. *Primitive Revolutionaries of China: A Study of Secret Societies in the Late Nineteenth Century.* Honolulu: University Press of Hawaii.

Davis, Natalie Zemon. 1984. *The Return of Martin Guerre*. Cambridge, Mass.: Harvard University Press.

————. 1990. *Fiction in the Archives: Pardon Tales and Their Tellers in Sixteenth-Century France*. Stanford: Stanford University Press.

De Certeau, Michel. 1984. *The Practice of Everyday Life*. Trans. Steven F. Rendall. Berkeley: University of California Press.

Decennial Reports on the Trade, Industries Etc. of the Ports Open to Foreign Commerce and on the Condition and Development of the Treaty Port Provinces. Chungking, 1891.

Deng Xihou. 1986. "Wozai Chuanxi qiyi de jingguo" [My experience in the West Sichuan uprising], in Zhengxie wenshi ziliao yanjiu weiyuanhui, ed., *Wenshi ziliao xuanji* [Selection of literary and historical materials], nos. 17–19: 15–25. Beijing: Zhongguo wenshi chubanshe.

Diamant, Neil Jeffrey. 2000. *Revolutionizing the Family: Politics, Love, and Divorce in Urban and Rural China, 1949–1968*. Berkeley: University of California Press.

Dittmer, C. G. 1918. "An Estimate of the Standard of Living in China." *Quarterly Journal of Economics* 33 (November): 107–28.

Du Daozheng. 2014. "Yeyi Zhou Yongkang an de genben qishi" [Basic inspiration behind Zhou Yongkang's case]. *Yanhuang chunqiu* [History of Yanhuang], no. 9: 9–12.

Duara, Prasenjit. 1988a. *Culture, Power, and the State: Rural North China, 1900–1942*. Stanford: Stanford University Press.

————. 1988b. "Superscribing Symbols: The Myth of Guandi, Chinese God of War." *Journal of Asian Studies* 47, no. 4: 778–95.

Eastman, Lloyd E. 1986. "Nationalist China during the Nanking Decade, 1927–1937," in John King Fairbank, Denis Crispin Twitchett, and Albert Feuerwerker, eds., *Cambridge History of China*, vol. 13, *Republican China, 1912–1949*, Part 2, 116–67. Cambridge: Cambridge University Press.

Edwards, Dwight W. 1959. *Yenching University*. New York: United Board for Christian Higher Education in Asia.

Fairbank, John King. 1983. *The United States and China*. Fourth edition. Cambridge, Mass.: Harvard University Press.

Fan Hongfei. 2003. "Heishehui fanzui gainian jieding jiqi duice xuanze" [Conceptual scope of underworld crimes and their response options]. PhD dissertation, East China Political Science and Law College.

Fan Shaozeng. 1982. "Huiyi wozai Sichuan paoge zhong de zuzhi shenghuo" [Recalling my life in the Sichuan Paoge organization], 148–60, in Wenshi ziliao bianzuan weiyuanhui, ed., *Wenshi ziliao xuanji* [Selection of literary and historical materials], no. 84: 204–22. Beijing: Wenshi chubanshe.

Fang Zhirong and Zhou Jianhua. 2011. "Renkou, gengdi, yu chuantong nongcun juluo zi zuzhi: Yi Chuanxi pingyuan linpan juluo tixi (1644–1911) weili" [Population, arable land, and traditional rural settlements: Concerning the example of the system of West Sichuan Plain bamboo-grove settlements, 1644–1911]. *Zhongguo yuanlin* [China gardens], no. 6: 83–87.

Fawu bianji xiaozu, ed. 2001. *Jiating hao liufa quanshu: Xianfa, minfa, xingfa* [Complete six laws for family use: Constitutional, civil, and criminal law]. Taipei: Huawenwang gufen youxian gongsi.

Fei Hsiao-tung (Fei Xiaotong). 1939. *Peasant Life in China: A Field Study of Country Life in the Yangzi Valley.* New York: Oxford University Press.

———. 1990. *Yunnan sancun* [Three villages in Yunnan]. Tianjin: Tianjin renmin chubanshe.

———. 1991. "Fifty Years Investigation in the Yao Mountains," in Jacques Lemoine and Chien Chiao, eds., *The Yao of South China: Recent International Studies,* 17–36. Paris: Pangu, Editions de l'A.F.E.Y.

———. 1992. *From the Soil: The Foundations of Chinese Society.* Berkeley: University of California Press.

———. 2006. *Liushang Yaoshan* [Six trips to the Yao mountains]. Beijing: Zhongyang minzu daxue chubanshe.

Fei Hsiao-tung (Fei Xiaotong) and Wang Tonghui. 1988. *Hualanyao shehui zuzhi* [Social organization of Hualanyao]. Nanjing: Jiangsu renmin chubanshe.

Feng Hefa. 1932. *Nongcun shehuixue dagang* [Outline of rural sociology]. Shanghai: Liming shuju.

Feng Weigang. 1991. *Zhang Lan* [Zhang Lan]. Chengdu: Sichuan renmin chubanshe.

Firth, Raymond, ed. 1957. *Man and Culture: An Evaluation of the Work of Bronislaw Malinowski.* London: Routledge & Kegan Paul Ltd.

Fong, Shiaw-Chian. 1997. "Fei Xiaotong's Theory of Rural Development and Its Application: A Critical Appraisal." *Issues and Studies* 33, no. 10 (October): 20–43.

Fu Chongju. 1987 [1909–10]. *Chengdu tonglan* [Investigation of Chengdu]. Originally 8 vols. printed by Chengdu tongsu baoshe in 1909–10. Reprinted in 2 vols. by Bashu shushe, Chengdu.

Fu Zengyang. 1989. "Shixi Sichuan junfa changqi hunzhan zhiyin" [A study of the causes of the extended, fierce warfare of the Sichuan warlords]. *Sichuan shifan daxue xuebao* [Journal of Sichuan Normal University], no. 6: 80–84.

Fung, Edmund S. K. 2010. *The Intellectual Foundations of Chinese Modernity: Cultural and Political Thought in the Republican Era.* New York: Cambridge University Press.

Gamble, Sidney D., and John Stewart Burgess. 1921. *Peking, a Social Survey.* First edition. George H. Doran. Reprint, Leiden: Global Oriental, 2011.

Gao Wangling. 2005. *Zudian guanxi xinlun: Dizhu, nongmin he dizu* [A new study of tenancy relations: Landlords, peasants, and land rent]. Shanghai: Shanghai shudian.

Geng Yunzhi and Chen Yuwu. 2009. *Kaifang de wenhua guannian ji qita: Jinian xin wenhua yundong jiushi zhounian* [Cultural concept of the opening up and related matters: Ninetieth commemoration of the New Culture Movement]. Beijing: Guojia tushuguan chubanshe.

Gilmartin, Christina K., Gail Hershatter, Lisa Rofel, and Tyrene White, eds. 1994. *Engendering China: Women, Culture, and the State.* Cambridge, Mass.: Harvard University Press.

Ginzburg, Carlo. 1982. *The Cheese and the Worms: The Cosmos of a Sixteenth-Century Miller.* Trans. John and Anne Tedeschi. New York: Penguin Books.

Golas, Peter J. 1977. "Early Ch'ing Guilds," 555–80 in G. William Skinner, ed., 1977. *The City in Late Imperial China.* Stanford: Stanford University Press.

Goldman, Merle. 1977. *Modern Chinese Literature in the May Fourth Era*. Cambridge, Mass.: Harvard University Press.

Grainger, A. 1917. "Chinese New Year Customs." *West China Missionary News*, no. 1: 5–11.

———. 1918. "Popular Customs in West China." *West China Missionary News*, no. 6: 5–8.

Gu Fu. 1924. *Nongcun shehuixue* [Rural sociology]. Shanghai: Shangwu yinshu guan.

Guan Hanqing. 1958a. "Dandao hui" [Single Broadsword meeting], in *Guan Hanqing xiquji* [A collection of Guan Hanqing's plays], 1–50. Beijing: Zhongguo jiju chubanshe.

———. 1958b. "Gantian dongdi Dou E yuan" [Dou E's injustice that moved the world], in *Guan Hanqing xiquji* [A collection of Guan Hanqing's plays], 487–924. Beijing: Zhongguo xiju chubanshe.

Guan Qun. 1948. "Chengdu de 'paoge'" [The So-called Gowned Brothers in Chengdu]. *Zhoumo guancha* [Weekend observer] 3, no. 7: 14.

Guan Zhigang. 1992. "Lun kangrizhanzheng shiqi de xin shenghuo yundong" [A study of the New Life Movement during the time of the War of Resistance against Japan]. *Kangri zhanzheng yanjiu* [Studies of the War of Resistance against Japan], no. 3: 143–59.

Guha, Ranajit. 1996. "The Small Voice of History," in Shahid Amin and Dipesh Chakrabarty, eds., *Subaltern Studies, IX: Writing on South Asian History and Society*, 1–12. Oxford: Oxford University Press.

Guo Hanming and Meng Guangyu. 1944. *Sichuan zudian wenti* [Tenant issues in Sichuan]. Chongqing: Shangwu yinshuguan.

Guo Jian et al. 1998. *Zhonghua wenhua tongzhi, zhidu wenhua dian, falü zhi* [General annals of Chinese culture; institutions and culture; laws]. Shanghai: Shanghai renmin chubanshe.

Guomin gongbao [Citizens' daily]. 1914.

Guomindang shengzhiwei. 1942. "Hanqing chaban Weiyuan xinchang gelaohui" [Request to investigate Gowned Brothers in Xinchang, Weiyuan county]. October 15. Sichuan Provincial Archives, file nos. 186–1385: 158–60.

Han Mingmo. 1997. "Zhongguo shehuixue diaocha fangfa he fangfalun fazhan de sange lichengbei" [Investigative methodologies of Chinese sociology and three milestones in the development of methodologies]. *Beijing daxue xuebao* [Journal of Peking University], no. 4: 5–15.

Harrison, Henrietta. 2005. *The Man Awakened from Dreams: One Man's Life in a North China Village, 1857–1942*. Stanford: Stanford University Press.

Hayford, Charles Wishart. 1990. *To the People: James Yen and Village China*. New York: Columbia University Press.

He Jianhua. 2008. "Yan Yangchu de pingjiao yundong jiqi xianzheng gaige shiyan" [James Yen's common education movement and the experience of county administrative reform]. *Dongnan xueshu* [Academic journal in Southeast China], no. 1: 61–68.

He Yimin, ed. 2002. *Biange yu fazhan: Zhongguo neilu chengshi Chengdu xiandaihua yanjiu* [Reform and development: A study of modernization in the Chinese interior city Chengdu]. Chengdu: Sichuan daxue chubanshe.

Hershatter, Gail. 1993. "The Subaltern Talks Back: Reflections on Subaltern Theory and Chinese History." *Positions* 1, no. 1: 117–18.

Hirayama Shu. 1911. *Shina kakumei oyobi himitsu kessha* [Revolutionaries organizations and secret societies in China]. *Nihon oyobi Nihonjin* [Japan and Japanese], no. 56. Tokyo: Seikyōsha.

Ho Ping-ti. 1966. "The Geographic Distribution of Huikuan (Landsmannschaften) in Central and Upper Yangtze Provinces." *Tsinghua Journal of Chinese Studies* 5, no. 2 (December): 120–52.

Hobsbawm, E. J. 1959. *Primitive Rebels: Studies in Archaic Forms of Social Movement in the 19th and 20th Centuries.* New York: Frederick A. Praeger.

———. 1981. *Bandits.* Revised edition. New York: Pantheon Books.

———. 1983. "Introduction: Inventing Traditions," in Eric Hobsbawm and Terence Ranger, eds., *The Invention of Tradition,* 1–14. Cambridge University Press.

Hu Guotai. 1993. "Jiapu suozai jiazu guifan yu qingdai lüling: Yi qianliang xingming yu shehui zhixu weili" [Clan regulations and Qing laws recorded by genealogies: Exemplified by money, grain taxes, criminal laws, and social order], in Lianhe bao wenhua jijinhui guoxue wenxian guan, ed., *Diliujie Yazhou zupu xueshu yantaohui huiyi jilu* [Record of the Sixth Symposium on Asian genealogy scholarship], 267–311. Taipei: Lianhe bao wenhua jijinhui guoxue wenxian guan.

Hu Hansheng. 1988. *Sichuan jindai shishi sankao* [Three studies of modern Sichuan]. Chongqing: Chongqing chubanshe.

Huang Manjun. 1980. "Sha Ting 'Zuolian' shiqi dui xianshi zhuyi de tansuo" [Sha Ting's exploring of realism during the period of the Left League]. *Zhongguo xiandai wenxue yanjiu congkan* [Studies of modern Chinese literature], no. 3: 100–21.

———. 1981. "Lun Sha Ting chuangzuo de xianshi zhuyi tese" [Special features of the realism in Sha Ting's works]. *Huazhong shifang daxue xuebao* [Journal of Central China Normal University], no. 3: 4–13.

———. 1993. "Lun Sha Ting de wenhua yishi yu xianshi zhuyi chuangzuo" [A study of Sha Ting's cultural consciousness and realist works]. *Zhongguo xiandai wenxue yanjiu congkan* [Studies of modern Chinese literature], no. 3: 117–37.

Huang Quansheng and Yang Guanghua. 2005. "Sichuan yimin diming yu 'Huguang tian Sichuan': Sichuan yimin diming kongjian fenbu he yimin de shengji bili tantao" [Migrant place-names and the flood of Hubei and Hunan migrants into Sichuan: Inquiry into spatial distribution of names related to migrants and ratios of provincial registrations]. *Xinan shifan daxue xuebao* [Journal of Southwest China Normal University], no. 3: 111–18.

Huang Tianhua. 2008. "Guojia tongyi yu difang zhengzheng: Yi Sichuan 'Er Liu dazhan' wei kaocha zhongxin" [National unity and local political struggles: A case study of the war between two Liu warlords in Sichuan]. *Sichuan shifan daxue xuebao* [Journal of Southwest China Normal University], no. 4: 94–101.

Huang Tinggui et al. 1733. *Sichuan tongzhi* (Yongzheng) [Comprehensive gazetteer of Sichuan (Yongzheng regime)].

Huang, Philip C. C. 1985. *The Peasant Economy and Social Change in North China.* Stanford: Stanford University Press.

———. 1996. *Civil Justice in China: Representation and Practice in the Qing.* Stanford: Stanford University Press.

———. 2001. *Code, Custom, and Legal Practice in China: The Qing and the Republic Compared*. Stanford: Stanford University Press.

Jaschok, Maria, and Suzanne Miers, ed. 1994. *Women and Chinese Patriarchy: Submission, Servitude, and Escape*. Hong Kong: University of Hong Kong Press.

Jiang Bo, ed. 2010. *Shenmi wenhua* [Secret cultures]. Beijing: Zhongguo wuzhi chubanshe.

Jinniuqu difangzhi bianzuan weiyuanhui, ed. 1996. *Chengdu shi jinniuqu zhi* [Gazetteer of Jinniu district of Chengdu]. Chengdu: Sichuan daxue chubanshe.

Kang Shuhua. 2004. "Zhongguo dalu heishehui xingzhi zuzhi fanzui de fazhan qushi" [Developmental trend in the organized crimes of mainland China's underworlds]. *Faxue zazhi* [Law journal], no. 3: 11–12.

Kaplan, Charles D., Helmut Kämpe, and José Antonio Flores Farfán. 1990. "Argots as a Code-Switching Process: A Case Study of the Sociolinguistic Aspects of Drug Subcultures," in Rodolfo Jacobson, ed., *Codeswitching as a Worldwide Phenomenon*, 141–58. New York: Peter Lang.

Kapp, Robert A. 1973. *Szechwan and the Chinese Republic: Provincial Militarism and Central Power, 1911–1938*. New Haven: Yale University Press.

Keehn, Martha McKee, ed. 1993. *Y. C. James Yen's Thought on Mass Education and Rural Reconstruction: China and Beyond: Selected Papers from an International Conference Held in Shijiazhuang, China, May 27–June 1, 1990*. New York: International Institute of Rural Reconstruction.

Ko, Dorothy Y. 1994. *Teachers of the Inner Chambers: Women and Culture in China, 1573–1722*. Stanford: Stanford University Press.

Kuang Shanji and Yang Guangyan, ed. 1991. *Sichuan junfa shi* [History of Sichuan warlords]. Chengdu: Sichuan renmin chubanshe.

Kuhn, Philip. 1990. *Soulstealers: The Chinese Sorcery Scare of 1768*. Cambridge, Mass.: Harvard University Press.

Kulp, Daniel H. 1925. *Country Life in South China*. New York: Columbia University.

Kuper, Adam, ed. 2004. *The Social Anthropology of Radcliffe-Brown*. London: Routledge.

Ladurie, Emmanuel. 1978. *Montaillou: The Promised Land of Error*. Trans. Barbara Bray. New York: G. Braziller.

Lan Bingkui et al. N.d. *Daxian zhi* [Gazetteer of Daxian county]. Republican period (1912–1949).

Lan Yong. 1996. "Qingdai xi'nan yimin huiguan mingshi yu zhineng yanjiu" [A study of names of Qing dynasty native place associations and their functions]. *Zhongguo shi yanjiu* [Researches in Chinese history], no. 4:16–26.

Lei Bing. 2005. "'Gaihang de zuojia': Shizhang Li Jieren juese rentong de kunjiong (1950–1962)" [The writer who changed his profession: A dilemma of Mayor Li Jieren's identity]. *Lishi yanjiu* [Historical research], no. 1: 20–33.

Lei Jieqiong and Shui Shizheng. 1989. "Yanjing daxue shehui fuwu gongzuo sanshi nian" [Thirty years of social service work at Yanching University], in Yanda wenshi ziliao bianweihui, ed., *Yanda wenshi ziliao* [Historical materials of Yenching University], no. 4: 49–58. Beijing: Beijing daxue chubanshe.

Leng Xueren. 1991. *Jianghu yinyu hanghua de shenmi shijie* [Argots and the secret world of the river and lake runners]. Shijiazhuang: Hebei renmin chubanshe.

Leslau, Wolf. 1964. *Ethiopian Argots.* London: Mouton & Co.

Li Anzhai, ed. 1936. *Wushu yu yuyan* [Witchcraft and language]. Shanghai: Shangwu yinshu guan.

———. 1934. *Meixue* [Aesthetics]. Shanghai: Shijie shuju.

———. 1935. *Yili yu liji zhi shehuixue de yanjiu* [A sociological study of the *Book of Rituals* and the *Book of Rites*]. Shanghai: Shangwu yinshu guan.

———. 1945. *Yiyixue* [Significs]. Chongqing: Shangwu yinshu guan.

Li Deying. 2006. *Guojia faling yu minjian xiguan: Chengdu pingyuan zudian zhidu xintan* [State laws and local practice: A new study of the tenancy system of the Chengdu Plain]. Beijing: Zhongguo shehui kexue chubanshe.

———. 2011. "Minguo shiqi Chengdu pingyuan xiangcun jizhen yu nongmin shenghuo: Jianlun nongcun jiceng shichang shequ lilun" [Rural markets and peasant life in the Chengdu Plain during the Republican era: A discussion of both rural low-level markets and community theory]. *Sichuan daxue xuebao* [Journal of Sichuan University], no. 3: 12–21.

Li Fuhua and Feng Zuozhe. 1994. *Zhongguo minjian zongjiao shi* [History of Chinese popular religions]. Taipei: Wenjin chubanshe.

Li Jieren. 1947 [1926]. "Shimin de ziwei" [Residents' self-protection], in Li Jieren, *Haoren jia* [The good family], 124–35. Shanghai: Zhonghua shuju.

———. 1980a [1936]. *Baofeng yuqian* [Before the storm], in *Li Jieren xuanji* [A selection of Li Jieren's works], vol. 1, 275–662. Originally published in Shanghai: Zhonghua shuju. Reprint, Chengdu: Sichuan renmin chubanshe.

———. 1980b [1936]. *Sishui weilan* [Ripple on stagnant water], in *Li Jieren xuanji* [A selection of Li Jieren's works], vol. 1, 3–271. Originally published in Shanghai: Zhonghua shuju. Reprint, Chengdu: Sichuan renmin Chubanshe.

———. 1980 [1937]. *Dabo* [The great wave], in *Li Jieren xuanji* [A selection of Li Jieren's works] vol. 2, Parts 1–3, 3–1631. Originally published by Shanghai: Zhonghua shuju. Reprint, Chengdu: Sichuan renmin Chubanshe.

Li Jinghan. 1929. *Beiping jiaowai zhi xiangcun jiating diaocha* [A survey of rural families past Beiping's suburbs]. Shanghai: Shangwu yinshu guan.

———, ed. 1933. *Dingxian shehui gaikuang diaocha* [Investigation of the social conditions in Ding County]. Originally published by Zhonghua pingmin jiaoyu cujinhui. Reprint, Beijing: Zhongguo renmin daxue chubanshe, 1986.

Li Mufeng. 1947. "Luetan Sichuan de 'paoge'" [A summary talk on the Gowned Brothers in Sichuan]. *Chahua* [Tea talk], no. 12: 81–84.

Li Rong. 1922. *Shisanfeng shuwu quanji* [Complete collections of the Shisanfeng study]. Pidu, vol. 1. Chengdu: Diyi shushe.

Li Weizhong. 2009. "Zhishi fenzi 'xiaxiang' yu jindai Zhongguo xiangcun biange de kunjing: Dui 1930 niandai xianzheng jianshe shiyan de jiexi" [Intellectuals who were sent to the countryside and the difficult situation of rural reform in modern China: Analysis of county administrative construction experiments of the 1920s and 1930s]. *Nankai xuebao* [Journal of Nankai University], no. 1: 115–25.

Li Wenhai, ed. 2005a. *Minguo shiqi shehui diaocha congbian: Hunyin jiating juan* [A series of social investigations of Republican China's society: Marriage and families]. Fuzhou: Fujian jiaoyu chubanshe.

————. 2005b. *Minguo shiqi shehui diaocha congbian: Shehui zuzhi juan* [A series of social investigations of Republican China: Social organization]. Fuzhou: Fujian jiaoyu chubanshe.

————. 2009. *Minguo shiqi shehui diaocha congbian: Xiangcun shehui juan* [A series of social investigations of Republican China: Rural society]. Parts 1–3. Fuzhou: Fujian jiaoyu chubanshe.

Li Yingfa. 1985. "Qingdai Chongqing diqu nongtian zudian guanxi zhong de jige wenti" [Several issues surrounding land tenancy relations in Qing Chongqing]. *Lishi dang'an* [Historical archives], no. 1: 81–90.

Li Yonghui. 2009. "Tian Jiaying zai Dafeng" [Tian Jiaying in Dafeng]. *Wenshi zazhi* [Journal of literature and history], no. 6: 17–19.

Li Zaiquan. 2006. "Guonan zhong de xiangcun shiye: Kangzhan shiqi Sichuan de xiangcun jianshe yundong-yi Pingjiao hui wei zhongxin de kaocha" [Rural programs in the national crisis: The Sichuan Rural Construction Movement during the War of Resistance against Japan, with an examination of the core of the Association for Common Education]. *Tianfu xinlun* [New studies of Sichuan], no. 2: 132–36.

Li Zhiqing et al. 1992. *Pixian zhi (Minguo)* [Gazetteer of Pixian (Republican period)]. Chengdu: Bashu shushe.

Li Zhuang. 2012. "Youren shuo Chongqing dahei moshou shangqianyi, guoku ruku cai 9.3 geyi" [It was said that Chongqing confiscated hundreds of billions when they beat the underworld, but only 903 millions were turned into the national treasury]. *Tencent news*. November 24, 2012. http://news.qq .com/a/20121124/000653.htm. Accessed September 15, 2014.

Li Zhuxi, Zeng Dejiu, and Huang Weihu, eds. 1987. *Jindai Sichuan wujia shiliao* [Historical materials concerning prices in modern Sichuan]. Chengdu: Sichuan kexue jishu chubanshe.

Li Zifeng, ed. 1940. *Haidi* [The bottom of the ocean]. Reprinted by Shanghai shudian in Republican series, Part 1, no. 16: 1–370.

Liang Shuming. 1936. *Xiangcun jianshe dayi* [General idea concerning rural construction]. Zouping: Xiangcun shudian.

————. 1937. *Xiangcun jianshe lilun* [The theory of rural construction]. Zouping: Xiangcun shudian.

————. 1941. *Da xiangcun jianshe pipan* [Answering criticisms of rural construction]. Shanghai: Zhongguo wenhua fuwushe.

————. 2011. *Xiangcun jianshe lilun* [Theory of rural construction]. Shanghai: Shanghai renmin chubanshe.

Liang Xisheng et al. 1999. "1950 nian Xinfanxian pingpan jiaofei shimo" [All aspects of the suppression of bandits in 1950 Xinfan county], in Zhengxie Sichuan sheng Xindu xian weiyuanhui wenshi ziliao weiyuanhui, ed., *Xindu wenshi* [Historical materials of Xindu county], vol. 15, 3–27.

————. 2008. "Qingdai Sichuan de tudi qingzhang yu yimin shehui de fazhan" [Land inspection and the development of migrant society in Qing dynasty Sichuan]. *Tianfu xinlun* [New studies of Sichuan], no. 3: 69–74.

Liao Taichu and Yang Shusheng. 1941. "Zhongguo jinri de xuetu jiaoyu" [Apprentice education in today's China]. *Jiaoyu xuebao* [Bulletin of education], no. 6: 163–76.

Liao T'ai-ch'u. 1947. "The Ko Lao Hui in Szechuan." *Pacific Affairs* 20 (June): 161–73.

Lin Shourong and Long Dai. 1984. "Sichuan junfa yu yapianyan" [Sichuan warlords and opium]. *Sichuan daxue xuebao* [Journal of Sichuan University], no. 3: 101–106.

Lin Yaohua. 1931. "Baizu" [Worshipping ancestors], in *Yixu zongzu de yanjiu* [A study of clans in Yixu], 244–48. Beijing: Sanlian shudian, 2000.

———. 1935a. *Yixu zongzu de yanjiu* [A study of clans in Yixu]. Master's thesis, Department of Sociology, Yenching University. Published by Sanlian shudian, 2000.

———. 1935b. "Zongfa yu jiazu" [The clan system and the family]. *Shehui yanjiu* [Social research], no. 79: 237–44.

———. 1936. "Cong renleixue de guandian kaocha Zhongguo zongzu xiangcun" [An anthropological examination of clans in rural China]. *Shehuixue jie* [Field of sociology], vol. 9: 125–42.

———. 1947a. *The Golden Wing: A Sociological Study of Chinese Familism.* London: K. Paul, Trench, Trubner.

———. 1947b. *Liangshan Yijia* [Yi families in Liangshan]. Shanghai: Shangwu yinshu guan.

———. 1977. *Jinchi* [The golden wing]. Trans. Song He. Taipei: Taiwan guiguan tushu gongsi.

———. 1985. *Minzuxue yanjiu* [Research in ethnology]. Beijing: Zhongguo shehui kexue.

———. 1989. *Jinyi: Zhongguo jiazu zhidu de shehuixue yanjiu* [The golden wing: A sociological study of China's clan system]. Trans. Zhuang Kongshao and Lin Zongcheng. Beijing: Sanlian shudian.

———. 1990. "New China's Ethnology: Research and Prospects," in Gregory Eliyu Guldin, ed., *Anthropology in China: Defining the Discipline,* 141–61. Armonk, N.Y.: M.E. Sharpe.

———. 1997. *Minzuxue tonglun* [General survey of ethnology]. Beijing: Zhongyang minzu daxue chubanshe.

———. 2003a. *Shehui renleixue jiangyi* [Teaching notes on social anthropology]. Xiamen: Lujiang chubanshe.

———. 2003b. "A Tentative Discussion of the Survival of the Concept of Rank in Contemporary Liangshan Yi Areas." *Chinese Sociology and Anthropology* 36, no. 1 (Fall): 46–62.

Ling Guangfu. 1949. "Sichuan gelaohui wenti zhi yanjiu" [Research into the issue of the Sworn Brotherhood Society in Sichuan]. Thesis, Department of Sociology, West China Union University. Housed at Department of History, Sichuan University.

Link, E. Perry. 1981. *Mandarin Ducks and Butterflies: Popular Fiction in Early Twentieth-Century Chinese Cities.* Berkeley: University of California Press.

Liu Chonglai. 2006. "Minguo shiqi xiangcun jianshe yundong shulue" [A review of the rural construction movement in Republican China]. *Chongqing shehui kexue* [Chongqing Social sciences], no. 5: 74–85.

———. 2007. *Zhongguo xibu xiangcun jianshe de xianqu zhe: Lu Zuofu yu minguo xiangcun jianshe yanjiu* [Pioneer of rural construction in West China: Lu Zuofu and rural construction in Republican China]. Beijing: Remin chubanshe.

"Liu Han, Liu Wei yishen beipanchu sixing" [Liu Han and Liu Weiyi are sentenced to death]. 2014. *Nanfang zhoumo* [Southern weekly]. May 23.

Liu Shiliang. 1975 [1939]. *Hanliu quanshi* [Complete history of the Hanliu]. Guting shuwu: n.p.

Liu Wennan. 2013. "Guixun richang shenghuo: Xin shenghuo yundong yu xiandai guojia de zhili" [Disciplining daily life: The New Life Movement and governance of the modern state]. *Nanjing daxue xuebao* [Journal of Nanjing University], no. 5: 89–102.

Liu Yuan. ca. 1790. "Shuzhong xinnian zhuzhici" [Bamboo-branch poetry on the Chinese New Year in Sichuan], in Lin Kongyi, ed., *Chengdu zhuzhi ci* [A collection on Chengdu bamboo-branch poems], 125–30. Chengdu: Sichuan renmin chubanshe, 1986.

Liu Zhenggang. 1991. "Qingdai Sichuan de Guangdong yimin huiguan" [Native place associations of migrants from Guangdong in Qing Sichuan]. *Qingshi yanjiu* [Research in Qing history], no. 4: 10–15.

Liu Zhengmei. 1997. "Kangzhan qianhou Guomindang zhongyang dui Sichuan de kongzhi" [The Nationalist Party's control of Sichuan before and after the War of Resistance against Japanese]. *Minguo yanjiu* [Research in Republican China], no. 3: 16–17.

Liu, Jianhong, Lening F. Zhang, and Steven Messner, eds. 2001. *Crime and Social Control in a Changing China*. Westport, Conn.: Greenwood Publishing Group.

Lu, Xinyu. 2010. "Rural Reconstruction, the Nation-State, And China's Modernity Problem. Reflections on Liang Shuming's Rural Reconstruction Theory and Its Practice" (trans. Zhu Ping and Adrian Thieret), in Tianyu Cao, Xueping Zhong, and Kebin Liao, eds., *Culture and Social Transformations in Reform Era China*, 235–56. Leiden: Brill.

Lu Xun. 1981. "Zhufu" [Blessings for New Year], in *Lu Xun quanji* [A complete collection of Lu Xun's works], vol. 2, 643–59. Beijing: Renmin wenxue chubanshe.

Lu Zhenxiang. 1987. "Sanshi niandai xiangcun jianshe yundong de chubu kaocha" [An examination of thirty years of the Rural Construction Movement]. *Zhengzhi xue yanjiu* [Research in political science], no. 4: 37–44.

Lü Pingdeng. 1936. *Sichuan nongcun jingji* [Rural economy in Sichuan]. Shanghai: Shangwu yinshuguan.

Lü Simian. 2011. *Zhongguo jindai shi, 1840–1949* [Modern Chinese history, 1840–1949]. Shanghai: Huadong shifan daxue chubanshe.

Lü Zuoxie. 1982. "Ming Qing shiqi de huiguan bingfei gongshangye hanghui" [Native place associations in Ming and Qing were not guilds]. *Zhongguo shi yanjiu* [Research in Chinese history], no. 2: 91–104.

Luo Xunan. 2012. "1935 nian 'Zhonghua minguo xingfa' dui Zhongguo chuantongfa de jicheng" [Criminal law of Republican China in 1935 concerning China's traditional laws of inheritance]. *Shehui kexue jia* [Social scientists], no. 1: 95–98.

Ma Xueyong. 2013. "Sha Ting dui xianshi zhuyi xiaoshuo de duoyuan tansuo" [Concerning Sha Ting's multivarious explorations in his realism novels]. PhD dissertation, Nanjing Normal University.

Malinowski, Bronislaw. 1926. *Crime and Custom in Savage Society*. New York: Harcourt, Brace & Company, Inc.

Malone, C. B., and J. B. Tagler. 1924. *The Study of Chinese Rural Economy*. Peking: China International Famine Relief Commission.

Mann, Susan. 1997. *Precious Records: Women in China's Long Eighteenth Century*. Stanford: Stanford University Press.

Maurer, David W. 1981. *Language of the Underworld*. Collected and edited by Allan W. Futrell and Charles B. Wordell. Lexington: University Press of Kentucky.

McIsaac, Lee. 2000. "'Righteous Fraternities' and Honorable Men: Sworn Brotherhoods in Wartime Chongqing." *American Historical Review* 105, no. 5: 1641–55.

Mühlhahn, Klaus. 2007. "Visions of Order and Modernity: Crime, Punishment, and Justice in Urban China during the Republican period," in David Strand, Sherman Cochran, and Wen-hsin Yeh, eds., *Cities in Motion: Interior, Coast, and Diaspora in Transnational China*, 182–215. Berkeley: Center for Chinese Studies, Institute of East Asian Studies, University of California.

Neighbors, Jennifer M. 2009. "The Long Arm of Qing Law? Qing Dynasty Homicide Rulings in Republican Courts." *Modern China* 35, no. 1 (January): 3–37.

Ng, Kenny K. K. 2009. "Temporality and Polyphony in Li Jieren's The Great Wave," in Dongfeng Tao et al., eds., *Chinese Revolution and Chinese Literature*, 197–224. Newcastle upon Tyne, England: Cambridge Scholars Publishing.

Novikov, Boris. 1972. "The Anti-Manchu Propaganda of the Triads, ca. 1800–1860," in Jean Chesneaux, ed., *Popular Movements and Secret Societies in China 1840–1950*, 49–64. Stanford: Stanford University Press.

Oldstone-Moore, Jennifer Lee. 2000. "The New Life Movement of Nationalist China: Confucianism, State Authority, and Moral Formation." Dissertation, Divinity School, University of Chicago.

Ou Shi. 1946. "Zhang Lan gufu paoge" [Zhang Lan letting down the Paoge]. *Kuaihuolin* [The joyful grove], no. 27: 2.

Ownby, David. 1996. *Brotherhoods and Secret Societies in Early and Mid-Qing China: The Formation of a Tradition*. Stanford: Stanford University Press.

———. 2001. "Recent Chinese Scholarship on the History of Chinese Secret Societies." *Late Imperial China* 22, no. 1 (June): 139–58.

Ownby, David, and Mary Somers Heidhues, eds. 1993. *"Secret Societies" Reconsidered: Perspectives on the Social History of Early Modern South China and Southeast Asia*. Armonk, N.Y.: M.E. Sharpe.

Pan, Naigu. 1992. "Vitality of Community Study in China: Professor Fei Xiaotong and Community Study," in Chie Nakane and Chien Chiao, eds., *Home Bound: Studies in East Asian Society: Papers Presented at the Symposium in Honor of the Eightieth Birthday of Professor Fei Xiaotong*, 33–43. Tokyo: Centre for East Asian Cultural Studies.

Pang Jin. 1993. *Baqiannian Zhongguo long wenhua* [Eight thousand years of Chinese dragon culture]. Beijing: Renmin ribao chubanshe.

Park, Robert Ezra. 1921. *Introduction to the Science of Sociology* (with Ernest Burgess). Chicago: University of Chicago Press.

———. 1925. *The City: Suggestions for the Study of Human Nature in the Urban*

Environment (with R. D. McKenzie and Ernest Burgess). Chicago: University of Chicago Press.

Peng Yaxin. 1988. "Wanjia youle dao xintou: Ji wei zhenli erzhan de Tian Jiaying" [Keeping everyone's happiness in his mind: A record of Tian Jiaying who fought for truth], in Qin Xiaoying et al., *Mingjianpian: Buxu chuan junzhuang de jiangjun* [History as a mirror: Generals who do not wear the uniform], 166–87. Beijing: Huaxia chubanshe.

Perry, Elizabeth J. 2013. "Managing Student Protest in Republican China: Yenching and St. John's Compared." *Frontiers of History in China* 8, no. 1 (March): 3–31.

Qiao Jian. 1996. "Meiguo lishi xuepai" [School of American historical anthropology], in Zhou Xing and Wang Mingming eds., *Shehui wenhua renleixue jiangyanji* [Extended collection of lectures on social and cultural anthropology], 137–56. Tianjin: Tianjin renmin chubanshe.

Qiao Zhaohong. 2005. "Lun kangzhan shiqi de xin shenghuo yundong" [A study of the New Life Movement during the War of Resistance against Japan]. *Tianfu xinlun* [New studies of Sichuan], no. 5: 120–23.

Qin Baoqi and Meng Chao. 2000. "Gelaohui qiyuan kao" [Study of the origin of the Elder Brothers Society]. *Xueshu yuekan* [Scholarship monthly], no. 4 (2000): 68–73.

Qin Gong. 2002. "Li Jieren lishi xiaoshuo yu Chuan wei xushi de duchuangxing" [Li Jieren's historical novels and the originality of Sichuan-flavored narratives]. *Xinan shifan daxue xuebao* [Journal of Southwest Normal University], no. 1: 132–35.

Qin Heping. 2000. "Ersanshi niandai yapian yu Sichuan chengzhen shuijuan guanxi zhi renshi" [Understanding the link between opium and urban taxes in 1920s and 1930s Sichuan], in *Chengshi shi yanjiu* [Research in urban history], vols. 19–20, 76–96. Tianjin: Tianjin shehui kexueyuan chubanshe.

———. 2001a. "Dui Qingji Sichuan shehui bianqian yu paoge zisheng de renshi" [On recognizing late-Qing Sichuan social transformations and the rise of the Gowned Brotherhood]. *Shehui kexue yanjiu* [Journal of socialsciences], no. 2: 120–25.

———. 2001b. *Sichuan de yapian wenti he jinyan yundong* [Problem of opium and the opium suppression movement in Sichuan]. Chengdu: Sichuan renmin chubanshe.

Qin Mu. 1983 [1943]. "Sixing, renshi, xuede shangwan" [Lynchings, human markets, and blood lust], in Zhongguo shehui kexue yuan wenxue yanjiu suo xiandai wenxue yanjiu shi, ed., *Zhongguo xiandai sanwen xuan, 1918–1949* [Selections of modern Chinese prose], 359–65. Beijing: Renmin wenxue chubanshe.

Radcliffe-Brown, A. R. 1931. *Social Organization of Australian Tribes.* Melbourne: Macmillan & Co.,

———. 1933. *The Andaman Islanders.* Cambridge: Cambridge University Press.

Ran Chongquan. n.d. "Cai Mengwei zai Tongnan" [Cai Mengwei in Tongnan], in Tongnan xian zhengxie wenshi ziliao yanjiu weiyuanhui, ed., *Tongnan wenshi ziliao* [Literary and historical materials of Tongnan], no. 2: 105–13.

Ran Jinhui and Li Huiyu. 2005. *Minguo shiqi baojia zhidu yanjiu* [Research on the baojia system in Republican China]. Chengdu: Sichuan daxue chubanshe.

Rankin, Mary B. 1986. *Elite Activism and Political Transformation in China: Zhejiang Province, 1865–1911.* Stanford: Stanford University Press.

———. 1990. "The Origins of a Chinese Public Sphere: Local Elites and Community Affairs in the Late Imperial Period." *Etudes Chinoises* 9, no. 2: 14–60.

Rowe, William T. 1984. *Hankow: Commerce and Society in a Chinese City, 1796–1889.* Stanford: Stanford University Press.

———. 1989. *Hankow: Conflict and Community in a Chinese City, 1796–1895.* Stanford: Stanford University Press.

———. 1990. "The Public Sphere in Modern China." *Modern China* 16, no. 3: 309–29.

———. 2007. *Crimson Rain: Seven Centuries of Violence in a Chinese County.* Stanford: Stanford University Press.

Sakai Tadao. 1992. *Chūgoku minshū to himitzukesya* [Chinese populance and secret societies]. Tokyo: Yoshikawa kobunkan.

Schlegel, Gustaaf. 1974 [1866]. *Thian Ti Hwui: The Hung-League or Heaven-Earth-League: A Secret Society with the Chinese in China and India.* Batavia: Lange & Co.. Reprint, New York: AMS Press.

Schoppa, R. Keith. 1973. "The Composition and Functions of the Local Elite in Szechwan, 1851–1874." *Late Imperial China* 10 (November): 7–23.

Scott, James C. 1985. *Weapons of the Weak: Everyday Forms of Peasant Resistance.* New Haven, Conn.: Yale University Press.

———. 1990. *Domination and the Arts of Resistance: Hidden Transcripts.* New Haven, Conn.: Yale University Press.

Sha Tiefan. 1936. "Sichuan zhi Gelaohui" [The Sworn Brotherhood Society in Sichuan]. *Sichuan xianxun xunkan* [Journal of County governance in Sichuan] 3, no. 67: 43–52.

Sha Ting 1982 [1940]. "Zai Qixiangju chaguan li" [In the Fragrant Chamber Teahouse], in *Sha Ting xuanji* [Selected Works of Sha Ting], vol. 1, 140–56. Chengdu: Sichuan renmin chubanshe.

Shen Baoyuan. 1946. "Yige nongcun shetuan jiating" [A family of the rural organization]. BA thesis, Department of Sociology, Yenching University.

Shi De. 1946. "Paoge zai Chongqing" [Gowned Brothers in Chongqing]. *Jipu* [The Jeep], no. 13: 10–11.

"Sichuan banghui diaocha" [A survey of gangsters in Sichuan]. 1949. Bureau of Sichuan Provincial Public Security.

Sichuan difang shiji wenti yanjiuhui, ed. 1940. *Sichuan Gelaohui gaishan zhi shangque* [A discussion of reform of Gelaohui in Sichuan]. Chengdu: Sichuan difang shiji wenti yanjiuhui.

Sichuan guanbao [Sichuan official gazette]. 1911.

Sichuan sheng Xindu xiangzhi bianzuan weiyuanhui, ed. 1994. *Xindu xianzhi* [Gazetteer of Xindu county]. Chengdu: Sichuan renmin chubanshe.

"Sichuan tongsheng jingcha zhangcheng" [Police regulations for Sichuan province]. 1903. From the Archives of Police Ministry, 1501-179, in the First Historical Archives (Beijing).

Sichuan xuebao [Bulletin of Sichuan education]. 1907.

Sichuan yuebao [Sichuan monthly]. 1930.

Skinner, G. William. 1964–65. "Marketing and Social Structure in Rural China." *Journal of Asian Studies* 24, no. 1: 3–43; 24, no. 2: 195–228; and 24, no. 3: 363–99.

Sommer, Mathew H. 2000. *Sex, Law, and Society in Late Imperial China.* Stanford: Stanford University Press.

Spence, Jonathan. 1978. *Death of Woman Wang.* New York: Viking Press.

Spivak, Gayatri Chakravorty. 1988. "Can the Subaltern Speak?" in Gary Nelson and Lawrence Grossberg, eds., *Marxism and the Interpretation of Culture,* 271–313. Urbana: University of Illinois Press.

Stanton, William. 1900. *The Triad Society or Heaven and Earth Association.* Shanghai: Kelly & Walsh, Ltd.

Stapleton, Kristin. 1996. "Urban Politics in an Age of 'Secret Societies': The Cases of Shanghai and Chengdu." *Republican China* 22, no. 1 (November): 23–64.

————. 2016. *Fact in Fiction: 1920s China and Ba Jin's Family.* Stanford: Stanford University Press.

Stuart, John Leighton. 1946. *Fifty Years in China.* New York: Random House.

Su Yu. 1993. "Lansede wuwangwo hua" [Blue forget-me-not flowers], in Huang Weijing and Xie Rixin, eds., *Choulaojiu, suanlaojiu, xianglaojiu: Suibi jingcui* [Stinky old nine, sour old nine, and fragrant old nine: Pithy jottings], 195–212. Guangzhou: Huacheng chubanshe.

Sun Jiang. 2000. "Sengo kenryoku saiken ni okeru chugoku kokuminto to hōkai, 1945–1949, I" [Relationship between the Guomindang and the secret societies during the power reconstruction after the war, 1945–1949, Part 1]. *Aichi daigaku kokusai mondai kenkyūjo* [Journal of Aichi University Institute of International Affairs], no. 114: 141–71.

————. 2001. "Sengo kenryoku saiken ni okeru chugoku kokuminto to hōkai, 1945–1949, II" [Relationship between the Guomindang and the secret societies during the power reconstruction after the war, 1945–1949, Part 2]. *Aichi daigaku kokusai mondai kenkyūjo* [Journal of Aichi University Institute of International Affairs], no. 116: 179–97.

————. 2007. *Kindai Chūgoku no kakumei to himitu kesya: Chūgoku kakumei no syakaisiteki kenkyu (1895–1955)* [The Revolution and secret societies in modern China: A social history of the Chinese revolution]. Tokyo: Kyūko shoin.

————. 2012a. *Kindai Chūgoku no shūkyō, kesya to kenryoku* [Religions, society, and power in modern China]. Tokyo: Kyuko Shoin.

————. 2012b. "Senjika no Karōkai: Jūkei kokuminseifu no syakai togo ni okeru Karōkai" [The Sworn Brotherhood Society during the wartime: The secret society and social integration under the Chongqing National Government]. *Aichi daigaku kokusai mondai kenkyūjo* [Journal of Aichi University Institute of International Affairs], no. 139: 129–56.

Sun Weike and Ji Wenjun. 2012. "Sha Ting, Zai qixiangju chaguan li" [Sha Ting: At Fragrant Chamber Teahouse]. *Wenyibao* [Journal of literature and art]. December 14.

Tadashi Negishi. 1906. *Shinkoku shōgyō sōran* [General information of commerce in the Qing], vol. 3. Tokyo: Maruzen.

Tang Xuefeng. 1990. "Sichuan junfa hunzhan pinfan zhi yuanyin" [The reasons for fierce fighting among Sichuan warlords]. *Xinan shifan daxue xuebao* [Journal of Southwest China Normal University], no. 2: 49–53.

Ter Haar, Barend J. 1998. *Ritual and Mythology of the Chinese Triads: Creating an Identity.* Leiden: E. J. Brill.

Thøgersen, Stig. 2009. "Revisiting a Dramatic Triangle: The State, Villagers, and Social Activists in Chinese Rural Reconstruction Projects." *Journal of Current Chinese Affairs* 38, no. 4: 9–33.

Tie Liu. 2007. "Wo suo jingli de xin Zhongguo" [My experience in the new China]. June 1, 2007. http://club.kdnet.net/dispbbs.asp?boardid=5&id=1715292. Accessed September 6, 2014.

Tongsu ribao [Popular daily]. 1909–11.

Tu Daozheng. 2014. "Fundamental Revelation from the Zhou Yongkang Case." *Yanhuang chunqiu* [Yanhuang annals], no. 9: 9–12.

Tu Minggao. 1980. "Guanyu Sichuan junfa geju hunzhan de jige wenti" [A few questions about Sichuan warlords and their fierce fighting]. *Xinan shifan daxue xuebao* [Journal of Southwest China Normal University], no. 1: 48–59.

Vale, J. 1906. "The Small Trader of Szechuan." *West China Missionary News* 10: 237–38; and 11: 255–62.

Wang Chonghui, ed. 2006. *Zhonghua minguo xingfa* [Criminal law in Republican China]. Beijing: Zhongguo fangzheng chubanshe.

Wang Chunwu. 1993. *Paoge tanmi* [Exploring the secrets of the Paoge]. Chengdu: Bashu shushe.

Wang Dayu. 1993. "Sichuan paoge" [Gowned Brotherhood in Sichuan]. *Sichuan wenshi ziliao xuanji* [Selections of Sichuan literary and historical materials], no. 41: 139–63.

Wang Dazhong. 2002. "Quanli fubai shi heishehui shengcheng de shehui jiegouxing turang" [Corruption of power is the structural soil for development of underworlds]. *Zhengfa xuekan* [Academic journal of political science and law], no. 6: 5–8.

Wang, Di. 1993. *Kuachu fengbi de shijie: Changjiang shangyou quyu shehui yanjiu, 1644–1911* [Striding out of a closed world: Social transformation of the upper Yangzi region, 1644–1911]. Beijing: Zhonghua shuju.

———. 2003. *Street Culture in Chengdu: Public Space, Urban Commoners, and Local Politics in Chengdu, 1870–1930.* Stanford: Stanford University Press.

———. 2008a. "Mysterious Communication: The Secret Language of the Gowned Brotherhood in Nineteenth-Century Sichuan." *Late Imperial China* 29, no. 1 (June, special issue in honor of William T. Rowe): 77–103.

———. 2008b. *The Teahouse: Small Business, Everyday Culture, and Public Politics in Chengdu, 1900–1950.* Stanford: Stanford University Press.

———. 2010. "Chi jiangcha: Chengdu chaguan, paoge yu difang zhengzhi kongjian" [Drinking negotiation tea: Teahouses, the Gowned Brotherhood, and local political space in Chengdu]. *Shixue yuekan* [Historiography monthly], no. 2: 105–14.

Wang Dongjie. 2008. "'Xiangshen' de jiangou yu chonggou: Fangzhi suojian Qingdai Sichuan diqu yimin huiguan chongsi zhong de diyu rentong" [Formation and reformation of the local gentry: What local gazetteers show us about regional correlations in the reverential ceremonies of native place associations in Qing dynasty Sichuan]. *Lishi yanjiu* [Historical research], no. 2: 98–118.

Wang Hui. 2003. "Zhongguo jindai minjian mimi zuzhi de yinyu chuanbo" [Spread of argots of secret societies in modern China]. *Zhejiang shehui kexue* [Social sciences in Zhejiang], no 2: 142–45.

Wang Jianchuan and Jiang Zhushan, eds. 1996. *Ming Qing yilai minjian zongjiao de tansuo: Jinian Dai Xuanzhi jiaoshou lunwenji* [Inquiries into popular religions since the Ming and Qing: Collection of essays on commemoration of Prof. Dai Xuanzhi]. Taipei: Shangding chubanshe.

Wang Jianmin. 2010. "Tianye minzuzhi yu Zhongguo renleixue de fazhan: Jinian Fei Xiaotong, Lin Yaohua xiansheng yibai zhounian danchen" [Field ethnography and the development of Chinese anthropology: Commemoration of Fei Xiaotong and Lin Yaohua on the 100th birthday]. *Zhongnan minzu daxue xuebao* [Journal of South-Central University for Nationalities], no. 6: 6–11.

Wang Jinxiang. 2005. *Zhongguo jindu shi* [History of drug suppression in China]. Shanghai: Shanghai renmin chubanshe.

Wang Kaiyun. 2007. *Xiangjun zhi* [History of the Hunan army]. Changsha: Human renmin chubanshe.

Wang Mingming. 1996. "Gongneng zhuyi yu Yingguo xiandai renleixue" [Functionalism and modern British anthropology], in Zhou Xing and Wang Mingming, eds., *Shehui wenhua renleixue jiangyanji* [A collection of lectures on social anthropology], vol. 1, 108–36. Tianjin: Tianjin renmin chubanshe.

Wang Qingyuan. 1944. "Chengdu pingyuan xiangcun chaguan" [Rural teahouses in the Chengdu Plain]. *Fengtu shi* [Folkways] 1, no. 4: 29–38.

Wang Shiliang and Diao Chunjin. 1990. "Baju Zhugao ji dang zheng jun fei pao yuyishen de fandong renwu He Song" [Reactionary figure He Song, who combined multiple identities in the party, military, politics, banditry, and Gowned Brothers of Zhugao], in *Jintang wenshi* [Literary and historical materials in Jintang county], 441–55. Chengdu: Bashu shushe.

Wang Shunwu. 1993. *Paoge tanmi* [Exploring the secrets of Paoge]. Chengdu: Bashu shushe.

Wang Xianming and Chang Shuhong. 2000. "Wanqing baojia zhi de lishi yanbian yu xiangcun quanli jiegou: Guojia yu shehui zai xiangcun shehui kongzhi zhong de guanxi bianhua" [Historical transformation and rural power structure in the late-Qing baojia system: Changes of relationships regarding state and society within rural social control]. *Shixue yuekan* [Historiography monthly], no. 5: 130–38.

Wang Xiaoting and Huang Wenyi, ed. 1993. *Zhandou de licheng, 1925–1949, Yanjing daxue dixiadang gaikuang* [History of struggling, 1925–1949: General situation of the CCP underground activities at Yenching University]. Beijing: Beijing daxue chubanshe.

Wang Yongqian. 1994. "Zhongguo de tudishen xinyang" [Chinese beliefs in patron dieties]. *Zhongguo minjian wenhua: Minjian wenxue tanyou* [Chinese folk culture: The deep recesses of folk literature], no. 3: 1–20.

Wang Youping. 1999. "Sichuan junfa geju zhong fangqu zhi de tedian" [Features of the defense districts during warlord separatism in Sichuan]. *Tianfu xinlun* [New studies of Sichuan], no. 2: 68–71.

Wang Yunzi. 1981. "Tongmenghui yu Chuanxi gelaohui" [The Chinese Revolutionary League and Sworn Brotherhood Society in West Sichuan], in Wenshi ziliao yanjiu weiyuanhui, ed., *Xinhai geming huiyi lu* [Memoirs of the 1911 Revolution], vol. 3, 218–23. Beijing: Wenshi ziliao chubanshe.

Wei Shouzhong. 1989. "Muqian guonei Zhang Henshui yanjiu xianzhuang gaishu" [A review of Zhang Hengshui studies]. *Xueshijie* [Academia], no. 3: 90–92.

Wei Yingtao and He Yimin. 1983. "Lun Tongmenghui yu Sichuan huidang" [A study of the Alliance League and Sworn Brotherhood] in *Jinian Xinhai Geming qishi zhounian xueshu taolunhui lunwenji* [Collection of essays from the Academic Conference on the 70th Anniversary of the 1911 Revolution]. Beijing: Zhonghua shuju.

Wei Yingtao and Zhao Qing, eds. 1981. *Sichuan xinhai geming shiliao* [Historical sources of the 1911 Revolution in Sichuan], 2 vols. Chengdu: Sichuan renmin chubanshe.

Wen Shu, Wu Jianzhou, and Cui Xianchang. 1984. "Jiu Chengdu de renshi" [Human markets in old Chengdu]. *Longmenzhen* [Folk tales], no. 2 (20): 15–27.

Wenjiang xianzhi bianzuan weiyuanhui, ed. 1990. *Wenjiang xianzhi* [Gazetteer of Wenjiang county]. Chengdu: Sichuan renmin chubanshe.

West China Missionary News. 1905.

West, Philip. 1976. *Yenching University and Sino-Western Relations, 1916–1952.* Cambridge, Mass.: Harvard University Press.

Wu Cang. 1946. "Sichuan paoge yu qinghongbang [Gowned brothers in Sichuan and the Green and Red Gang]. *Kuaihuo lin* [The happy grove], no. 22: 9.

Wu Fuhui. 1990. *Sha Ting zhuan* [Biography of Sha Ting]. Beijing: Shiyue wenyi chubanshe.

Wu Hanchi, ed. 1924. *Quanguo gejie qiekou dacidian* [Jargons of all professions in China]. Shanghai: Donglu tushu gongsi.

Wu Jialun and Wang Jinhou. 1981. "Lun Li Jieren he tade Sishui weilan" [A study of Li Jieren and his ripple on stagnant water]. *Shehui kexue yanjiu* [Journal of social sciences], no. 3: 91–96.

Wu Jinhang. 1981. "Sichuan xinhai geming jianwenlu" [Records things seen and heard of the 1911 Revolution], in *Xinhai geming huiyi lu* [Memoirs of the 1911 Revolution], vol. 3, 99–110. Beijing: Wenshi ziliao chubanshe.

Wu Qiyuan. 1934. *Zhongguo xin wenhua yundong gaiguan* [A brief overview on China's New Cultural Movement]. Shanghai: Xiandai shuju.

Wu, Shugang, and Binchang Tong. 2009. "Liang Shuming's Rural Reconstruction Experiment and Its Relevance for Building the New Socialist Countryside." *Contemporary Chinese Thought* 40, no. 3 (Spring): 39–51.

Wu Wenzao. 1934. "Xiandai shequ shidi yanjiu de yiyi he gongyong" [Significances and functions of modern community field work research]. *Beiping chenbao* (Shehui yanjiu zhoukan). [Beijing morning news, social research weekly], no. 66 (December 26).

———. 1935. "Zhongguo shequ yanjiu de xiyang yingxiang yu guonei jinkuang"

[Western influences and recent internal developments in community studies in China]. *Beiping Chenbao* (Shehui yanjiu zhoukan) [Beijing morning news, social studies weekly], nos. 101 and 102 (January 9).

———. 1936. "Gongneng pai shehui renleixue de youlai yu xianzhuang" [The origin and current state of the Functionalist school in social anthropology]. *Minzuxue yanjiu jikan* [Series on ethnological research], no. 1.

Wu Yu. 1984. *Wuyu riji* [Diary of Wu Yu], vols. 1 and 2. Chengdu: Sichuan renmin chubanshe.

Wu Yue. 2010. *Teshu jiangjun de dubai: Zhonggong mishi Du Zhongshi* [Monologue of a special general: CCP's secret agent Du Zhongshi]. Beijing: Dongfang chubanshe.

Wu Zelin. 1930. *Shehui yuezhi* [Social control]. Shanghai: Shijie shuju.

Xia Yan. 1949. *Fangcao tianya* [Fragrant grass at the edges of the sky]. Shanghai: Kaiming shudian.

Xiang Qifen. 2003. "Ji zai Chuanxi minsu zhong de gongyong ji xingcheng chutan" [Function and form of the chicken in folk traditions of western Sichuan]. *Xinan minzu daxue xuebao* [Journal of Southwest University for Minorities], no. 9: 65–69.

Xiao Tiezhui. 1946. "Tan banghui" [Discussion about gangsters]. *Xinxin xinwen* [The newest news]. August 16.

Xie Zaosheng. 1996. "Yi Sichuan yanhuo" [Recalling the opium disaster in Sichuan], in Sichuan wenshi ziliao bianzuan weiyuanhui, ed., *Sichuan wenshi ziliao xuanji* [Selection of Sichuan literary and historical materials], no. 10: 137–63. Chengdu: n.p.

———. 2002. "Sichuan yapian wenti" [Problems concerning opium in Sichuan], in Quanguo zhengxie wenshi ziliao weiyuanhui, ed., *Wenshi ziliao cungao xuanbian* [Draft selection of literary and historical materials], vol. 25, 585–96. Beijing: Zhongguo wenshi chubanshe.

Xie Zengshou, ed. 2011. *Zhang Lan* [Zhang Lan]. Beijing: Qunyan chubanshe.

Xin shenghuo yundong cujin zonghui. n.d. *Xin shenghuo yundong* [New Life Movement]. Nanchang: Xin shenghuo yundong cujin zonghui.

Xinfanxian gonganju. 1950. "Xinfanxian paoge gaikuang" [General situation of the Gowned Brothers in Xinfan county]. Manuscript copy, no archival category number. Bureau of Sichuan Provincial Public Security.

Xingdao ribao [Sing Tao Daily]. 1950.

Xinhua ribao [Xinhua daily]. 1945.

Xu Yongshun. 1931. "Dongsansheng zhi yimin yu fanzui" [Migrants and crimes in Northeastern China]. *Shehuixue jie* [Sociology], no. 5: 147–65.

Yamamoto Shin. 2008. "Chongzhou Yuantongzhen Paoge diaocha" [A report on an investigation of the Gowned Brothers in Yuantong township, Chongzhou].

———. 2010. "1940 nendai shisenshō ni okeru chihō mingi kikan to himitzukesya" [Local social organizations and secret societies in 1940s Sichuan], in Ishizuka Jin, Nakamura Motoya, and Yamamoto Shin, eds., *Kensei to kingendai chūgoku: Koka, syakai, kojin* [Constitutional politics and modern China: State, society, and individules], 103–26. Tokyo: Gendai jinbunsya.

Yan Xinzhe. 1934. *Nongcun shehuixue gailun* [Introduction to rural sociology]. Shanghai: Zhonghua shuju.

Yan, Yunxiang. 1996. *The Flow of Gifts: Reciprocity and Social Networks in a Chinese Village*. Stanford: Stanford University Press.

Yanda wenshi ziliao bianweihui, ed. 1989. *Yanda wenshi ziliao* [Literary and historical materials of Yenching University], vol. 4. Beijing: Beijing daxue chubanshe.

Yang Daixin. 2011. "Li Jieren bixia de chuancai yu chuancai wenhua de fazhan" [Sichuan cuisine and development of cuisine culture in Li Jieren's novels]. *Wenshi zazhi* [Journal of literature and history], no. 2: 9–11.

Yang Haitao. 2012. "Lun Li Jieren bixia de Chengdu" [Chengdu in Li Jieren's writings]. PhD dissertation, Sichuan Normal University.

Yang Kaidao. 1929. *Nongcun shehuixue* [Rural sociology]. Shanghai: Shijie shuju.

Yang Shuyin. 1944. "Yige nongcun shougongye de jiating: Shiyangchang dujia shidi yanjiu baogao" [A rural handcraft family: A research report on Du family in Shiyangchang]. Thesis, Department of Sociology, Yenching University. Library of Peking University.

Yanjing daxue Chengdu xiaoyou hui. 2007. "Kangzhan shiqi qian Rong de Yanjing daxue" [Yenching University in the evacuation to Chengdu during the War of Resistance against Japan], in Chengdu shi zhengxie wenshi ziliao xuexi weiyuanhui, ed., *Chengdu wenshi ziliao xuanbian: Kangri zhanzheng juan* [Selection of Chengdu literature and historical material: War of Resistance volume], part 1, 339–56. Chengdu: Sichuan renmin chubanshe.

Ye Shengtao. 2004. *Ye Shengtao ji* [A collection of Ye Shengtao's works], vol. 19. Nanjing: Jiangsu jiaoyu chubanshe.

Yen-ching ta hsüeh, Shê hui hsüeh hsi. 1930. *Ching Ho: A Sociological Analysis: The Report of a Preliminary Survey of the Town of Ching Ho, Hopei, North China 1930*. Beijing: Department of Sociology and Social Work, Yenching University.

Yu Songqing. 1994. *Minjian mimi zongjiao jingjuan yanjiu* [Research on scriptures of folk secret religions]. Taipei: Lianjing chuban shiye gongshi.

Yuan Tiangang. n.d. *Xinkan zhinan taisi Yuan Tiangang xiansheng wuxing sanming Daquan* [New edited guide to Yuan Tiangang's fortunetelling works], 2 vols. N.p.

Yuan Tingdong. 2010. *Chengdu jiexiang zhi* [History of streets and alleys in Chengdu], 2 vols. Chengdu: Sichuan jiaoyu chubanshe.

Yun Tao. 1933. "Sichaun gelao hui de neirong dagang" [Substantiave outline of Sichuan Brotherhood Society]. *Shishi zhoubao* [Current affairs weekly] 4, no. 15: 15–16; and 4, no. 17: 15.

Zeng Xianyi, ed. 2011. *Shenfen yu qiyue: Zhongguo chuantong minshi falü xingtai* (Zhongguo chuantong falü wenhua yanjiu 3) [Identities and contracts: Civil law in traditional China (Studies of traditional Chinese law, vol. 3). Beijing: Zhongguo renmin daxue chubanshe.

Zhang Dezeng. 1992. "Jiaoyu yuandi de xinqin gengyunzhe: Liao Taichu" [A hardworking educator—Liao Taichu], in Yanda wenshi ziliao bianweihui, ed., *Yanda wenshi ziliao* [Literary and historical materials of Yenching University], vol. 6, 263–73. Beijing: Beijing daxue chubanshe.

Zhang Fengzhu. n.d. *Pengshan xianzhi* [Gazetteer of Pengshan county]. Qianglong period (1735–1795).

Zhang Guanghai and Liang Hongou. 1987. "Qiantan paoge jiqi zai Nan'an de gai-kuang" [A chat on the Gowned Brotherhood in Nan'an]. *Nan'an qu wenshi ziliao xuanji* [Selections of literary and historical materials in Nan'an], no. 2: 107–28.

Zhang Guoqi. 2004. "Dangdai Zhongguo heishehui (xingzhi) fanzui chengyuan de xinli tezheng" [Psychological features of underworld criminals in comtemporary China]. *Zhongzhou xuekan* [Academic journal of Zhongzhou], no. 5: 200–202.

Zhang Haiyang. 2001. "Lin Yaohua jiaoshou yu Zhongguo de shaoshu minzu he minzu yanjiu" [Lin Yaohua and studies of Chinese minorities and ethnicities]. *Xinan minzu xueyuan xuebao* [Journal of Southwest College for Minorities], no. 1: 28–31.

Zhang Ji et al. n.d. *Wenjiang xianzhi* [Gazetteer of Wenjiang county]. Republican period (1912–1949).

Zhang Jianji. 2003. "Chuanxi junfa de xingcheng" [Formation of Sichuan war-lords]. *Junshi lishi yanjiu* [Research in military history], no. 3: 84–94.

Zhang Jing, Gui Tao, and Yu Li. 2014. "Liu Han heijin'an beihou de paoge zuzhi: Huoyou Chen Jinnan kaichuang" [The paoge organization behind Liu Han's black gold case: It might be founded by Chen Jinnan]. *Tencent news*. May 24, 2014. http://news.qq.com/a/20140524/013020.htm. Accessed September 9, 2014.

Zhang Renshan. 2001. "Lun dangdai Zhongguo heishehui xingzhi zuzhi shengcheng de shehui jizhi" [A study of the nature of contemporary Chinese secret societies and the social mechanism of their emergence]. *Nanjing daxue xuebao* [Journal of Nanjing University], no. 4: 62–69.

Zhang San. 1946. "Chongqing de canyiyuan" [Counselors of Chongqing]. *Xing-guang* [Starlight], no. 3: 4.

Zhang Weiying, Wang Baiqiang et al., ed. 1999. *Yanjing daxue shigao* [Draft history of Yenching University]. Beijing: Zhongguo renmin daxue chubanshe.

Zhao Li and Zhu Hu. 2007. "Yanda shehui diaocha yu Zhongguo zaoqi shehuixue bentuhua shijian" [Social surveys of Yenchjing University and the practice of localization in China's early sociology], in Li Changli and Zuo Yuhe, eds., *Jindai Zhongguo shehui yu minjian wenhua* [Modern Chinese society and folk culture], 88–106. Beijing: Shehui kexue wenxian chubanshe.

Zhao Qing. 1990. *Paoge yu tufei* [Gowned Brothers and bandits]. Tianjin: Tianjin renmin chubanshe.

Zhao Xudong. 2008a. "Fei Xiaotong duiyu Zhongguo nongmin shenghuo de ren-shi yu wenhua zijue" [Fei Xiaotong concerning the understanding of peasants' lives and cultural consciousness]. *Shehuikexue* [Social sciences], no. 4: 54–60.

———. 2008b. "Xiangcun chengwei wenti yu chengwei wenti de Zhongguo xiangcun yanjiu: Weirao 'Yan Yangchu moshi' de zhishi shehui xue fansi" [The rural area becoming an issue and the studies of rural China that have become an issue: An intellectual sociological revisit of James Yen's model]. *Zhongguo shehui kexue* [Journal of Chinese social sciences], no. 3: 110–17.

Zhao Ying. 2011. "Dangdai Zhongguo heishehui xingzhi zuzhi fanzui de chengyin jiqi fazhan qushi" [Factors and developmental trends of organized crime in contemporary Chinese underworlds]. *Shehui kexue jikan* [Journal of social sciences], no. 2: 84–87.

Zheng Dahua. 2000. *Minguo xiangcun jianshe yundong* [The rural construction movement in Republican China]. Beijing: Shehui kexue wenxian chubanshe.

Zheng Ling. 2000. "Jiushi niandai Zhang Henshui yanjiu shuping" [Review of Zhang Hengshui studies in the 1990s]. *Anhui daxue xuebao* [Journal of Anhui University], no. 6: 88–90, 99.

Zhengxie Chengdu shi Xindu qu wenshi ziliao bianji weiyuanhui, ed. 2006. *Xindu kejia yanjiu* [Research on the Hakkas of Xindu]. Chengdu: n.p.

Zhongguo diyi lishi dang'an guan and Beijing shifan daxue lishi xi, eds. 1986. *Xinhai geming qian shinian jian minbian dang'an shiliao* [Archival materials of mass uprisings during the ten years before the 1911 Revolution]. Beijing: Zhonghua shuju.

Zhongguo shehui kexueyuan yuyan yanjiu suo ed. 1997. *Xiandai hanyu cidian* [Dictionary of modern Chinese]. Beijing: Shangwu yinshuguan.

Zhou Lei. 2009. "Guomin zhengfu dui nüxing de suzao he xunlian: Yi kangzhan qian xin shenghuo yundong wei zhongxin de kaocha, 1934–1937" [The Nationalist government's shaping and training of women: A study of the New Life Movement before the War of Resistance against Japan]. *Funü yanjiu luncong* [Series on women's studies], no. 3: 49–53.

Zhou Xun. 1936 [1987]. *Furong huajiu lu* [Talking about Chengdu's past]. Chengdu: Sichuan renmin chubanshe.

Zhou Yong, ed. 2006. *Xi'nan kangzhan shi* [A history of the War of Resistance against Japanese in Southwest China]. Chongqing: Chongqing chubanshe.

Zhou Yumin and Shao Yong. 1993. *Zhongguo banghui shi* [History of Chinese gangsters]. Shanghai: Shanghai renmin chubanshe.

Zhuang Jifa. 1994. *Qingdai mimi huidang shi yanjiu* [A history of secret societies in the Qing dynasty]. Taipei: Wenshizhe chubanshe.

Zhuo Tingzi. 1991. *Xinke jianghu qieyao* [New edition of the language of river and lake runners], in Leng Xueren, *Jianghu yinyu hanghua de shenmi shijie* [Argots and the secret world of the river and lake runners], 243–74. Shijiazhuang: Hebei renmin chubanshe.

Zuo Yuhe. 1990. "Lun Jiang Jieshi fadong de xin shenghuo yundong" [A study of the New Life Movement launched by Chiang Kai-shek]. *Shixue yuekan* [Historiography monthly], no. 4: 70–75.

Zuo Zongtang. 2009. *Zuo Zongtang quanji* [Complete collection of Zuo Zongtang's works]. Zougao 4. Changsha: Yuelu shushe.

———. n.d. *Zuo kejingbo zougao* [Zou Zongtang's memos to the emperor]. N.p.

Index